FACIAM VOS PISCATORES HOMINUM

SAINT JOHN FISHER

Humanist ✠ Reformer ✠ Martyr

by
E.E. Reynolds

Edited by Ryan Grant

Mediatrix Press
MMXV

ISBN: 978-1-953746-39-9
© Mediatrix Press 2015

All rights reserved. This work may not be reproduced in electronic or physical format without the express permission of the publisher except for quotations for review and classroom use.

Reprinted from
St. John Fisher
Originally published 1955

All images are in the public domain.

Nihil Obstat:
Joannes M. T. Barton, S.T.D., L.S.S.
Censor Deputatus

Imprimatur:
E. Morrogh Bernard   *Vicarius Generalis Westmonasterii*
Die XVIII Junii MCMLV

Table of Contents

PREFACE. 1

CHIEF REFERENCES.. 7

CHAPTER I
    YOUTH.. 9

CHAPTER II
    THE LADY MARGARET. 18

CHAPTER III
    THE PREACHER.. 27

CHAPTER IV
    CHRIST'S COLLEGE. 38

CHAPTER V
    THREE PANEGYRICS. 47

CHAPTER VI
    ERASMUS. 57

CHAPTER VII
    ST. JOHN'S COLLEGE. 73

CHAPTER VIII
    THE BISHOP IN HIS DIOCESE—I. 83

CHAPTER IX
    FROM WYCLIFF TO LUTHER. 99

CHAPTER X
    FIRST CONTROVERSIES. 110

CHAPTER XI
    LUTHER. 126

CHAPTER XII
    FURTHER CONTROVERSIES. 139

JOHN FISHER'S LATIN. 152

CHAPTER XIII
    ROBERT BARNES. 154

CHAPTER XIV
    THE BISHOP IN HIS DIOCESE—II. 164

CHAPTER XV
    THE KING'S CONSCIENCE. 179

CHAPTER XVI
    KING AND POPE. 195

CHAPTER XVII
    BLACKFRIARS. 207

CHAPTER XVIII
    THE KING'S ANGER. 217

CHAPTER XIX
    PRÆMUNIRE. 230

CHAPTER XX
    THE KING HAS HIS WAY. 255

CHAPTER XXI
    THE NUN OF KENT. 266

CHAPTER XXII
    TEN WEEKS' WORK. 289

CHAPTER XXIII
    THE OATH. 296

CHAPTER XXIV
    IN THE BELL TOWER. 325

CHAPTER XXV
    FOR HIS SISTER. 335

CHAPTER XXVI
    THE RED HAT. 347

CHAPTER XXVII
    INTERROGATIONS. 359

CHAPTER XXVIII
    THE TRIAL. 369

CHAPTER XXIX
    THE MARTYRDOM. 377

CHAPTER XXX
    FOUR HUNDRED YEARS
    385

APPENDIX A
    A PRAYER COMPOSED BY ST. JOHN FISHER
    397

APPENDIX B
    SAINT JOHN FISHER'S RELATIVES. 402

Introduction to the Mediatrix Press Reprint

WHEN we look to the reign of Henry VIII, one figure stands out in the popular imagination and feeling: St. Thomas More. We have countless centers of law, references and other things to place More as the predominant figure in the struggle. This may be because More was a layman, and at a certain level we identify more with him because he seems closer to us, and his wit and merriment are attractive.

One of the major figures in the Church during Henry's reign, however, is forgotten today, namely St. John Fisher. Fisher was a far better theologian than St. Thomas More, and like More was a humanist, a reformer and a martyr. Thus I have added this subtitle to the current work, which the author, Reynolds, did not use. Fisher, more than anyone else (including St. Thomas Aquinas), was cited in the Council of Trent's decree on Justification. He was the greatest pre-Tridentine opponent of Luther and, keen to reform the life of the clergy, he instituted the seminary system at St. John's Cambridge, before it had that name. He was a famous preacher, and no respecter of persons no matter how great, even those who normally terrified opponents with their power such as Wolsey. Lastly, he was the great defender of the marriage between Henry and Catherine, far more so than Sir Thomas More. More, as the successor to Cardinal Wolsey, was formally in a position to advocate for the divorce policy. He did so as long as he operated within the law, though he became quite convinced of the validity of the marriage to Catherine and resigned. This is not to attack More, who was also a great man, but to bring out the fact that it was St. John Fisher who took the active role of defending the

Editor's Introduction

Queen, where as More supported her in secret. The great irony is that a decade earlier, More had suggested to Henry that he drop the valiant defense of the Papacy in his treatise on the Sacraments against Luther, because More did not believe the Papacy was a divine institution, Henry did. The shift comes when More begins to read St. John Fisher's tracts against Luther, most specifically in the first *Confutatio*, where the scriptural and patristic argumentation is so clear, that More had to distance himself from the opinions of Erasmus, which he had espoused, and accept that the Papacy was a divinely established office, no matter how unworthy the occupant.

In that conflict, it is Fisher who was the most outspoken, and the one who clearly argued Catherine's case.

Reynolds, in this monumental historical treatment, paints for us the picture of this reforming preacher, bishop, and ultimately the Church's only Cardinal martyr. In doing so, he based his work entirely on primary sources, state papers, and previous works having done the same. Herein, Reynolds provides us with a historical work rather than hagiography that crashes into the secular history of today; a history which has tried to insulate itself from anything religious. More can be celebrated because he can be secularized, not because he wasn't a fervent Catholic, but because he was a lawyer who wrote with wit and argued by law. How does a modern secularize one such as John Fisher? Reynolds' work challenges the neglect of such a truly great man, showing from the primary sources his great achievements.

In reproducing this work, we have made the choice not to alter anything in the work, including the UK spelling, save for modernizing the system of quotation marks in use in Reynolds' time. The only change we have

Editor's Introduction

ventured is to change the order of the pictures. The original editors placed portraits of individuals at times many chapters before they actually appear. We have kept all the original portraits, save for Katherine of Aragon which we have substituted with a portrait of her at the time of the divorce. We have also added portraits of the other major figures, *e.g.* the original lacked even a portrait of Sir Thomas More! Perhaps they determined such a portrait was already well known.

In like manner, Reynolds wrote his narrative with the assumption that anyone picking up this book was already acquainted with the main points at issue in Henry VIII's reign. At different points it was very tempting to make additions of information in regard to Henry or Henry's reign, but we have preferred to leave the work as it is, for the simple reason that this is a work of St. John Fisher, not so much of Henry, or of Wolsey or Anne Boleyn. It is Fisher's life in the most important moment of English history, and Fisher who signally stands out as the great defender of the sacrament of Marriage and the Papacy, two institutions which again in the modern world are under attack, though in circumstances far removed from Henry's reign. It is my hope that the republication of Reynolds' treatment may lead to further studies of St. John Fisher and a renewed interest in his central role in the conflict.

Ryan Grant
Post Falls, ID
September 2015

PREFACE

FATHER THOMAS E. BRIDGETT'S *Blessed John Fisher* (1888) was the first full-scale biography to be based on a careful study of state papers; the result was a work that, once and for all, established the position and stature of John Fisher. When that book was published, Froude's reputation was at its height; he had derided John Fisher as "a miserable old man", and had scoffed at his "babbling tongue". Not the least of Bridgett's services was that he confuted Froude, not so much by argument, as by an accurate presentation of evidence taken from primary sources. He believed that "the best answer is the simple record of historic facts."

Two generations have passed since this pioneer work; Bridgett was scrupulously careful not to go beyond the available evidence; since he wrote, other material has become accessible that strengthens the portrait given in Blessed John Fisher.

The publication in *Analecta Bollandiana* (1891 and 1893) of Fr. Van Ortroy's edition of the manuscript of the earliest life of John Fisher, was an event of first importance; this work of fine scholarship must be the basis of all study of John Fisher's life.

Fr. Bridgett was unaware of the existence of copies of three of John Fisher's sermons—the one preached in 1525, and the two printed in 1532 by William Rastell. Nor does he seem to have examined the episcopal registers at Rochester.

The first printed biography of John Fisher was written by Dr. Thomas Bailey and published in 1655. It made use, without any acknowledgment, of the early manuscript life, but the book contained many inaccurate additions by the author. Fr. Bridgett went back to the original manuscript and so was able to strip away what Van Ortroy called Bailey's "*sottes interpolations*".

The next published biography appeared exactly two hundred years later and was the work of the Rev. John Lewis; he uncritically accepted Bailey's work, but he made use also of such state documents as he could find. His careful summaries of John Fisher's Latin works and his collection of documents are still useful. It is however an ill-made book containing some irrelevant material. Lewis had evidently seen the Rochester registers, but, beyond extracting one or two cases of abjuration, he made little use of them.

There are eleven manuscript copies of the earliest biography, and also five copies of a Latin translation. The most important of the English manuscripts is Arundel 152 (B.M.); another, Harleian 6382 (B.M.) was used as the text for the E.E.T.S. version in 1921.[1]

Until Van Ortroy made his meticulous examination of these manuscripts, it was customary to ascribe (as did Fr. Bridgett) the original version to Dr. Richard Hall (d. 1604), who for many years was a professor at Douai. Van Ortroy argued, I think convincingly, that Hall was not the author of the English life, but that he was responsible for the translation into Latin (Barberini Library); this contains one or two additional statements that could have come within his experience, e.g. the fact that Richard Wilson, John Fisher's servant in the Tower, fled to the Low Countries and became a priest.

The author of the English life remains anonymous. Van Ortroy tentatively put forward the claims of Dr. John

---

[1] Fr. Philip Hughes edited another edition in 1935, *The Earliest Life of St. John Fisher.*

Young who was vice-chancellor of Cambridge under Queen Mary. In the following pages, I have referred to this unidentified author as "the early biographer".

The evidence suggests that the material for this early life was collected during the reign of Queen Mary and put into narrative form early in Elizabeth's reign, at a time when publication was out of the question.

Not the least of Van Ortroy's services was his analysis of the material out of which the life was constructed. The early biographer got into touch verbally or by correspondence with many who had known John Fisher. His best informant was someone who "was but a young scholar of St. John's College' when Fisher died. Amongst this material are some extracts from a life of Sir Thomas More by his nephew William Rastell; he had witnessed John Fisher's execution, and, as a lawyer, was in a good position to collect information about the trial even if he himself was not present, as he may have been. It is a tragedy that the complete manuscript of this biography has not been preserved, but these few pages are a precious remnant.

The early biographer also made use of a manuscript of the life of Wolsey by George Cavendish.

In the following pages I have given extracts from William Rastell (as given in E.E.T.S. *Harpsfield*), and from George Cavendish direct from their text and not in the rewritten versions of the early biographer.

Amongst those who had known John Fisher, the early biography had information from Robert Truslove (a chaplain in the bishop's last years), Thomas Watson (Fellow and Master of St. John's, Bishop of Lincoln under Queen Mary, and for twenty-five years under restraint during Elizabeth's reign), Walter Phillips (last prior of Rochester), a priest named Buddell of Cuxton (scribe to

John Fisher), as well as from servants and others of the Rochester household.

Van Ortroy does not exaggerate when he writes of this early biography, "*elle a été préparée et composée avec un soin jaloux et avec une sollicitude constante de la vérité, a une époque où la memoirs des travaux et des épreuves de l'illustre martyr était encore vivace parmi les contemporains survivants de trois règnes successifs.*"

The Registers for the years during which John Fisher was Bishop of Rochester have been preserved, as well as the Act Book of his Consistory Court. The information in the first is largely of a routine character—ordinations, institutions, professions, and so on. Unfortunately the Visitation records have not been preserved. While the Registers do not add substantially to our knowledge of John Fisher, they throw light on the administration of the diocese and confirm the reputation he left of being a pastoral bishop. Of each year, particular interest for our purpose are the cases of abjuration. It is possible, also, to follow his movements during many months of each year.

Here I must acknowledge my debt of gratitude to the Rev. L. E. Whatmore[2] who most generously placed at my disposal his full notes from the *Register*. It is to be hoped that he may be given the opportunity of editing the Registers as their publication is much to be desired.

All existing letters of John Fisher are here given in full from fresh transcripts from the originals. Spelling has been modernized in these letters and in all quotations from sixteenth-century sources.

Like all who make extensive use of the calendars of state papers, I have had to face the problem of trying to

---

[2] Editor of *Archdeacon Harpsfield's Visitation*, 2 vols. (Catholic Record Society, 1950-1.) References will be found in the footnotes to other writings of Fr. Whatmore.

distinguish between summaries of documents and full transcripts. I have chosen to adopt the method used by A. F. Pollard, who, in the Preface to his Wolsey, wrote:

> When one quotes The Letters and Papers of Henry VIII one may be reproducing written or spoken *ipsissima verba*, or merely a summary of a third hand report of words which have passed through as many languages and as many fallible processes of dictation, transcription, calendaring and printing. All one can do, it appears, is to mark a simple distinction between one's own words and those which are taken from some source indicated in the text or footnotes; and I have tried to meet what seems to me the most elementary requirement of scholarship, namely to provide the critical reader with the means of checking the evidence on which my statements are based. For this reason I have given specific references in footnotes to the text instead of collecting them at the end of the volume, or compiling a general bibliography which is more useful as an advertisement than as a means of verification.

The reader should also be aware that speeches quoted from the early biographer, or from Cavendish, or from Rastell, are not verbatim reports; they are in the nature of reconstructions based on memory and not on accounts written down when the speeches were made.

I have not attempted a bibliography of John Fisher's writings. The general reader will find all he wants in the text. Scholars will refer to the full bibliography published in 1955 by the Oxford Bibliographical Society; the research for this was made by the Rev. J. F. McMahon, M.S.C., of Australia.

The most accessible edition of Saint John Fisher's vernacular sermons and writings is the one volume English Works, published by the Early English Text Society (1876; reprint, 1935). There is need for a new and more comprehensive edition in modern spelling.

E. E. R.

CHIEF REFERENCES

Allen. "Opus Epistolarum Des. Erasmi Roterodami," ed. P. S. Allen. vols.

Bridgett. "Life of Blessed John Fisher," by the Rev. T. E. Bridgett (1888).

Cal. Span. "Calendar of State Papers, Spanish."

Cavendish. "The Life and Death of Thomas Wolsey," by George Cavendish. Temple Classics (1908).

Ehses. "Römische Dokumente zur Geschichte der Ehescheidung Heinrichs VIII," Paderborn, 1893.

E.W. "The English Works of John Fisher," ed. J. E. B. Mayor. E.E.T.S. (1876).

G. & H. "Documents Illustrative of English Church History," ed. H. Gee and W. J. Hardy (1896).

Harpsfield. "The Life and Death of Sir Thomas More" ed. E. W. Hitchcock and R. W. Chambers. E.E.T.S. (1932).

L.P. "Calendar of Letters and Papers Foreign and Domestic of the reign of Henry VIII."

Lewis. "The Life of Dr. John Fisher," by the Rev. John Lewis. 2 vols. (1855).

Ortroy. "Vie du bienheureux martyr Jean Fisher," ed. Fr. Van Ortroy, S. J., Bollandiste. (Brussels, 1893).

Rogers. "The Correspondence of Sir Thomas More," ed. E. F. Rogers. (1947).

Roper. "The Lyfe of Sir Thomas More, knighte," by William Roper, ed. E. V. Hitchcock. E.E.T.S. (1935).

S.P. "State Papers of the reign of Henry

CHAPTER I
YOUTH

BEVERLEY lies at the foot of the eastern slopes of the wolds of East Yorkshire. In the fifteenth century it was at the height of its prosperity as one of the leading cloth-making and marketing towns of the country. Its liberties were jealously preserved by its merchant governors, and the town itself was evidence of their civic pride. The surrounding mote was guarded by five gates and within that protection there had grown up a pleasant town of fine houses and public buildings, of market places and paved streets.

Dominating the town was the Minster, the Collegiate Church of St. John of Beverley. In addition there was the parish church of St. Mary, the houses of the Dominicans and Franciscans, a commandery of the Knights Hospitallers, and the hospitals of St. Giles and St. Nicholas. For its population of five thousand, Beverley was well served by the Church.

During the Wars of the Roses, the town managed to avoid committing itself to either side. Edward IV led his army through Beverley in 1461 on his way to Towton, but that was a quiet passage. Both Lancastrians and Yorkists were careful not to alienate the great trading towns.

It was at Beverley that John Fisher was born in 1469. His father, Robert, was a mercer, and the terms of his will show that he was prosperous. He made bequests to a number of churches and almshouses and to two priests. To a monastery at Hagnaby in Lincolnshire he left ten shillings for a trental of Masses for the repose of his soul, and to a church at Holtoft not far away in the same county, he left a small sum for the upkeep of the fabric.

These two bequests suggest that he may have been a native of that part of Lincolnshire. Four children are referred to in the will but not named. We know the names of two, John and his brother Robert who was later steward at Rochester. One of the other, children was a daughter who married an Edward White. The fourth child may have been the Ralph Fisher whose name comes in a list of debts owing to John Fisher at his attainder. The name, however, of Fisher was not uncommon in Yorkshire so it is no wise to go further than suggest a possible relationship. An early manuscript version[1] of John Fisher's life says that he was the eldest son, but this too lacks confirmation.

Robert Fisher died in 1477 and was buried in St. Mary's, the parish church, whose vicar witnessed the will on 17th June; it was proved on the 26th.[2] John was then eight years old. His mother, Agnes, married as her second husband a man named White; neither his Christian name nor his occupation is known. He may have been a relation of the Edward White who married his step-daughter.

There were four children of this second marriage. John and, Thomas became merchants, and Richard a priest. Elizabeth White entered the Dominican nunnery at Dartford, Kent.[3]

John Fisher went to the school attached to the Minster. The history of this school[4] can be traced back to the tenth

---

[1] *Arundel*, 152 (B.M.).

[2] Both *Bridgett* (p. 8 and p. 10n.), and *Lewis* (I, 3, and II, 253) have confused the dates. A fresh examination of the original will at York showed that the year was 1477 (17th and 26th June).

[3] See Appendix B.

[4] A. F. Leach, V. C. H. Yorkshire, I, p. 424. The earlier history of the school is well documented, but unfortunately there is a break in the records from 1456 until the Reformation.

century and at one period there were three schoolmasters in charge of it. It enjoyed a high reputation as a grammar school. If his later distinction as a Latinist may be taken as evidence, John Fisher must have had a thorough grounding in the language.

Apart from the fact that he went to the Collegiate school, there are no records or legends of his boyhood. He was an impersonal writer and only two or three definite references are to be found to his own experiences. We can picture him growing up in a bustling medieval town. He no doubt watched the completion of the building of the great west front of the Minster.

The town was famed for its miracle plays which were produced by the gilds. There was the Corpus Christi play, the riding on the Feast of the Purification, and the Paternoster play on the Sunday after the feast of St. Peter ad Vincula. These would give delight to any boy and John Fisher may have taken his part in them. The liturgy of the Minster and of St. Mary's and the preaching of the friars would strengthen his devotion to the Church. The great emphasis he was later to put on the need for good preaching and instruction may reflect a boy's impressions, good or bad.

References in his sermons and writings to country scenes need not always be memories of his early years; no one lived beyond the reach of fields and woods in the fifteenth century; rather they may be taken as reflecting his own delight in the countryside.

His aptitude for learning was so apparent that his mother, with the encouragement of his friends and no doubt with the approval of the boy's schoolmaster, decided to send him to the University of Cambridge. The family was sufficiently well-off for him to enter as a student without having to earn his keep as a sizar,[5] or, as was sometimes necessary, as a mendicant. So, at the age of twelve or thirteen, he set out on the hundred and fifty mile journey along the old Roman road through Lincoln down to Cambridge, a full week's journey.

The Cambridge to which the boy John Fisher went about the year 1482 was showing signs of stirring from the sluggishness into which it had declined after a period of intellectual brilliance. New hostels and colleges were being built and gradually a more ordered society was forming. The riotous and sometimes dissolute days of unguided youth were passing. This change was necessary if scholarship was to advance. John Fisher himself was to carry this reform further and to impose the discipline of life as well of studies on the students.

In an oration made before Henry VII in 1506, John Fisher referred to the state of the University as he knew it in his youth.

> At the time when your majesty first showed your concern for us, learning had begun to decline among us—this may have been the result of constant litigation with the town, or of the frequent plagues that beset us so that we lost many of our leading scholars, or of the lack of patrons of learning. Whatever the cause, we should indeed have been reduced to despair had not your majesty shone down upon us like the rising sun itself.[6]

To this may be added the comment of Erasmus in a letter (1516) to his old pupil Henry Bullock of Queens'

---

[5] Someone on financial aid. –Editor.

[6] *Lewis*, II, p. 269.

College: "About thirty years ago," he wrote, "nothing was taught at Cambridge but Alexander [de Villa Dei], the *Parva Logicalia*, as they are called, those old dictates of Aristotle, and the questions from Scotus."[7]

Sir Thomas More could also look back with a smile to the old ways; in Utopia, he wrote, "they have not discovered one of those rules about restrictions, amplifications, and suppositions so ingeniously devised, which our children everywhere learned in the *Parva Logicalia*."[8]

One indication of the decline in learning is that in 1491 the University found it necessary to engage an Italian to compose Latin orations as there were no resident scholars capable of doing so.[9]

The impulse of the New Learning was not felt at Cambridge as early as in Oxford. William Grocyn, after having studied in Italy, was teaching Greek at Oxford in 1491; several younger scholars from the University also went to Italy and were influenced by the revived study of classical Latin and by the new enthusiasm for Greek studies. There was no similar movement at Cambridge at that period.

There had been, indeed, little change in the mode or manner of learning since the previous century. The first stage of study consisted of the Trivium (Grammar, Rhetoric, Logic or Dialectic). Of these grammar was the foundation subject and probably the most efficiently taught. Oral methods were a necessity as books were few and expensive. It may be noted that John Fisher was eight

---

[7] *Allen*, II, No. 456.

[8] *Utopia* (tr. Richards), p. 69. Several of the text-books of logic were entitled *Parva Logicalia*.

[9] C. H. Cooper, *Annals*, I, p. 240. This statement seems incredible.

years old when Caxton printed his first book in England. Disputation was an essential part of the training method; students sharpened their wits and proved their knowledge in public disputation. The method can be seen by reference to the works of St. Thomas Aquinas. A question is first posed; for example, "Whether there is in us a Natural Law?" First three objections are fairly stated; then follow three replies to these objections. It was an exercise of considerable benefit to the disputants, but during the fifteenth century it had become stereotyped and pedantry had taken the place of creative thought. The ridicule[10] directed at the debased form of dialectic was deserved, and after the Reformation, the work of the schoolmen fell into neglect; during the past hundred years their great constructive achievement has come to be recognized and appreciated anew.

The second stage of university training was the Quadrivium (Astronomy, Music and Geometry), and after successfully disputing his way for seven years the student became a Master (or in continental parlance, a doctor, or professor) of Arts. A Bachelor of Arts was one who had accomplished half the course. Comparatively few students got even as far as that, and but a small proportion of these became Masters. For most students, a sound knowledge of Latin was all that they needed to begin clerical or administrative careers. It will be noticed that theology was not part of this course, though its subject matter often supplied questions for discussion.

---

[10] It was Dr. Arbuthnot (1667-1735) who invented the question, "How many angels could dance on the point of a needle without jostling one another?" The unwary have sometimes quoted this as actually discussed by the schoolmen.

YOUTH

Such was the course of study that John Fisher followed as a student of Michaelhouse[11] where he was fortunate to come under the guidance of William de Melton (d. 1528), a scholar and preacher of repute. His pupil referred to him as "a very eminent theologian," and recalled in one of his rare autobiographical notes that his master,

> used often to admonish me when I was a boy and attended his lectures on Euclid, that if I looked on the least letter of any geometrical figure as superfluous, I had not seized the true and full meaning of Euclid.[12]

He took his degree in Grammar in 1483 at the age of fourteen. This did not show exceptional precocity but proved that he must have been a diligent student. This qualification was simply for proficiency in the first subject of the Trivium and it carried with it a licence to teach in a Grammar School.[13] This was emphasized by the new grammarian being invested with rod and birch; at the ceremony a victim was supplied who was recompensed for his pains.

John Fisher took his B.A. in 1488 and his M.A. in 1491, and became a Fellow of Michaelhouse. In June of that year a papal dispensation[14] was granted for him to take priest's orders while under canonical age. The register states that

---

[11] *Bridgett*, p. 12, refers to the "uncertain tradition" that John Fisher was at first a student of Godshouse; there is no evidence for this.

[12] *Proemium* to *De Veritate* (1527)

[13] The French Baccalauréat of today suggests a parallel. It was probably this degree and not the B.A. that Wolsey took at the age of fifteen.

[14] The discovery of this dispensation by A. H. Lloyd (*Early History of Christ's College, Cambridge*, p. 391) settled the controversy as to the year of John Fisher's birth.

he was then in his twenty-second year. He was ordained on the title of his fellowship. The entry in Archbishop Rotherham's Register reads:

> 17 Dec. 1491.
> Presbiteri.
> Mr. Joh. Fysher atrium M. Socius domus sive hospicii Sancti Michaelis Cantibrig. ad titulum societas suæ.[15]

No doubt he visited Beverley at this time; there is no record of any later visit but his close association with his brother Robert and his half-sister Elizabeth suggests an enduring family affection.

Thomas Rotherham, Archbishop of York, may well have been personally interested in John Fisher. Lincoln College, Oxford, claims Rotherham as its second founder, but he had been a student of King's College, Cambridge, and was elected Chancellor of the University during the reign of Edward IV. He was munificent in his gifts to the University. From 1480 he was Master of Pembroke Hall for at least six years. In what was then a small society, the Archbishop may have noted the young scholar from his own county.

After taking his Master's degree, John Fisher began the course of theology which normally lasted ten or twelve years. He took his doctorate in 1501, the earliest year in which he could have done so.

As his life was to be so closely associated with Cambridge it is necessary to know something of the government of the University at that period. The supreme

---

[15] I am indebted to the Revd. Dr. J. S. Purvis for the transcription. There is no record that John Fisher took any of the other orders at York, or elsewhere.

officer from 1246 was the chancellor; he was elected for a period of two years by the house of regents who were the teachers. As he was sometimes a bishop or statesman, his duties were often delegated to the vice-chancellor. He was responsible for discipline and had his own court; after long disputes, his independence of ecclesiastical control was established. Two proctors were elected annually; they were the executive and administrative officers of the University; they supervised the disputations and all ceremonies, managed the finances, kept order in the streets and controlled market supplies to the students. They usually represented the University in any negotiations with the town authorities. The proctors played an important part in university life.

John Fisher was first elected senior proctor in 1494.

CHAPTER II
THE LADY MARGARET

THE election of John Fisher to be senior proctor at the age of twenty-five is evidence that his fellow regents had recognized certain of his outstanding abilities. The series of university appointments that followed confirmed their opinion. He was as much an administrator and man of affairs as a scholar and he gained the trust and confidence of his colleagues.

He must have been a familiar figure in the streets of Cambridge. He was tall, big-boned but lean; his hair was auburn; the grey eyes were prominent; the strong jaw was that of a man not easily turned from his purpose. His speech was as spare as his person, but these appearances were belied by the mildness and modesty of his demeanour. He probably did not invite easy acquaintanceship, but once the outward defences had been penetrated, men found in him a warm friend and a trustworthy guide.

Amongst the friends he made was John Syclyng, the Proctor or Master of Godshouse, the college founded by William Byngham in 1439 "for the free herbigage of poor scholars of Grammar."[1] The first recorded association of the two men was in 1494 when the perennial controversies between the University and the Town were exceptionally acute. Each claimed rights that were

---

[1] A. F. Leach described it as "the first secondary school training college on record." (*Schools of Medieval England*, p. 257). For a fuller account of John Syclyng, see A. H. Lloyd's *Early History of Christ's College, Cambridge.*

disputed by the other; royal grants of privileges were often capable of conflicting interpretations. The university proctors had to make many visits to London for appeals at the courts and to seek the aid of influential protectors at the king's court. John Syclyng was a leader in such negotiations and he found a reliable colleague in John Fisher.

One such visit marked an epoch in John Fisher's life. In the Proctor's Accounts, recorded in his own neat handwriting, is this entry for the year 1494.

> For hire of two horses for II days . . . 7s.
> For breakfast before crossing to Greenwich . . . 3 d.
> For the crossing by boat . . . 4d.
> I dined with the lady-mother of the king.
> I supped with the Chancellor.

The journey from Cambridge usually took two days by way of Barkway, Ware and Waltham, the first night being spent at Barkway. The accounts include the cost of lodgings and refreshments as well as of the hire and care of horses. Thus, "for wine and fruit at the sign of St. John's Head . . . is. 3d." suggests that they were entertaining guests. Another entry reads, "for the use of altars at St. Bride, and bread, wine and candles . . . is. 8d." So, on at least one occasion, John Fisher said Mass at St. Bride's in Fleet Street.[1]

The chancellor mentioned in the last line of the 1494 entry was Cardinal Morton (d. 1500) who was both chancellor of England and of the University of Oxford.

The "lady-mother of the king" was the Lady Margaret Beaufort, Countess of Richmond and Derby; such was the respect with which she was held, both the University and

---

[1] *Grace Book B.*, Part I, pp. 68 et seq.

Town of Cambridge submitted their differences to her arbitration. This was the first recorded meeting between John Fisher and the Lady Margaret; its consequences were momentous for the future of the University and for John Fisher himself.

There have been many great ladies named Margaret, but to mention the Lady Margaret at once calls to mind one of the remarkable women in our history; her influence in religion and culture and learning was enduring. It was through her that the Tudors derived that acuteness of mind and power of governance so marked in her son Henry VII, in her grandson Henry VIII, and not least in her great-grand-daughter Elizabeth I. The way in which her abilities and influence were used during the last fifteen years of her life, was, as we shall see, largely directed by John Fisher who spoke of her "singular wisdom far passing the common rate of women."

Margaret Beaufort, daughter and heiress of the first Duke of Somerset, was born in 1443. At the age of twelve she married, or was married to, Edmund Tudor, Earl of Richmond, whose father had married the widow of Henry V.[2] Edmund Tudor died in November 1456, and his son, the future Henry VII, was born two months later. In a speech in the presence of the Lady Margaret and Henry VII, John Fisher said that the king, like Moses, was "wonderfully born and brought into the world by the most noble princess, his mother, who at the time of the king's birth, was not above fourteen years of age, and very small

---

[2] Twelve was the earliest legally permissible age to marry in those times, but it was generally frowned upon. Normally such marriages were merely arranged and not completed until the girl attained 14. King Henry V subdued the Church to compliance, and thus Henry VI found it very accommodating to an arrangement for Edmund Tudor which even contemporaries considered distasteful, and we moderns would classify as pedophilia. -Editorial note.

of stature, as she was never a tall woman; it seemed a miracle that at that age, and of so little a personage, any one should be born at all, let alone one so tall and of so fine a build as the king."[3]

She married Henry, Lord Stafford, as her second husband, and after his death in 1481, she married Thomas Lord Stanley. John Fisher tells us that "in her husband's days long time before he died (1504), she obtained of him license and promised to live chaste, in the hands of the reverend father my Lord of London [FitzJames] which promise she renewed after her husband's death into my hands again."[4]

The record of the renewal of this vow concludes with the following passage:

> And also, for my more merit and quietness of soul in doubtful things pertaining to the same, I avow to you, my Lord of Rochester [Fisher], to whom I am and hath been, since the first time I see you, admitted, very determined (as my chief trusty councillor) to own mine obedience in all things concerning the well and profit of my soul.[5]

With patient skill Margaret Beaufort safeguarded and promoted the interests of her only son, Henry Tudor. She was a direct descendant of Edward III through John of Gaunt by his mistress Katherine Swynford. The Beauforts had been legitimated by Acts of Parliament, and, with the murder of Edward Prince of Wales on Tewkesbury field in 1471, Margaret succeeded to the Lancastrian claims. She

---

[3] MS. Bodl. 13; *Lewis*, II, p. 265.

[4] *E.W.*, p. 294.

[5] *Lewis*, II, p. 258.

does not seem, however, to have had any pretensions to the crown herself, but to have willingly made way for her son.

During the reign of Richard III, she lost her titles and possessions; her husband, Lord Stanley, was granted her lands as he was too powerful to be alienated by the king. She remained in seclusion, but she found means to further her absent son's cause, and it was her husband's desertion of Richard at Bosworth Field that proved decisive.

Her position when her son became Henry VII was unique; on purely hereditary grounds she had as much right to be queen as he to be king, but this anomaly in no way impaired their strong affection for each other. The respect and tenderness with which Henry regarded his mother were amongst the more attractive traits in his character. In a letter to him of 1500 she calls him "my own sweet and most dear king and all my worldly joy."

The Lady Margaret's deep devotion to the Church and her love of learning gave meaning to her life and excluded those worldly ambitions that might have poisoned the feelings of any other woman standing so close to the throne.

She was an early patron of the printing press, and it was at her wish that Wynkyn de Worde printed Walter Hilton's *The Scale of Perfection*.

> This mighty Princess hath commanded me
> To imprint this book, her grace for to deserve.

She herself translated the French *The Mirror of Simple Souls*, and the fourth book of the *Imitatio Christi* which was printed in 1503 with the translation of the first three books by William Atkinson which he had made at her request. Even here the influence of John Fisher may be suggested, for the two scholars were almost exact contemporaries at Cambridge. At the beginning of Henry VIII's reign, Wynkyn de Worde described himself as "printer unto the most excellent princess my lady the king's grandame."

Such works show the direction of her interests, and her patronage of a number of religious houses emphasizes this devotion. Yet, combined with this piety, was an almost masculine sense of the practical. She was noted for the efficient way in which she managed her household and her widespread worldly affairs. John Fisher likened her to Martha.

> First her own household with marvellous diligence and wisdom, this noble princess ordered providing reasonable statutes and ordinances for them, which by her officers she commanded to be read four times a year. . . . If any factions or bands were made secretly amongst her head officers, she with great policy did bolt it out and likewise if any strife or controversy, she would with great discretion study the reformation thereof.[6]

John Fisher's reputation was probably known to the Lady Margaret before they met. She chose him as one of her chaplains and later as her confessor in place of Richard FitzJames who had become Bishop of Rochester in 1497. The early life reads:

> After he was awhile established, he ordered himself so discreetly, so temperately and so wisely, that both she and all her family were governed by his

---

[6] *E. W.*, p. 296.

high wisdom and discretion. Whereby at last he became greatly reverenced and beloved, not only of that virtuous lady and all her household, but also of the king her son with whom he was in no less estimation and credit all his life than with his mistress.[7]

In a dedicatory letter written in 1527 to Richard Fox then Bishop of Winchester, John Fisher paid this tribute to the Lady Margaret:

> My debts were indeed great. Were there no other besides the great and sincere love which she bore to me above others (as I know for a certainty), yet what favour could equal such a love on the part of such a princess? But besides her love, she was most munificent towards me. For though she conferred on me no ecclesiastical benefice, she had the desire, if it could be done, to enrich me, which she proved not by words only, but by deeds; among other instances, when she was about to leave the world. . . . This only I will add, that though she chose me as her director to hear her confessions and to guide her life, yet I gladly confess that I learned more from her great virtue than ever I could teach her.[8]

It is difficult to give exact dates for John Fisher's residence in the Lady Margaret's household. He succeeded William de Melton as Master of Michaelhouse in 1497, the same year in which her confessor, Richard FitzJames became Bishop of Rochester. The early biography states

---

[7] *Ortroy*, p. 88.

[8] 1 *Letters of Richard Fox*, pp. 153-4.

that "he resigned the mastership of Michael-house and left the University for that time" in order to enter the Lady Margaret's household. He was appointed vice-chancellor of his university in July 1501, and the duties of that position would not have permitted much absence. If we allow two to three years for his mastership of Michaelhouse, the year 1500 seems the most likely for his period as spiritual director to the Lady Margaret.

Another problem of chronology is posed by John Fisher's later references to his great indebtedness to Richard Fox who "had taken so affectionate an interest in me." He was at least twenty years older than John Fisher, and was lord privy seal throughout the reign of Henry VII. He spent much of his time in diplomatic negotiations, and at the end of 1494, the year of John Fisher's attendance on the court at Greenwich, he became Bishop of Durham. He had previously held the sees of Exeter and of Bath and Wells, neither of which had he even visited. His appointment to Durham was more a political than an ecclesiastical move, and he lived in the north for about six years to deal with the Scots. In 1500 he succeeded Bishop Blythe as Chancellor of Cambridge University, and in the following year he exchanged Durham for Winchester, but it was not until 1517 that he resigned the privy seal and decided at last to devote himself to his long neglected duties as a bishop. From 1509 to 1519 he was Master of Pembroke, but he could rarely have been in residence.

His love of learning is shown in his munificent foundation of Corpus Christi College, Oxford, to which he devoted his declining years.

Such a crowded life would seem to have left little time for any close association between the statesman-bishop and the young scholar of Michaelhouse who had no ambitions for a political career. Richard Whitford, "the wretch of Syon,"⁹ may supply one link. He was a fellow of Queens' College about 1495, and later became chaplain to Fox. The puzzle of time and opportunity must remain. John Fisher's tribute, however, is so positive that it cannot be doubted that Richard Fox was his patron and influenced his career to an even greater extent than the Lady Margaret herself.

---

⁹ *Roper*, p. 8, tells a story of Fox, Thomas More and Whitford that is not to the credit of the Bishop.

CHAPTER III
THE PREACHER

IT might have been expected that the Lady Margaret's munificence and patronage would find their natural outlet in promoting the welfare of such royal foundations as Eton College, or King's College and Queens' College at Cambridge, or in furthering her son's plans for a new chapel at Westminster. Her devotion to the memory of Henry VI might well have been the deciding factor in her consideration when she thought of how best she could use her great wealth. The fact that she followed a different course was entirely due to the influence of John Fisher.

A common purpose can be traced in the projects he commended to her; he wished to promote the study of theology and to raise the standard of preaching. He recognized two weaknesses in the state of the Church; few priests, and even few bishops, were theologians or had a sound grounding in the "queen of sciences". There had also been a decline in the art and practice of preaching and teaching amongst the secular clergy. In far too many parishes there was need for careful instruction in the faith.

It was these ordinary parishioners that John Fisher had in mind; he was not thinking of academic scholarship as an end in itself; but he hoped that, gradually, the secular clergy would be more fitted for their high calling.

On 8th September, 1503, the Nativity of our Lady, readerships in divinity were instituted at Oxford and Cambridge by the Lady Margaret with lands granted for this purpose to the Abbot and Chapter of Westminster. These yielded an annual sum of £27 13s. 4d., half of which was to be paid to each university. Dr. John Fisher was the first Lady Margaret Reader at Cambridge, and Dr. John Roper at Oxford.

By the terms of the foundation, the reader was elected biennially by the chancellor, doctors and regents; he was obliged to read and expound daily to all who attended such works of divinity as the university authorities selected. No fee could be charged as his salary of £13 6s. 8d. was considered sufficient; it compared favourably with other incomes at the universities. There were strict regulations limiting the number of days on which reading could be omitted; even part of the long vacation was included in the required period; during Lent the reader was allowed, with the approval of the chancellor, to preach instead of reading. Periodically the terms of the foundation were to be read publicly (as the Lady Margaret's own household regulations were read), and certain psalms and collects were to be said for the souls of the foundress and her relatives; so too she was to be remembered in all Masses said by the reader.

Such detailed regulations were typical of John Fisher's methods; he tried to forestall any temptation to laxity or neglect. To us such conditions may seem too restrictive, but they are a measure of the state into which the University had fallen.

In the following year, 1504, the Lady Margaret founded and endowed a chantry in the University of Cambridge for the maintenance of a preacher. He had to preach six sermons annually at Paul's Cross or at St. Margaret's, Westminster, and once during the two years of his appointment at each of the churches of Ware and Cheshunt in Hertfordshire, Bassingbourn, Orwell, and Babraham in Cambridgeshire, Maxey, St. James Deeping, St. John Deeping, Bourn, Boston and Swineshead in

Lincolnshire. All these places were associated with the Lady Margaret; some were her manors, of others she owned the advowsons and some were near monasteries of which she was the benefactress. The preacher had to be an unbeneficed priest, a perpetual Fellow of a college, and to be either a bachelor or doctor of divinity. His annual stipend of £10 was to be paid from endowments given by the Lady Margaret to the monastery at Westminster.

It was in connexion with this endowment that Henry VII wrote to his mother:

> By your confessor the bearer [Fisher] I have received your good and most loving writing, and by the same have heard at good leisure such credence as he would show unto me on your behalf, and thereupon have sped him in every behalf without delay according to your noble petition and desire, which resteth in two principal parts; the one for a general pardon for all manner causes; the other is for to alter and change part of a licence which I had given unto you before to be put unto mortmain at Westminster, and now to be converted unto the University of Cambridge for your soul health. All which things according to your desire and pleasure I have with all my heart and good will given and granted unto you.[1]

John Fisher's concern for the increase of good preaching was also shown by the Papal Bull obtained in 1502 during his vice-chancellorship (Bishop Richard Fox being chancellor) which granted the privilege to the University of appointing "twelve Doctors, Masters, or Graduates, who shall be in Priest's Orders, to preach throughout the whole kingdom of England, Scotland, and

---

[1] Cooper, *Lady Margaret*, p. 91.

Ireland, under the common seal of the University, without any other licence from a Bishop." It is stated in the Bull that it was granted at the request of Dr. John Fisher. A licence granted under this privilege by John Fisher in 1522 makes it clear that the last phrase "without any other licence from a Bishop" did not mean freedom to preach anywhere; the consent of the bishop of the diocese and of the rector of the parish had to be obtained.

John Fisher was not the man to advocate for others what he himself refrained from doing; he was a preacher and teacher all his life. Fortunately a series of sermons he preached on the Penitential Psalms were published[2] at the request of the Lady Margaret before whom they had been preached. She had asked him to write them down so that they could reach a wider audience. In the published form these sermons are printed as if preached on seven occasions, but a closer examination shows that the central three were each divided into two parts, giving ten sermons in Each lasted about an hour and a half. They were preached on Sundays in August and September 1508; in the first part of the third, the Psalm was used as the basis for a sermon on the Nativity of our Lady.

The Penitential Psalms are numbered 6, 31, 37, 50, 101, 129 and 142 in the Vulgate.[3] The designation of this group as "Penitential" goes back to at least the sixth century, and it was on these that St. Augustine meditated in his last days. They were an accepted form of devotion throughout the Middle Ages and were included in the Primers that were amongst the earliest and most popular productions of the printing press. St. Thomas More recited them daily,

---

[2] Printed by Wynkyn de Worde, 12th June, 1509. It was a popular book, being reprinted seven times between 1509 and 1530.

[3] In modern editions, 6, 32, 38, 51, 102, 130, 143.

and the Lady Margaret evidently felt a similar devotion to them when she asked John Fisher to expound them to her household.

The form adopted is of interest. The preacher probably had in mind the *Enarrationes in Psalmos of St. Augustine*, but he did not follow this pattern closely, for instead of first giving a running commentary followed by a sermon, he combined both commentary and sermon in one discourse, weaving the two together with considerable skill. All the verses of each Psalm are quoted in their right sequence, first in Latin and then in translation or by paraphrase in the vernacular in which the sermons were given.

As an example his translation-paraphrase of the *De Profundis* is here pieced together.

1. *Lord I have cried to thee from my very heart-root.*
2. *I beseech thee, hear my voice. Good Lord, I beseech thee, give heed to the voice of my prayer with the ears of thy pity and mercy.*
3. *Lord, if thou bear in mind our sins and will not forgive us, who may keep him from despair?*
4. *The ordinance of his law cannot withstand nor fear us ever to have forgiveness if we ask it.*
5. *My soul is succoured from despair by steadfast hope and trust in the promise of almighty God.*
6. *The hope and trust of my soul is all whole in our Lord.*
7. *Every true penitent trust in our Lord both early and late.*
8. *For the mercy of God is infinite; our redemption is performed to the uttermost.*
9. *He shall make every penitent person partaker of his redemption.*

The fourth verse is a good example of John Fisher's paraphrase method. In his exposition he interprets "Israel" as "the penitent." The simplicity of the wording will be noted.

These sermons do not rigidly follow the schemes laid down in medieval treatises on preaching. There is a bidding prayer at the opening of the first sermon.

> I beseech thee, almighty God, for his great mercy and pity, so to help me this day by his grace that whatever I shall say may first be to his pleasure to the profit of mine own wretched soul, and also for the wholesome comfort to all sinners which be repentant for their sins and hath turned themselves with all their whole heart and mind unto God, the way of wickedness and sin utterly forsaken.[4]

Apart from this prayer, there are few traces of the medieval style of sermon. There are no elaborate rhetorical devices, nor is the meaning forced into strange shapes, "Allegorik, tropologik, anagogik."[5]

John Fisher preached as St. Augustine did, out of the Bible, and his regular hearers must have become familiar with the Scriptures from the numerous quotations he used. Two verses from the Hymn for the Feast of St. Augustine, might be applied to John Fisher himself.

> *Frangis nobis favos mellis*
> *De Scripturis disserens.*

---

[4] *E.W.*, p.2.

[5] G. R. Owst, *Preaching in Medieval England* (1926), p. 312. See also Charles Smyth, *The Art of Preaching* (1940).

THE PREACHER

Quae obscura prius erant
Nobis plana faciens.

Tu de verbis Salvatoris
Dulcem panem conficis,
Et propinas potum vitae
De Psalmorum nectare.[6]

In this series of sermons there are, apart from the Psalms, some one hundred and sixty quotations from the Bible; forty of these come from the Old Testament; sixty from the Gospels, forty of which give the words of Christ, and fifty-five from the Epistles, including thirty-six from St. Paul. In addition the preacher recounted the parables of the Good Samaritan, and of the Prodigal Son, and the story of the meeting between Jesus and the woman of Samaria. Bible incidents are used as illustrations, such as the story of David and Goliath, and of Jonas.

Quotations from the Fathers and Schoolmen are not numerous. It is significant that the most frequently quoted is St. Augustine (ten times), followed by St. Jerome (four times); others are St. John Chrysostom (three times), St. Anselm and William of Auvergne (twice), with one quotation from Origen, and from St. Thomas Aquinas. Of classical writers, Demosthenes is twice quoted, and there are single references to Cicero, to Plato (*Gorgias*), and to Ovid.

Such lists may give the impression that these sermons were overloaded with quotations. It should be remembered that frequent use of sentences from the

---

[6] You break for us the honeycomb in expounding the Scriptures, making plain what was at first obscure. You offer us sweet bread from the words of the Saviour and give us the drink of life from the nectar of the Psalms."

Scriptures was an important part of the accepted method of instruction in times when comparatively few could read and when manuscripts and printed books were expensive. The skill with which John Fisher wove together these several strands in his exposition can be appreciated only by a full reading; extracts would fail to bring out the art of the preacher.

The general theme of the sermons is sin, repentance, and the mercy of God. There is inevitably some repetition as the seven Psalms suggest similar themes, but this would not be so obvious to a listener attending from Sunday to Sunday as it is to us if we read the sermons as a whole. Even so, it does not become tedious as the preacher varies his treatment and brings in fresh illustrations of the points he wishes to make. While he warns us of the perils of hell in plain terms, the predominant note is his emphasis on the boundless mercy of God to all who truly repent of their sins.

John Fisher's style has been rightly praised for its "craftsman-like methods of work."[7] It lacks, however, the range of St. Thomas More's prose with its light touches of humour and flashes of wit. The occasional similitudes are not far-fetched but call to mind familiar things—millstones, sore eyes, mending a clock, or the snaring of birds.

What may seem comic was to his hearers matter-of-fact. We may smile as we read this account of how to capture monkeys.

> Like as men say apes be taken by hunters by doing on shoes, for the property of an ape is to do as he seeth a man do. The hunter therefore will lay a pair of shoes in his way, and when he perceiveth the hunter

---

[7] George Saintsbury, *Short History of English Literature*, p. 212. 79.

doing on his shoes he will do the same, and so after that it is too hard for him to leap and climb from tree to tree as he was wont, but falleth down, and anon is taken.[8]

That would be accepted by his hearers as a piece of established natural history.

The special congregation to which these sermons were addressed would have appreciated the following commendation of the use of the Psalms.

> That these holy Psalms be like as letters of supplication the which we may give unto almighty God as ready movers and stirrers of his infinite mercy for us, shall be made open on this wise. If peradventure any person have a matter or business with the king's highness and in his cause greatly desire his goodness and pity, will he not shortly go unto some wise man in such matters and desire a letter of supplication for to be made diligently, whereby he may cause the king's pity in his business to be obtained and had. Truly his trust is not only in his own wisdom for to be so bold in handling his matter and to purpose it only by his own words or his own wit. We sinners be in like condition. For truly we have many matters in the high court of the most high king almighty God, for the which it should be profitable and necessary the pity of God to be purchased for us. And who is more wise in that court for our business to be sped, that is to say for forgiveness to be obtained, than is our prophet David that committed before the peril and danger of the same thing in himself. Verily he was a sinner as we be and a busy follower for

---

[8] E.W., p. 79.

forgiveness. With great diligence [he] made these holy Psalms which he daily offered up unto almighty God with great devotion as letters of supplication, by which he moved greatly his goodness for to forgive him. Therefore we knowing the virtue and efficacy of these holy Psalms, let us use them in our like business and doubt not to have forgiveness if we do it so lovingly as he did in his time.[9]

The simplicity of the language will at once be apparent to the reader. The phrasing is at times strange to our ears; stranger, indeed, than the style of St. Thomas More, but this may be explained by the fact that John Fisher was a Yorkshireman and Thomas More was a Londoner, and it is the London dialect that has determined our modern speech.

John Fisher carried out in practice his own desire that preaching should be in language understood by the ordinary people. Here are no displays of learning for learning's sake. The style is that of a deeply serious and devout man who wished to speak to the hearts of his congregation.

The early biographer of John Fisher wrote of his great "diligence in preaching the word of God; which custom he used not only in his younger days when health served, but also even to his extreme age, when many times his weary and feeble legs were not able to sustain his weak body standing, but forced him to have a chair and so to teach sitting."[10]

His everyday sermons were probably seldom written down in full, and it is to our loss that so few of them were

---

[9] *E. W.*, p. 73.

[10] *Ortroy*, p.99.

printed or have survived. His funeral sermons on Henry VII and on the Lady Margaret come within a different category; these must be considered separately. So too his sermon at Paul's Cross "against the pernicious doctrine of Martin Luther" calls for special treatment. A sermon "preached on a Good Friday" has also been preserved. There is no indication of when it was delivered. This discourse must have taken nearly three hours to deliver. Perhaps it is made up of two sermons, or was a long meditation for Good Friday. It is notable for an elaborate and somewhat strained analogy between the making of a manuscript book and the crucifixion of Christ, but its general characteristics are those of the sermons on the Penitential Psalms. Two sermons preached in 1520 will be considered in a later chapter.

CHAPTER IV
CHRIST'S COLLEGE

JOHN FISHER was already Chancellor of the University of Cambridge and Bishop of Rochester when he delivered his sermons on the Penitential Psalms. He was elected chancellor in 1504 and was re-elected each year until 1514 when, as will be seen, the unique distinction was conferred on him of being elected for life.

On 24th November 1504, he was consecrated Bishop of Rochester by Archbishop Warham at Lambeth. Two days later he was present in the Star Chamber as a member of the King's Council; this was probably his formal introduction.[1] Henceforth we must think of him as bishop, as chancellor of a university,[2] and as a member of the King's Council. He was installed in his cathedral by proxy on 24th April 1505 in the person of Dr. Thomas Head, Vicar-General.[3]

John Fisher acknowledged that he owed his preferment to Richard Fox, Bishop of Winchester. "You also," he wrote,

> recommended me to King Henry VII, who then, with the greatest prudence, held the reins of this kingdom, so that by the esteem he had for me from

---

[1] Cal. Pat. Rolls. *Henry VII*, II, p. 388.

[2] It may be noted that of the eight chancellors that followed John Fisher during the 16th century, four were executed.

[3] *Register*, f. 42r.

your frequent commendations, and of his own mere motion, without any obsequiousness on my part, without the intercession of any (as he more than once declared to me) he gave me the bishopric of Rochester, of which I am now the unworthy occupant. There are, perhaps, many who believe that his mother, the Countess of Richmond and Derby, that noble and incomparable lady, dear to me by so many titles, obtained the bishopric for me by her prayers to her son. But the facts are entirely different, as your lordship knows well.[4]

The king himself announced his decision in a letter to his mother.

> Madam,
> An' I thought I should not offend you, which I will never do wilfully, I am well minded to promote Master Fisher, your confessor, to a bishopric; and I assure you, Madam, for none other cause, but for the great and singular virtue that I know and see in him, as well in cunning [knowledge] and natural wisdom, and specially for his good and virtuous living and conversation. And by the promotion of such a man I know well it should encourage many others to live virtuously and to take such ways as he doth, which should be a good example to many others hereafter. Howbeit, without your pleasure known I will not move him nor tempt him therein. And therefore I beseech you that I may know your mind and pleasure in that behalf which shall be followed as much as God will give me grace. I have in my days promoted many a man unadvisedly, and I would now make some

---

[4] *Letters of Richard Fox*, pp. '53-4.

recompense to promote some good and virtuous men which I doubt not should best please God, who ever preserve you in good health and long life.[5]

Henry had reason to feel uneasy in his conscience when he recalled the grounds on which the appointments of bishops had been made since he won the throne. John Fisher recorded that, in his last illness, the king assured his confessor that "the promotions of the church that were of his disposition should from henceforth be disposed to able men such as were virtuous and well-learned."[6]

It has already been noted that the lack of effective preachers was one of the defects of the Church at this period; the want of pastoral bishops was an even more serious defect, for the state of the Church depends to a large extent on the care with which the bishops watch over the spiritual welfare of their people. Milton's lines, written more than a century later, applied to many of the bishops of the sixteenth century.

> *Blind mouths! that scarce themselves know how to hold*
> *A Sheep-hook, or have leaned ought else the least*
> *That to the faithful Herdman's art belongs . . .*
> *The hungry Sheep look up, and are not fed.*[7]

The Reformation had not reformed this abuse!

Of the sixteen bishops in 1504 when John Fisher was appointed, two were non-resident Italians, and of the others, seven were not theologians but canonists whose main concern was the ecclesiastical courts, and the

---

[5] Cooper, *Memoir*, pp. 95-6.

[6] E. W., p. 278.

[7] *Lycidas*, ll. 119-25.

majority were chiefly occupied with state duties as administrators or diplomatists. They were able men and, for the most part, decent living, and a few were patrons of learning. Some in their old age, or in disgrace, tried to make up for the lost years by going to live in the dioceses they may not have visited previously. They had been appointed for reasons of state and their incomes as bishops provided a simple means of rewarding them. Henry VIII followed his father's example, and not his father's belated resolution.

Rochester was the smallest and poorest diocese in England; the bishop's revenue was about 350 a year, a tenth of that received by the Bishop of Winchester. Rochester was regarded as the first rung of the episcopal ladder; Thomas Savage, for instance, was bishop there from 1492 to 1496, when he was translated to York; his successor at Rochester, Richard Fitzjames, was translated to Chichester in 1504 and to London in 1506. John Fisher, had the opportunity been offered him, might have later accepted a more valuable see. In the preamble to his statutes for St. John's College, Cambridge, he stated that

> the noble princess, Lady Margaret, Countess of Richmond, the foundress of this college, in her great condescension had a great desire to procure me a richer bishopric. But when she saw that her approaching death would frustrate this desire, she left me a no small sum of money to use for my own purposes, which I mention lest anyone think that I have made this large endowment with other people's money.[8]

---

[8] J. E. B. Mayor, *Statutes of St. John's College* (1859), p. 238.

During the remaining years of Henry VII's reign, only three bishoprics fell vacant, and these were within two years of John Fisher's appointment to Rochester. Between the accession of Henry VIII and John Fisher's death, there were sixteen vacancies, but there is no record of the Bishop of Rochester having been considered for translation to a greater see. Perhaps he was not regarded with favour by Henry VIII even in the halcyon years of the reign, or was it Wolsey's opposition that barred the way? It would be difficult to think of two men more antithetic in their conceptions of the good life. John Fisher lacked the art of self-advancement, and he was more at home in the university than at court.

Two Cambridge colleges, Christ's College, and St. John's, look back with gratitude to the services he rendered them in their foundations. Here we are concerned with Christ's College.

By an indenture dated 22nd February 1525, the Master and Fellows of Christ's College accepted an endowment from John Fisher for Masses and prayers for his soul and for the souls of his parents. The preamble of the deed contains these sentences:

> Whereas the reverent Father and Lord in Christ Lord John Fisher by divine favour Bishop of Rochester of his own mere motion and pious liberality of mind or rather by divine instinct and paternal affection has by his counsels and exhortations caused this College of Christ to be instituted by our excellent Foundress . . and has aided by his assistance and resources in its erection and completion and has advanced adorned and embellished it in all ways in which he was able as

well as by establishing laws and institutes of right living as by acquiring and confirming estates ....[9]

Here are three statements; John Fisher persuaded the Lady Margaret to bestow her wealth on the College; he made its statutes, and he himself added to its endowments.

The history of Christ's College begins with the decision of William Byngham, Rector of St. John Zachery, London, to establish a college at Cambridge for the purpose of providing masters in grammar for schools. In 1448 he was granted a charter by Henry VI for the foundation of the College of Godshouse. Hopes that the king would sufficiently endow the college were not fulfilled; the unhappy king's troubled reign defeated many of his dearest wishes. The college struggled along but was not, as has been said, in desperate straits. When the need for further development became urgent, it was natural to turn to Henry VI's near relative, the Lady Margaret Beaufort, "heir to all King Henry's godly intensions."

John Syclyn, the Proctor or Master of Godshouse, found a warm advocate in his friend John Fisher, and it was through his influence that the Lady Margaret's bounty was bestowed on Godshouse. In 1501 John Fisher was vice-chancellor and John Syclyn was senior proctor, and, as we have seen, both were frequently with the Lady Margaret at that period when her mediation was being sought in the university-town dispute.

All the records of her various transactions show that she was what we should call a good business-woman. She insisted on careful inquiries before making any decisions. The information obtained was considered by her and her

---

[9] H. Rackham, *Early Statutes of Christ's College* (1927), p. 127. The remainder of this chapter is based upon A. H. Lloyd, *Early History of Christ's College* (1934).

council of which John Fisher was the leading member from about 1502. The composition of that council reflects her own disposition; it included the Masters of two colleges and the future Master of another; another member was Hugh Oldham, known to us as the founder of Manchester Grammar School.

The letters patent of Henry VII, dated 1st May 1505, gave permission for the development of Godshouse with a change of name to "Christ's College in the University of Cambridge by Henry the sixth King of England first begun and after his decease by Margaret Countess of Richmond Mother of King Henry and seventh augmented finished and stablished." The name was changed at the desire of the Lady Margaret "on account of her singular devotion to the most glorious and most holy name of Jesus Christ." These letters patent required the acceptance of the Master and Fellows of Godshouse before they could be effective; the necessary legal process was completed by 3rd October 1506.

It is impossible to say what part any one person had in framing the statutes; John Fisher, in spite of the later commendation from the Master and Fellows, was not solely responsible for the statutes. It is reasonable to suggest that certain provisions were included at the wish of the Lady Margaret herself; John Fisher was to have the use of her rooms in the college; he was to be visitor for life; a woman nurse was to be engaged; provision was to be made in case of plague; and there were domestic details that would probably not have occurred to the academic mind. Some of the statutes which were formerly ascribed to John Fisher as innovations, have now been shown to have been taken from William Byngham's provisions for Godshouse. The appointment of a regular college lecturer, for instance, was an existing requirement; so too the inclusion of the "study of the poets and orators of antiquity" can be found in the earlier Godshouse statutes. Erasmus himself has been credited with the last requirement in the Christ's Church statutes, but there is no evidence that he had any voice in the matter.

One unusual provision may have been directly due to John Fisher. The Master had to give his bond "for observing the Foundresses Statutes, by not procuring or causing to be procured, or not using when procured, any Dispensation from the Apostolic See, or (as much as in him was) not suffering his Fellows to make them." John Fisher evidently regarded this bond as important for he included a similar safeguard in the later statutes of St. John's for which he was responsible. The bond was designed to prevent abuses such as had often led in the past to the modification of statutes and even to their abrogation. Thus the wishes of founders and benefactors had often been set aside. The scandal was recognized by all earnest churchmen and scholars, but effective remedies had not been applied. John Fisher was evidently determined that the statutes for which he had some responsibility should not be evaded in this manner.

The portrait of him that emerges so far is that of a scholar and preacher who had the gift of government and the strength of will to impose discipline in studies and conduct. He had won the trust and confidence of those older than himself; they valued his prudent judgment and his lack of self-interest. His outlook, however, was not limited to university life; he saw beyond that the spiritual needs of ordinary folk; his desire was to educate priests and teachers who could minister to those needs as devoted pastors. He was not a radical reformer; his cast of mind was conservative. He built on well-proved foundations, retaining what was sound in the past but rejecting what had proved defective. As we have seen, some of the statutes that have been thought to be his innovations, have proved to be of older date. He recognized the good work of his predecessors and made it part of the fabric which was under his care. He made his own contributions to the building and did not refuse new materials if they seemed likely to be serviceable.

The tragedy was that time was against him; the too-long delayed reform of abuses and scandals in the Church had created a spirit of impatience and agitation that was to prove calamitous.

Bishop—chancellor—councilor—"What time," asked the early biographer, "can you think was left him to pray or to write?" No detailed answer is given to this question, but, as the same writer noted, there were many time-wasting usages that John Fisher avoided.

> For who had at any time seen him idle, walk or wander abroad? When did he frequent the courts and houses of princes and noblemen to the intent (as the old proverb saith) to see and be seen? Where did he use to banquet and feast?
> What noble men or others hath he for pleasure invited? What company hath used to resort unto him for idle talk and driving away of time? Whom hath he excluded from him that in any wise he might profit? If you will call that man occupied that is still occupied in worldly business, then cannot that be verified in him, for he lived most commonly alone, calling himself to a daily account of his life, using the church as a cloister and his study as a cell.[10]

---

[10] *Ortroy*, p. 97.

CHAPTER V
THREE PANEGYRICS

ON 12th April 1505, the Fellows of Queens' College, Cambridge, wrote to their president, Dr. Thomas Wilkinson, accepting his resignation and announcing that they were "fully determined" to elect in his place the Lord Bishop of Rochester. They referred to a letter from "the most excellent princess my Lady the king's mother" in which she had proposed this appointment.[1] Dr. Wilkinson had been an easy-going and frequently absent president, and the lack of warmth in the Fellows' letter may have been due to a fear that the new president would require of them a closer attention to their duties.

The Lady Margaret had a natural interest in the college; one of the queens associated with it was Margaret of Anjou, the wife of Henry VI.

Since he had resigned from Michaelhouse in 1502, John Fisher had had no official residence at Cambridge, and this appointment to Queens' College may have been made so that he could more closely watch the building of Christ's College. The old Godshouse buildings were not adequate for the larger foundation, but they were incorporated in the new plans.[2] The three years during which John Fisher was president of Queens' saw the building of the president's lodge, the first floor rooms of which were for the Lady Margaret's own use, and, in her absence, for John Fisher himself.

---

[1] *Lewis*, II, p. 260.

[2] *Lloyd*, Chap. XVIII.

When the Lady Margaret visited Cambridge in 1505 she was met by the chancellor and other university dignitaries at Caxton, and escorted to Queens' College where she lodged. This visit cost the University sixty shillings and twopence, while the college spent one shilling and fivepence in preparing her lodging. The last item suggests that her rooms must have been in good condition as so little was needed to get them ready for her. It may have been on this visit that she thought of making Queens' the residence of John Fisher.

On the 22nd April of that year, the king with his son Henry also lodged at the college while on a pilgrimage to Our Lady of Walsingham. As this was the eve of the feast of St. George, the king in his Garter robes went to the unfinished chapel at King's College for solemn vespers. On the next day the chancellor, Bishop Fisher, officiated at High Mass. The king remained at Cambridge for a few days and listened to the disputations in the schools. John Fisher later said "that this visit had not been a mere formality but was of some length, such an honour as no one, king, prince, lord or even knight had ever before paid the University."[3] This was done, as John Fisher, believed, in order to encourage students to apply themselves with greater enthusiasm to their studies. Before he left, the king gave a banquet to the members of the University.

He returned the next year with his mother and Prince Henry for Commencement. This was held in the old Grey Friars church; the Latin oration was delivered by John Fisher. Two quotations have already been given from this panegyric.[4] The orator surveyed the events of the king's life and extolled his temperance, prudence and wisdom.

---

[3] *Lewis*, II, p. 270.

[4] See above, pp. 11 and 20, and previous paragraph.

"So greatly is your wisdom to be admired that not only do we your subjects marvel, but indeed all foreign princes, kings and the governors of all nations, strive which of them shall be the most intimate, the most closely allied, and the most united in friendship." The chancellor went on to review the benefits conferred on the University by the king's predecessors and praised his generosity to it and his interest in its welfare. "May God grant to thee great king, long, happy and prosperous days, and that your son here present, an illustrious prince and worthy of such a father, may succeed you on the throne, that your family may increase, that your nobles may be dutiful, your soldiers loving, your people obedient; may your friends honour you, your enemies fear you, your allies prove constant. May you suffer no sickness on earth, and in heaven may you have everlasting happiness."

The hope that son would succeed father would not be regarded as a tactless remark to make in front of the king; to establish a strong reigning dynasty was one of his earnest desires; the Tudor wish for male heirs was to prove the cause of many troubles.

This oration may seem somewhat fulsome to us in its praise of the king, but it was not all flattery for which Henry had little liking. On a similar occasion he asked the Archbishop of Dublin, Walter Fitzsimons, what he thought of the unctious address they had just heard. "Excellent, saving that I think he flattered your majesty too much." "In good faith," said the king, "we are greatly of that opinion ourselves."

Whatever their thoughts may have been when John Fisher was made their president, the Fellows of Queens' were distressed to receive his letter of resignation in June 1508; it was, they said, "to the right heaviness of them all," and they asked him to nominate a successor. "The

Bishop," they wrote, "was a man that, without flattery, was very dear to them all, not only on account of his ingenuous humanity, but for his excellent learning and prudence."[5]

Henry VII died at Richmond on 21st April 1509, and on 9th May at St. Paul's, John Fisher preached the funeral sermon, "the body being present", at the request of the Lady Margaret who afterwards had it printed by Wynkyn de Worde.

The sermon was of about an hour's length; of this time some twenty minutes were devoted to the dead king; the panegyric itself occupied only a few minutes; far more time was given to a description of the king's repentance, "a true turning of his soul from the wretched world unto the love of Almighty God."

The brief "laud and commendation" of the king reads:

> Let no man think that mine intent is for to praise him for any vain transitory things of this life, which by the example of him, all kings and princes may learn how sliding, how slippery, how failing they be. Albeit he had as much of them as was possible in manner for any king to have, his politic wisdom in governaunce it was singular, his wit always quick and ready, his reason pithy and substantial, his memory fresh and holding, his experience notable, his counsels fortunate and taken by wise deliberation, his speech gracious in divers languages, his person goodly and aimiable, his natural complexion of the purest mixture, his issue fair and in good number, leagues and confederacies he had with all Christian princes, his mighty power was dread everywhere, not only within his realm but without also, his people were to him in as humble subjection as

---

[5] *Lewis*, I, p. 26.

ever they were to king, his land many a day in peace and tranquility, his prosperity in battle against his enemies was marvellous, his dealing in time of perils and dangers was cold and sober with great hardness. If any treason was conspired against him it came out wonderfully, his treasure and riches incomparable, his buildings most goodly and after the newest cast all of pleasure. But what is all this now as unto him, all be but *fumus et umbra*, a smoke that soon vanisheth and a shadow soon passing away. Shall I praise him then for them? Nay forsooth.[6]

John Fisher here selected those characteristics of Henry that historians of a later age have recognized as his distinctive qualities. Indeed one authority has recently suggested that Henry VII "has some claim to be regarded as the greatest of the Tudors."

Apart from this short passage, the sermon might be described as a pendant to the series on the Penitential Psalms. The text was the 114th[7] Psalm, and again the preacher called up the figure of David, "albeit he had been an adulterer and murderer, yet with one word speaking, his heart was changed saying, *Peccavi*." It may seem a strange theme for such an occasion, but it was certainly in the tradition of the medieval church. Nor did the preacher hesitate to point the moral to his listeners.

Ah, my lords and masters that have this worldly wisdom, that study and employ your wits to cast and compass this world, what have ye of all this business at the last but a little vanity. The spider craftily spinneth her threads and curiously weaveth and joineth her web, but

---

[6] *E.W.*, p. 269

[7] *Modern Editions*, no. 116

cometh a little blast of wind and disappointeth all together.

Perhaps the warning did not reach the ears of those who most needed it, for, during the sermon, some of the mourners took the opportunity to refresh themselves."[8]

Henry's will was as business-like as his life; it provided for many works of charity and included large bequests for the completion of King's College, Cambridge, and for his new chapel at Westminster.

The Lady Margaret did not long survive her son. She was present at the coronation of her grandson and his queen, Catherine of Aragon; she died on 29th June 1509. Henry VII and his mother were both buried in the chapel at Westminster.

John Fisher was one of her executors. She left him as a personal gift "a pair of gilt pots compassed about like a hoop graven with portcullis and marguerites; a small salt of gold covered, chased chevron-wise, garnished with pearls and on the height of the cover resteth a sapphire."

A month after her death, John Fisher preached a commemorative sermon. This too was printed[9] by Wynkyn de Worde; he thriftily used the same woodcut as for the funeral sermon of Henry VII by cutting out the portion showing the body of the king and substituting a coffin covered with a pall and with four guttering candles at the corners. The bishop is shown in his mitre and with crossed stole.

This sermon is almost entirely a panegyric in which the preacher likened the Lady Margaret to "the blessed woman Martha," basing his remarks on the gospel of the commemorative Mass said on the thirtieth day after a

---

[8] *L. P.*, I, 20.

[9] *E. W.*, pp. 289-310. The editor incorrectly gives the text as Luke x, 38-9.

funeral, St. John xi, 21-27, the conversation of Martha and Jesus before the raising of Lazarus.

The comparison is at times rather strained; thus "the blessed Martha was a woman of noble blood to whom by inheritance belonged the castle of Bethany."

In spite of this tendency to force a parallel, the sermon gives a convincing portrait of a great woman by one who knew her intimately in her later years. It is not an oratorical performance such as Bossuet achieved in the next century in his *oraisons funèbres* on less admirable women.. There is no glowing rhetoric nor is the meaning obscured by far-fetched figures of speech or by the devices of the schools. A short passage will illustrate the style, which, plain as it is in wording, has the grace of a deeply felt tribute.

> All England for her death had cause of weeping. The poor creatures that were wont to receive her alms, to whom she was always piteous and merciful. The students of both universities to whom she was as a mother. All the learned men of England to whom she was a very patroness. All the virtuous and devout persons to whom she was as a loving sister, all the good religious men and women whom she so often was wont to visit and comfort. All good priests and clerks to whom she was a true defendress. All the noble men and women to whom she was a mirror and exemplar of honour. All the common people of this realm for whom she was in their causes a common mediatrix, and took right great displeasure for them, and generally the whole realm hath cause to complain and to mourn her death.

54   THE LIFE OF ST. JOHN FISHER

The contrast between the commemoration of Henry VII and that of the Lady Margaret is striking. The first placed emphasis on the need for penitence; it was as if, while recognizing the great qualities of Henry and his right disposition at death, the preacher refrained from noting some of the less admirable characteristics of the king. There is no hint of any such reservation in his eulogy of the Lady Margaret, and all that is recorded of her confirms the estimate of her life as here given by her former confessor.

II - Lady Margaret Beaufort,
Countess of Richmond and Derby

III - Lady Margaret Tomb
Westminster Abbey

CHAPTER VI
ERASMUS

IT is not known when John Fisher and Erasmus first met. The bishop was not closely connected with the group of scholars who have been misleadingly called "The Oxford Reformers." Until he became Bishop of Rochester in 1504, his adult life was spent at Cambridge or in attendance on the Lady Margaret. University affairs took him to London from time to time, but there are no indications that he was brought into contact with such scholars as Grocyn, or John Colet, or with the much younger Thomas More. His chosen manner of life did not allow for easy social relations outside the needs of his work. When he became Bishop of Rochester and a member of the King's Council as well as chancellor of his university, his standing was advanced in the eyes of all who, like Erasmus, were looking for patrons.

It seems unlikely that the two men formed a close acquaintanceship during the first visit to England by Erasmus in the last half of 1499. Much of that time was spent by him either at Lord Mountjoy's house, or at Oxford. There is, however, a possibility that Erasmus brought an introduction from his pupil in Paris, Robert Fisher (d. 1511), who is described as a cousin (kinsman) of John Fisher.

When Erasmus returned to England towards the end of 1505 there were more opportunities for meeting the Bishop of Rochester and it was during this period that they became acquainted. This may have come about through the services of Richard Whitford. In 1498 he had received permission to be absent from Queens' College in order to go to Paris as chaplain to Lord Mountjoy who there became the devoted pupil of Erasmus. By about 1505, Richard Whitford had become chaplain to Richard Fox, Bishop of Winchester, one of the most influential councilors of Henry VII. Erasmus was probably introduced to Fox by Whitford. Two letters written by Erasmus at the end of 1505 are addressed "At London, from the bishop's palace." Which bishop? There is nothing to connect Erasmus with William Barnes, Bishop of London, who died in October 1505; the see was vacant for ten months. John Fisher's palace was by Lambeth Marsh; from his register we know that he was at his manor at Bromley towards the end of December 1505 and in January 1506. This does not exclude the possibility that he may have been at Lambeth Marsh before that period, but he was also very busy at this time with Cambridge affairs. Richard Fox, however, was more frequently in London, so it was probably from his palace that Erasmus wrote. Is it a misreading of his character to feel that he would be more drawn to the powerful and wealthy bishop than to the relatively impecunious Bishop of Rochester?

Erasmus was certainly at Cambridge at least once, possibly twice during this period. He was entered at Queens' College as a pensioner of Henry VII sometime between August 1505 and April 1506.[1] Here perhaps we may see the influence of Richard Fox, and the choice of College suggests either Bishop Fisher who was then Master, or Richard Whitford. Dr. John Caius, who became a student of Gonvile College in 1529, recorded a tradition that Erasmus was present when Henry VII visited Cambridge for the Feast of St. George in 1506. This seems possible as Erasmus had applied for admission to the Doctor's degree before Easter of that year. Presumably he

---

[1] *Allen*, I, Ap. VI.

planned to go into residence, but an opportunity of getting to Italy made him give up this intention, and he left England in June 1506.²

So far the indications of any association between him and John Fisher are meagre and any conclusions must be speculative.

The third visit of Erasmus from about June 1511 to July 1514 tells another story. Richard Fox, high in the council of the young king, was a fellow executor with John Fisher of the Lady Margaret, and this must have brought them together frequently, though the main part of the responsibility was left to Bishop Fisher. Erasmus had an exaggerated idea of the funds at John Fisher's disposal and this may have raised his expectations; his motives were not always above reproach, but one thing is clear; when he came to know John Fisher he recognized in him a man of holy life and he regarded him with a respect that he rarely paid to any man.

Erasmus arrived in London towards the end of June 1511 and an almost fatal attack of the sweating sickness kept him there for some weeks. He was in residence at Queens' College by 24th August when he dated a letter from there to John Colet.³ In this he wrote, "I see before me the footprints of Christian poverty. There is so little hope of profit that I realise I shall have to use up whatever I have extracted from my patrons." Caution should be used in accepting at their face value any reference made by Erasmus to poverty; the tradition grew up that he was in serious straits at Cambridge, but there is no evidence of this. He was paid by the University for lectures in Greek

---

² It was on this occasion that the officials at Dover confiscated the scholar's money, a proceeding that before 1939 seemed harsh, but we are now accustomed to such happenings.

³ *Allen*, I, no. 225.

and he had an allowance from Lord Mountjoy. He had good rooms in the college, probably part of the Master's lodging; later he decided to move into the town and lived in the house of a bookseller named Garrett. Nor need too much concern be felt at his grumblings: the bad beer, the draughty rooms, the incivilities of the people (his English was rudimentary), and the dishonesties of carriers: all these and similar complaints were part of his established behaviour; he had a cat-like ability to make himself comfortable. More serious was the outbreak of plague that drove him into the country for a time.

A letter to John Colet written a month[4] later announced that Erasmus had begun to translate Basil on Isaias. "I am going to show a specimen to the Bishop of Rochester, and see if he is prepared to lighten my labours with a small reward." John Fisher however showed no enthusiasm for the project.

A direct request for financial help at the end of 1511 brought the following reply from the Bishop.[5]

> Greetings to you, Erasmus. I beg you, don't be too offended that I did not write when I sent to you recently. The messenger was in a hurry to leave town, and I met him just as I was going out. So, as I was unable to write, I gave him the small gift you asked for; it was not, however, from the fund you assume to be at my disposal and to be of some size. Believe me, Erasmus, whatever may be said, I have no funds that I can use at my sole discretion. The use of that money is restricted and cannot be varied just as we wish. I feel that you are so much needed in our University that I

---

[4] *Allen*, I, no. 227.

[5] *Allen*, I, no. 242.

will not let you be in want as long as there is anything to spare out of my own modest resources. At the same time, I will do all I can, whenever an opportunity comes, to beg help from others when my own means are insufficient. Your Mountjoy, nay, mine also, will I am sure remember you if he has promised to do so, and I will gladly encourage him since he is now at court. The best of health, Erasmus. From London.

Probably Erasmus thought that a grant could be made to him out of the funds bequeathed by the Lady Margaret.

It has been said that Erasmus was Lady Margaret Professor of Divinity; there is, however, no evidence of this beyond the fact that at the end of 1511 he undertook to lecture on St. Jerome. Had he been receiving the stipend of £13 6s. 8d. in addition to his fees as lecturer in Greek, he could hardly have pleaded poverty. Moreover his absences from Cambridge made it impossible for him to observe the very strict requirements of the appointment. He was in London for a good part of 1512 and again early in 1513.

John Fisher invited Erasmus to accompany him to Rome in 1512 to attend the fifth Lateran Council. It had been decided that England should be represented at the Council by Silvestro de Gigli, Bishop of Worcester, who was already in Rome, and by John Fisher, Sir Thomas Docwra, Prior of St. John's and premier baron, and Richard Kidderminster, Abbot of Winchcombe. An allowance of £800 for one hundred and sixty days was granted.[6] Erasmus was unable to accept the invitation, but he wrote to friends of his at Rome to commend John Fisher to them. Thus to Thomas Halsey, English Penitentiary, he wrote;

---

[6] *L. P.,* I, I no. 1048.

Unless I am sadly mistaken, he is the one man at this time who is incomparable for uprightness of life, for learning, and for greatness of soul.[7]

The Council lasted from May 1512 to March 1517 with frequent intervals. John Fisher was again hoping to go in 1514, and had even appointed the Priors of Rochester and of Leeds (Kent) to act for him during his absence from the diocese.[8] Again he was disappointed; the reason for this change is not known.

It was on this occasion that John Fisher suggested that he should resign his position as Chancellor of Cambridge University. He had been re-elected regularly for ten years. He now suggested that the University should invite the Bishop of Lincoln (Thomas Wolsey) to become chancellor. Wolsey was now growing in power and his patronage would have been of great value to the University. It was with some reluctance that the University accepted John Fisher's suggestion. A letter was written to Wolsey who, however, declined the honour in terms of humility that read strangely out of tune with his pretensions. Perhaps it was in relief at this escape that the University at once elected John Fisher as chancellor for life, a unique distinction. Even when he was attainted and imprisoned, the University remained faithful to him and did not hasten to win favour by rejecting him in his time of trial.

England was represented at the Lateran Council only by the Italian Bishop of Worcester. The ineffectiveness of the Council was a tragedy; with determination it might have done much to reform the admitted abuses in the

---

[7] *Allen*, 1, no. 254; also, 242 and 253 for similar testimonials.

[8] *Lewis*, II, p. 286.

Church; its few notable decisions were stultified by the Medici Pope Leo X.

John Fisher and Erasmus probably saw little of each other at Cambridge. The bishop fulfilled his many obligations scrupulously. However much he may have preferred, as one may suspect, life in the University to life at the court, he could not reside regularly at Cambridge; the King's Council, Parliament and Convocation all made demands on his time. Overriding these duties there would be, for him, the paramount needs of his diocese, and, as we shall see, he was a pastoral bishop who devoted himself to his spiritual charge. In one respect he was fortunate; Rochester, London and Cambridge were within comfortable reach of one another, and the tall, gaunt figure of the bishop on his horse must have been a familiar sight on the roads linking the three towns.

The periods during which Erasmus was at Cambridge were not sufficiently continuous to admit of regular teaching. He rendered two services to the University; he established Greek as a subject of study, and he inspired a small band of students to devote themselves to that language.

The indications are that he received small encouragement from the older generation, and, it may be that without the support of the chancellor, the experiment would have collapsed. So little favour did he gain that an appeal had to be made in 1512 to Lord Mountjoy for help in paying the scholar's stipend.

While at Cambridge Erasmus was working on his edition of the New Testament in Greek with a new Latin translation, and on his edition of the works of St. Jerome. He also completed a book on Latin composition, *De Copia*, which he dedicated to John Colet who had suggested such a book for the use of his new school at St. Paul's; it became a widely used school text-book.

Erasmus left England in July 1514;[9] he was back again in May 155. John Fisher then wrote to him a letter in which he said, "When the time for your journey to Basle comes, do arrange to come here as I need your advice. I beg you not to let this slip your memory. Long may you be happy and healthy."[10] The letter was written at Hailing and is signed, "Tuus Io. Roffensis."

It is not known if the scholar accepted this invitation.

On his return to Basle, Erasmus saw his *Novum Instrumentum* (his edition of the New Testament) through the press; it was published in 1516. The Greek text was accompanied by a new translation into Latin. A copy must have been sent to John Fisher at once for in June of that year he wrote to give his first impressions.[11]

> Although I am up to the eyes in business—in fact I am just setting out for Cambridge for the opening of the College[12] [St. John's] which is at last to take place—I could not let your Peter [Meghen] return without a letter. You have put me greatly in your debt by the gift of your *Novum Instrumentum* translated from the Greek. As soon as I received it and had seen some of the notes in which you extol your Canterbury Maecenas [Warham] with many compliments, I hurried to him to show him these passages. When he had read them, he promised he would do much for

---

[9] When he left, John Fisher gave him a rose-noble: *Allen*, I, no. 295.

[10] *Allen*, II, no. 336.

[11] *Allen*, II, no. 432 (June 1516).

[12] Actually for the consecration of the restored chapel. The college had opened in the old buildings in 1511.

you, and begged me, if I should write to you, to urge you to return. Indeed I do not doubt if you do he will be more generous to you than ever.

The *Novum Instrumentum* prompted John Fisher at the age of, forty-eight to learn Greek. Erasmus himself gave him some preliminary instruction during a ten days' visit in August 1516 when he was again in England. He stayed at the bishop's Palace at Rochester. He grumbled "I have repented ten times over,"[13] but this seems to have been on account of the unhealthy site, as he regarded it. Writing some years later, Erasmus warned the bishop of the dangers. "The near approach of the tide, as well as the mud which is left at every ebb of the water, makes the climate unwholesome. Your library, too, is surrounded with glass windows which let the cold air through the crevices. I know how much time you spend in the library which is to you a very paradise. As for me, I could not live in such a place three hours without being ill."[14] One compensation for the stay at Rochester in 1516 was that Thomas More came down to see Erasmus. On this occasion at least we can picture the three friends together, each a remarkable man, two of them saints, and all three destined to leave imperishable names.

It is not known who supervised the bishop's further study of Greek. Both Erasmus and Thomas More did their best to persuade William Latimer, an eminent scholar who had studied in Italy, to become the bishop's tutor, but he had other engagements.[15] Erasmus did not frighten him off

---

[13] *Allen*, II, no. 452; letter to Ammonius; also no. 455.

[14] *Allen*, V, no. 1489.

[15] *Allen*, II, nos. 468, 520, 540. It may be noted that John Colet also decided to learn Greek at this time. *Allen*, II, no. 423.

by talking of the Medway mud! John Fisher certainly gained a working knowledge of Greek and in his turn encouraged its study at Cambridge.

A year later he gave a more considered verdict on the Erasmus version of the New Testament. This reads rather like a testimonial, as it may well have been, for Erasmus was gathering support against those critics who, to his astonishment, regarded his work with distaste and even horror. He had been in England for a brief stay in April 1517, and, as the opening shows, had stopped at Rochester on his way to Dover. This was the last meeting between the two friends. John Fisher wrote:[16]

> Just as I was distressed to hear of the dangers of your voyage, so I was glad that you had escaped safe and sound. It was only right that you should pay the penalty for having hurried away from me with whom you could have rested safe from all tossing on the sea . . . . No sensible person could be offended at your translation [into Latin] of the New Testament for the common benefit of everyone, since not only have you made many passages clear by your learning but have indeed provided a full series of comments on the whole work; thus it is now possible for everyone to read and understand it with more gratification and pleasure . . . I owe it to you, Erasmus, that I can to some extent understand where the Greek does not quite agree with, the Latin. Would that I could have had you as my tutor for a few months.

His only criticism was that there were a number of misprints and obvious omissions. The book was indeed faulty according to modern standards of scholarship, but it was pioneer work.

---

[16] *Allen*, II. no. 592.

The letter was signed, "Discipulus tuus."

Erasmus not only inspired John Fisher to learn Greek, but, indirectly, Hebrew as well. John Reuchlin (1455-1522) was one of the truly great scholars of the day; his work in Hebrew studies was admired and encouraged by Erasmus who sent his books to John Fisher. One of these *Caballistica* took some time to reach the bishop as both Thomas More and John Colet found it so interesting that they retained it before passing it on.[17] Reuchlin had to suffer much harsh treatment for promoting the study of Hebrew and John Fisher gladly joined in his defence; he asked Erasmus to put him in correspondence with Reuchlin, but no letters between them have survived. A letter from Erasmus to Reuchlin in August 1516 shows that John Fisher had hoped to go to Stuttgart to see the great scholar.

> I cannot find words to express in what affection and veneration your name is held by that great leader of learning and piety, the Bishop of Rochester, insomuch that, whereas Erasmus has been hitherto in high esteem, he is now almost despised in comparison with Reuchlin. This is so far from being an occasion of jealousy, that I am rather disposed to spur on, as they say, the willing horse. I never have a letter from him (often as he writes) without some honourable mention of you. He had made up his mind to put off his episcopal garb, I mean the linen vest, which the bishops always wear in England (except when they are out hunting) and to cross the sea, mainly in order that he might have an opportunity of talking with you. And on this account, as we were hurrying to the ship, he detained us for ten days on purpose that we might

---

[17] *Allen*, II, nos. 592, 593.

make the passage together. Some later incident made him change his plan, but if he has put off its accomplishment, he has not changed his purpose.[18]

John Fisher's tutor in Hebrew was Robert Wakefield (d. 1537), a Cambridge scholar who had studied Hebrew and oriental languages abroad. He left Louvain, where he was a teacher of Hebrew, at the end of 1519, and the following year would seem to have been the most likely time for his tuition of John Fisher in Hebrew.

It was recognized that John Fisher had considerable influence with Erasmus. When John Siberch of Cologne was printing at Cambridge, 1521-1523, he published the scholar's *Libellus de Conscribendis Epistolis* without the author's permission. In dedicating the book to John Fisher, the printer wrote, "This book was dedicated a long time ago to one of your kinsmen [Robert Fisher] by Erasmus. Now I beg you that you be my protector with him, that he may not bear me ill-will for having published it without his consent." He made this plea because "you are all-powerful with Erasmus."

Siberch was brought to Cambridge by Henry Bullock and Richard Croke; the latter had studied at Cologne and succeeded Erasmus as Reader in Greek at Cambridge. The enterprise was also supported by Robert Wakefield. There is no evidence that Erasmus was directly concerned. These scholars were all friends of John Fisher at that period, and he may have given his approval when the University made a loan of £20 to Siberch.[19]

The letter quoted above is the last preserved of those written by John Fisher to Erasmus. There are eleven later

---

[18] *Allen*, II, no. 457.

[19] See E P. Goldschmidt, *The First Cambridge Press* (1955).

letters, the last dated 4th September 1524, from Erasmus to John Fisher; in these there are references to letters received. Several deal with the affairs of John Reuchlin, and one (1st September 1522) gives news of Robert Wakefield who was then on the Continent again. Of their later relations little is known; a letter from Erasmus reached John Fisher when he was imprisoned in the Tower, but it has not been preserved.[20] Erasmus did eventually carry out a task that had been suggested to him by John Fisher. It was to write a book on the art of the preacher. This, under the title *Ecclesiastes*, was not completed until 1535, and would have been dedicated to John Fisher but, by the time it was published, he had perished on the scaffold.

It has been said that "in later years their relations were perhaps somewhat less friendly."[21] There is no decisive evidence of this; certainly the letters written by John Fisher increase in the warmth of their tone and are evidence of the affection with which he could follow the career of a friend. On the other hand the letters from Erasmus show that he stood in some awe of the bishop; perhaps he recognized the essential saintliness of John Fisher and any display of affection was restrained by veneration.

---

[20] See below, p. 338.

[21] *Allen*, I, p. 469.

IV - Erasmus of Rotterdom
Hans Holbein the Younger

V - Sir Thomas More
Hans Holbein the Younger

VI - St. John's College, Cambridge

One can see at the left the Tudor Rose of Henry VII, and also on the right the Portcullis, which was the emblem of Lady Margaret Beaufort. The founding of this college was due solely to the efforts of John Fisher.

CHAPTER VII
ST. JOHN'S COLLEGE

THE last chapter has taken us rather ahead in the main narrative of the events of John Fisher's life, and we must now retrace our steps to give an account of one of his great achievements, the foundation of St. John's College, Cambridge. Without doubt, but for his dogged pertinacity, that College would not have been established.

There is no mention in the Lady Margaret's will of her intention to found a second college at Cambridge; the only reference was in an undated codicil written in the third person. After Christ's College had been founded, a group of Oxford Fellows had tried to interest her in the proposal to establish a new college in their university, and it was only at the earnest intervention of John Fisher that she was persuaded to continue her benefactions to Cambridge.[1] He pointed out that the ancient hospital of St. John the Evangelist had greatly decayed; its finances were in a desperate state, and the prior and two brethren left were living in a manner that brought disrepute to the University. The proposal was that permission should be obtained from Rome to dissolve the hospital and to found and endow a college for a Master and fifty scholars.

An account of the difficulties and discouragements met with after the Lady Margaret's death was recorded by

---

[1] *Red Book*, St. John's, pp. 61 ff.; Lewis, II, p. 293. For the early history of the college, see Thomas Baker, History of the College of St. John, ed. J. E. B. Mayor (1869), vol. I.

John Fisher,[2] and from this it is possible to realize how irksome the delays must have been; a less determined man would have given up what must have seemed a hopeless task.

The first step had to be the dissolution of the old hospital, and this depended on the action of the Bishop of Ely, James Stanley, a step-son of the Lady Margaret, but a man of irregular life. In spite of his promises to her, he refused to move in the matter until a compromise had been effected that was favourable to himself: Having at length obtained his consent, the executors had next to get the papal licence. The first granted was defective owing to the stupidity (or dishonesty) of their agent, so the negotiations had to be reopened. The amount of the endowment was another problem; as the codicil to the will was not sealed, the full provision could not be granted by the courts. At this point the reluctance of Henry VIII to part with any of his grandmother's lands caused more delay, but eventually John Fisher secured a reasonable interpretation from the courts. "If this had not been obtained," he said, "here would have been but a poor college."

Out of the lands given to him by the Lady Margaret he gave the college nearly 1,1500 acres as well as the sum of £500.[3] His endowment provided for four Fellows and two scholars; three of the Fellows were to come from the diocese of York and one from Rochester. Masses were to be said in perpetuity for the souls of the Lady Margaret and her executors.

---

[2] *Red Book*, pp. 38-40; Lewis, II, 277-282.

[3] H. F. Howard, *Finances of the College of St. John the Evangelist* (1935), p. 7 and Ap. III.

A further cause of delay was that her servants put in claims that at first were supported by the king who was, said John Fisher, "a very heavy lord against me." This trouble was overcome by sacrificing some of the lands intended for the endowment. "Forsooth," wrote John Fisher, "it was sore laborious and painful unto me that many times I was right sorry that ever I took that business upon me."

In place of the lost lands, the executors (and that really meant John Fisher) appealed to the king for permission to appropriate the decayed hospital, or Maison Dieu, of Ospringe and two small nunneries in Kent. There was nothing unusual or reprehensible such proceedings. When a foundation had decayed for want of support or members, or had lost its original character, or, more seriously, had become a scandal, it was permissible after thorough investigation and with the approval of Rome, to divert the resources to other church or educational purposes. The wholesale confiscation carried out at a later date by Henry VIII and Thomas Cromwell was of a very different nature, and the sale of buildings and lands to laymen for purely secular purposes was iniquitous.

Ospringe had been founded by Henry III for a Master, three brethren and two clerks, but by the time Henry VIII came to the throne there was only a Master in occupation. After the official inquiry, the Archbishop of Canterbury gave his judgment on 13th October 1519[4] in favour of appropriation; the deed was executed in the presence of John Fisher, Robert Fisher, his brother, and Edward White, his brother-in-law. The Master was granted a pension of £30 a year and a priest was appointed to teach grammar. The sum of £500 was paid to the king "by commandment of my lord cardinal." Two small nunneries, one at

---

[4] Cooper, *Memoir*, pp. 158-61.

Brornhall in Berkshire and another at Higham (Lillechurch) in Kent were also appropriated. The one at Higham had been a constant source of trouble and the bishop's orders for a strict observance of the rule had been ignored. The original foundation had been for sixteen nuns, but in 1521 there were only three, and two of these were convicted of immorality. The decree of suppression was read in public in Rochester Cathedral on 19th May 1523.[5] St. John's College undertook to maintain the charity for poor people, to provide for the teaching of the children and to maintain prayers for the souls of the benefactors of the nunnery.

The Priory of Bromhall was suppressed in 1521 by the Bishop of Salisbury; there were then only a prioress and two nuns; it was described as a "profane place". The property was transferred by the Crown in 1522 to St. John's College.

It will be noticed that the last date is seven years after the opening mentioned in the last chapter and fourteen years after the death of the Lady Margaret. When John Fisher told Erasmus in June 1510 that he was just off to Cambridge for the consecration of the college chapel,[6] he was rejoicing at the achievement of part of his labours. The chapel of the old hospital had been restored and adapted and at least part of the first court had been built and perhaps the great gate as well. Four chantry chapels were added one of which John Fisher had intended as his last resting place.

As we have seen, he had taken on his shoulders the greater part of the wearisome business of getting the college established and well endowed. He had been

---

[5] *Register*, f. 121V.

[6] The chapel was pulled down in the 19th century.

obliged to contend with the Bishop of Ely and with the king himself; there is some evidence that Cardinal Wolsey had also been obstructive.

His fellow executors empowered John Fisher to frame the statutes and to elect the first Fellows. Provisional statutes were based on those of Christ's College, but he was not satisfied with these and revised them in 1524 and again in 1530. He adopted sonic provisions from the statutes of Corpus Christi College, Oxford which had been drawn up by his friend Bishop Richard Fox.[7]

The aims of the college were stated to be, the worship of God, training in uprightness of life, and the strengthening of the Christian faith. Every priest had to say Mass at least four times a week and emphasis was laid on the duty of preaching. Both Fellows and students were bound on oath not to seek any dispensations from the statutes. The emphasis of the studies was on theology. Indeed it would be true to say that John Fisher regarded St. John's as a seminary for priests rather than as a centre of secular studies. There were to be disputations on philosophy on one day, and on theology on two days in the week. Two questions from Duns Scotus were to be the subjects of disputation. This choice of the "doctor subtilis" throws light on John Fisher's own predilection. It is doubtful if Erasmus would have approved of this course of study. A recent judgment may be quoted:

> The philosophy of Scotus looks backward as well as forward. . . . A triumph of dialectical skill and of careful patient thought the philosophy of Scotus is the work of man who was, though impregnated with tradition, a powerful vigorous and original thinker, a

---

[7] *Early Statutes of St. John's College*, ed. J. E. B. Mayor (1859); the 1530 and 1545 Statutes are printed in parallel columns.

man who really belonged to the closing epoch of "dogmatic philosophy" but who at the same time heralded the new movement.[8]

"Looks backward as well as forward" can be equally well applied to John Fisher himself. His statutes not only provided for disputations on Duns Scotus, but also for regular teaching in Greek for the junior students and in Hebrew for the seniors.

These statutes were modified under Henry VIII in 1545. St. John's also lost the valuable library given to it by the bishop who had retained its use during his lifetime. Unfortunately the books were at his palace at Rochester at the time of his martyrdom, and so fell an easy prey to the despoilers. The Fellows were not in a position to dispute the possession of the library with their new chancellor, Thomas Cromwell.

Some letters preserved at St. John's give us a few glimpses of other sides of John Fisher's life.[9] Trivial as they may seem, they are precious because so little is known of his personal life. One letter can be dated as it refers to his projected attendance at the Lateran Council in 1512. It is to Henry Hornby (d. 1518), Master of Peterhouse, and a fellow executor of the Lady Margaret's will. The bishop had asked him to lend his servant, Henry Dey, for the journey. The request was granted and the writer added, "a gelding of mine, one of the best and surest I have, which I shall leave unto your lordship to bear my said servant." Readers of the letters of Erasmus will appreciate the importance of a good horse.

---

[8] F. Copleston, S. J., *A History of Philosophy*, II, p. 485.

[9] Printed in Sir R. F. Scott, Notes from the Records of St. John's College (1889).

ST. JOHN'S COLLEGE

There is a batch of letters from Dr. Richard Sharpe,[10] the bishop's chaplain, to Nicholas Metcalfe, a former chaplain and Archdeacon of Rochester, who became Master of St. John's in 1518. These letters can probably be dated about 1518 to 1520. One says that the bishop's hat is being sent. "You shall receive my lord's hat again which is too narrow in the head by two inches or more," so another hat was to be made but without a fringe. The letter also requested the loan of the works of St. John Chrysostom.

Another note reports that the bishop was in good health "and uses the baths. I pray God they do him good; he says that they do him much good." A later letter states that he is "very sorry that the last part of his sermon [the bishop's] is lost; it will cost him some labour for I think he have not the copy; also my lord desireth you to send him *annotationes Erasmi*[11] left with Arnold to mend the binding of them. My lord taketh great labour against Luther. I think verily that his work shall pass all other means." The reference to Luther suggests that this letter was written about 1522 when John Fisher would be engaged in writing his *Confutatio*.[12]

The next note refers to a relative of Thomas More whose first wife was Jane Colt. "At the desire of Mr. More my lord commanded me to pay to Mr. Colt's daughter and her husband on Sunday last 5 marks for certain money and stuff of hers that was left at Higham." Perhaps this

---

[10] First mentioned in the *Register* at Kemsing in 1517 where he succeeded N. Metcalfe who had been appointed in 1509. The latter was appointed archdeacon 26th Nov. 1512 (*Register*, f. 6iv; not 1515 as in D.N.B.). He had carried out the negotiations about Bromhall (*Lewis*, II, p. 281). According to the *Register*, f. 62v., he was born in 1470.

[11] Perhaps the *Paraphrases*.

[12] See below, p. 130.

has some bearing on the dissolution of the nunnery at Higham and can be dated in 1522 or 1523.

A friendly note assures the Master of St. John's that "my lord liked the sturgeon that you sent him very well, and likewise fed well of it."

Amongst these papers is a request to William Bolton, Prior of St. Bartholomew-the-Great in Smithfield, to pay over to the bearer money due to "my lady's poor folk at Hatfield."[13] The Lady Margaret had maintained twelve poor men and women there and this charity was to be continued after her death. This first part of the note is in the formal handwriting of a scribe and is signed "Io. Roffs." After which the bishop added in his own distinctive script, "And I pray you do so much to see Peter's work for my lady's tomb and when you have once seen I will come myself thither."

The year is not given. William Bolton was a great builder and in Henry VII's will he was described as Master of the Works for the new chapel at Westminster. "Peter" was Pietro Torrigiano, the Florentine sculptor; the gilt-bronze figure of the Lady Margaret on her tomb is regarded as one of his great achievements.[14] Erasmus composed the epitaph for which he received a fee of twenty shillings from John Fisher. The iron screen round the tomb was given by St. John's College in 1529.[15]

One other letter suggests an unfamiliar aspect of John Fisher. It is an invitation to hunt from George Neville, Lord Bergavenny (d. 1535), Keeper of Ashdown Forest, and owner of several manors in Kent and Sussex.

---

[13] See Plate VIII.

[14] See Plate II.

[15] This screen was removed during Wyatt's "restoration" in 1822. It was happily found nearly a century later and put back where it belonged.

If it shall please you to see your greyhounds run at any time either within or without, I have commanded my keeper to give you attendance and make you such disport as if I were there present.

Strange as it may be to think of John Fisher as a huntsman, one has only to read his "comparison between the life of hunters and the life of religious persons"[16] to feel that he knew what he was talking about.

Lord Bergavenny evidently had a high regard for the bishop; in 1531 he presented the advowson of Ibstock, Leicestershire, to the Bishops of Rochester.[17]

---

[16] *E. W.*, p. 365.

[17] *Register*, f. 16iv.

VII - William Warham, Archbishop of Canterbury
Hans Holbein the Younger

CHAPTER VIII
THE BISHOP IN HIS DIOCESE—I

CAMBRIDGE affairs were only part of the business that occupied John Fisher's days and thoughts. He was summoned to the Parliaments and Convocations of 1510, 1512 and 1515. Nothing is recorded of the part he played on those occasions. We get glimpses of him at great functions; thus on 15th November 1515 he was crosier to Archbishop Warham at Westminster Abbey when Wolsey received the Cardinal's hat, "in so solemn wise," wrote George Cavendish, "as I have not seen the like unless it had been at the coronation of a mighty prince or king."[1] In the following year, the Bishop of Rochester christened the son of Mary, the king's sister, who was now Duchess of Suffolk after having been Queen of France.[2]

Pope Leo X urged the princes of Europe to war against the Turks who were threatening to carry their power north of the Danube. He proposed in 1518 to send Cardinal Campeggio as his legate to England to advance this intention. Henry and Wolsey objected that it was contrary to English practice to receive a cardinal legate; this difficulty could be overcome, however, if Wolsey were granted the same powers as Campeggio. So on 17th May Wolsey became cardinal *a latere*, an exceptional appointment that he skillfully made permanent. Campeggio was kept waiting at Calais until further, and more profitable, concessions were granted to Wolsey. John Fisher was one of the prelates who received

---

[1] *Cavendish*, p. 20.

[2] *L.P.*, II, i, no. 1652.

Campeggio at Canterbury on 23rd July 1518, and, no doubt, joined the cardinal's train as far as Rochester.

Shortly afterwards, Wolsey called a synod of the clergy; in this way he demonstrated that his new powers were greater than those of the Archbishop of Canterbury. The early biographer of John Fisher gives an account of this synod which needs to be read with the caution that it does not report speeches verbatim, but as historical reconstructions. The words he puts into the mouth of John Fisher no doubt expressed the bishop's real opinions though it may be questioned if he would have used some of the phrases given to him.

> This council was called by my lord Cardinal rather to notify to the world his great authority and to be seen sitting in his pontifical seat, than for any great good that he meant to do, which this learned and wise prelate [Fisher] perceived quickly. Wherefore having now good occasion to speak against such enormities as he saw daily rising among the spirituality, and much the rather for that his words were among the clergy alone, without any commixture of the laity, which at that time began to hearken any speaking against the clergy. He there reproved very discreetly the ambition and incontinency of the clergy, utterly condemning their vanity in wearing of costly apparel, whereby he declared the goods of the Church to be sinfully wasted and scandal to be raised among the people seeing the tithes and other oblations given by the devotion of them and their ancestors to a good purpose so inordinately spent in indecent and superfluous raiment, delicate fare and other worldly vanity.
>
> Which matter he debated so largely and framed his words after such sort that the Cardinal perceived

himself to be touched to the very quick. For he affirmed this kind of disorder to proceed through the example of the head and thereupon reproved his pomp, putting him in mind that it stood better with the modesty of such a high pastor as he was, to eschew all worldly vanity, specially in this perilous time, and by humility to make himself conformable and like to the image of God. "For in this trade of life," said he, "neither can there be any likelihood of perpetuity with safety of conscience, neither yet any security of the clergy to continue, but such plain and imminent dangers are like to ensue as never were tasted or heard of before our days."

"For what should we," said he, "exhort our flocks to eschew and shun worldly ambition, when we ourselves, that be bishops do wholely set our minds to the same things we forbid in them? What example of Christ our Saviour do we imitate, who first exercised doing and after fell to teaching? If we teach according to our doing, how absurd may our doctrine be accounted? If we teach one thing and do another, our labour in teaching shall never benefit our flock half so much as our examples in doing shall hurt them. Who can willingly suffer and bear with us in whom (preaching humility, sobriety and contempt of the world) they may evidently perceive haughtiness in mind, pride in gesture, sumptuousness in apparel and damnable excess in all worldly delicates? Truly, most reverend fathers, what this vanity in temporal things worketh in you I know not; but sure I am that in myself I perceive a great impediment to devotion and so have felt a long time, for sundry times when I have settled and fully bent myself to the care of my flock committed unto me, to visit my diocese, to govern my church, and to answer the enemies of Christ, straightways hath come a messenger for one cause or another sent from higher authority by whom I have been called to business and so left of my former purpose. And thus by tossing and going this way and that ways, time hath passed and in the meanwhile nothing done but attending after triumphs, receiving ambassadors, haunting of princes' courts and such like, whereby great expenses rise that might better be spent many other ways."[3]

That last passage may well have been spoken from the heart of one who regarded himself first as a bishop and to a less degree as a statesman.

The early biographer went on to lament that "few were persuaded by his counsel. . . . So that (excuses never wanting to cover sin) this holy father's words spoken with so good a zeal were all lost and came to nothing for that time."

As Rochester lay on the road from Canterbury to London, visitors of distinction who were travelling from or to Dover would expect to be received by the Bishop of Rochester.

The letter he received from the Council in 1514 when the sword and cap presented by Leo X to Henry VIII arrived in England, is typical of others.

> . . . the prior of Christ's Church of Canterbury shall meet with the said ambassador and . . . shall conduct him to some place convenient between Sittingbourne and Rochester, where the king hath appointed that your lordship, the Master of the Rolls, and Sir Thomas

---

[3] *Ortroy*, pp. 135-9.

Bolyn shall meet with him and so conduct him to London.[4]

So too in 1522 when Charles V came to England, the Bishop of Rochester had to be at Canterbury with the archbishop to meet him, and, on the way to London, to entertain the emperor at Rochester during a Sunday.

The early biographer said that "if any strangers came to him, he would entertain them according to their vocations with such mirth as stood with the gravity of his person, whose talk was always rather of learning or contemplation than of worldly matters."[5]

John Fisher could easily have allowed affairs of state and the prestige and allurements of court life to draw him more and more away from the care of his diocese, nor would anyone have thought this surprising; he was peculiar in that he never allowed secular matters to overwhelm his primary duty to the Church as a bishop. William Rastell recorded the opinion of a young contemporary.

> He was in holiness, learning and diligence in his cure and in fulfilling his office of bishop such that of many hundred years England had not any bishop worthy to be compared unto him. And if all countries of Christendom were searched, there could not lightly among all other nations be found one that hath been in all things like unto him, so well used and fulfilled the office of bishop as he did. He was of such high perfection in holy life and strait and austere living as

---

[4] *Lewis*, II, p. 297.

[5] *Ortroy*, p. 102.

few were, I suppose, in all Christendom in his time, religious or other.[6]

The diocese of Rochester, it has already been noted, was the smallest in the kingdom, but it was even smaller than a map suggests; there were thirty-four parishes belonging to Canterbury and forming the deanery of Shoreham; these therefore did not come under the jurisdiction of the Bishop of Rochester.

There were two episcopal palaces and several manors belonging to the bishop. In those days of horseback travel and of bad, and, in winter, sometimes impassable roads, it was necessary for the bishop to have several centres from which he could carry out his duties. This also met the problem of supplies as the produce of each manor could be used in turn. The palace of Rochester, which had been built during the previous century, was between the monastery (the present cathedral) and the river. The site today seems more removed from the Medway mud than Erasmus suggested,[7] but the banks of the river have been built up and there may have been inlets up which the tide could wash. There are no substantial remains of the buildings.

The bishop's London palace was by Lambeth Marsh adjoining the archbishop's palace to the east, so it was simple for John Fisher to hurry off to show William Warham the complimentary passages in the *Novum Instrumentum*. From the Register we learn that John Fisher built a brick wall round the palace and repaired the buildings.[8] It ceased to be a palace of the Bishops of

---

[6] *Harpsfield*, p. 249.

[7] See above, p. 64.

[8] *Register*, f 55v.

Rochester in 1540; after many changes of use and occupation it was demolished in 1827.[9]

There were manors at Hailing (between the church and the river), at Bromley, at Stone (near Dartford), and at Trottescliffe (near Wrotham), but John Fisher does not seem to have used the last two.

The Register for the period of John Fisher's episcopate has been preserved; so too has the Act Book of his Consistory Court.

Unfortunately the records of his visitations have not survived. The first began on 15th May 1505. The early biographer gives us:

> And first, because there is small hope of health in the members of that body where the head is sick, he began his visitation at his head church of Rochester, calling before him the priors and monks exhorting them to obedience, chastity and true observation of their monastical vows; and where any fault was tried, he caused it to be amended. After that he carefully visited the rest of the parish churches within his diocese in his own person; and sequestrating all such as he found unworthy to occupy that high function, he placed other fitter in their rooms; and all such as were accused of any crime, he put to their purgation, not sparing the punishment of simony and heresy with other crimes and abuses. And by the way he omitted neither preaching to the people, nor confirming of children, nor relieving of needy and indigent persons; so that by all means he observed a due comeliness in the house of God.[10]

---

[9] Carlisle Lane passes over the site.

[10] *Ortroy*, p. 96.

During the first half of his episcopate, he carried out visitations in 1508, 1511, 1514 and 1517. His archdeacon no doubt shared this important work but to what extent we cannot now determine.

From the Register we can follow the bishop's movements about the diocese from year to year. Occasional intervals of a month or two indicate when he was away on state or university business but without giving information of what occupied him.

A survey of one year, 1513, will give a typical record of his official acts.[11] There is much more we should like to know, but these bare facts add something to the picture.

The first entry is dated 5th March; it records an abjuration of heresy before the bishop in his chapel at Hailing. Henry Potter of West Mailing was accused of saying publicly that he would not believe in the Last Judgment "till I see it." He promised to avoid suspect persons in the future, also books of Scripture in English, and to give information about them as soon as possible. The bishop absolved him from excommunication and ordered him as penance to walk in procession in his parish church with the faggot on his back, and to do so again in the cathedral on the following Sunday unless dispensed from this by the bishop. In addition he was to see that no harm came to those who had testified against him. Finally he was not to leave the diocese for two years, during each of which he must present himself to the bishop. Henry Potter made his cross on the record.

On 12th March, also at Hailing, the bishop ordained a deacon. He was at Rochester on 4th April when he collated one priest and admitted another to vicarages. On the same day he confirmed the election of the new abbot of Lesnes, William Ticehurst, formerly Prior of Bilsington.

---

[11] *Register*, ff. 62r-70v.

The bishop, vested in pontificals, received the profession of obedience of the abbot elect. There is a long account of the proceedings, including testimonies that William Ticehurst was of legitimate birth, and discreet and circumspect. On 27th June at Lambeth, the bishop admitted a cleric to a vacancy in Cobham College in conformity with the king's wishes.

The bishop collated three priests to livings on 20th August at Bromley, and on 7th October, two others at the same place. There is then a copy of a letter from the bishop instituting Richard Clarke to the vicarage of Hailing vacant by the deprivation of John Cotton. Here the Acts of the Consistory Court explain the circumstances. On 17th September at Hailing the bishop had dealt with five cases of correction of his clergy. One of these was John Cotton who had again fallen into adultery; he said, "I would my lord had put me in prison when he commanded Joan Hubbard to prison."[12] The investigation took several sittings and was not concluded until 27th September.

There is also the copy of a letter dated 1st October. This is from the bishop to the Barons of the Exchequer stating what arrangements he was making to collect the four-tenths ordered by the king.[13] The Augustinian canons of Tonbridge and of Lesnes, and the prior of Rochester were to be responsible for making the collection by stated dates. A list of nearly forty benefices follows which he described as too poor to be taxed.

---

[12] An interesting reference to one of the bishop's prisons is in the Patent Rolls, Henry VII, pt. II. On 11th December 1506 a pardon and release was granted to John Bishop of Rochester for the escape of two men indicted for murder from his prison at Bromley.

[13] This was part of the heavy taxation of 1512 to pay for the French war.

This summary of one year of the Register shows the pattern of the normal diocesan business. A similar account could be given for any one of the other years of John Fisher's long episcopate, the only noticeable variation being that in the later period he seems to have spent more time at Rochester; this may have been due to declining health.

Some particular entries may be noted from the other years for the first half of his rule. One instance of an abjuration has been given. Two earlier cases give other examples of heretical opinions before the onset of the full tide of Lutheranism.

The first is dated May 1505.[14] John Mores (or Wener) of St. Nicholas Parish, Rochester, was accused of saying, in addition to expressing "divers doubts concerning Scripture":

1. that Christ did not die in perfect charity on Good Friday because he did not die to redeem Lucifer as well as Adam and Eve;
2. that our Lady "is butt a sakk", and the Son of God desired the Father to come to middle earth[15] to take a sack upon his back.

It is impossible to make sense of the last statement. Mores made his cross to a document in which he promised to have no further dealings with heretics, nor to use any suspect books of Scripture in English, and to denounce such books and persons as soon as possible.

The abjuration was made in the Lady Chapel of the Cathedral before the bishop. Mores was freed from

---

[14] *Register*, 41v.

[15] The place between heaven and hell.

excommunication and had to do penance in the usual form. He was not to leave the diocese for seven years. He made his cross on the record.

Another case of heresy was brought before the bishop in 1507.[16] This concerned a Richard Gavell of Westerham who said that:

1. the feast of St. Thomas the Apostle [sic: of Canterbury?] should not be observed;
2. it was not necessary to take holy water "of the priest's hand";
3. offerings and offering days were only ordained by priests and curates "by their own covetous minds and singular avayles [advantages]"; on one such day he had caused Joan Harries to withhold her offering "to the evil example of the people".

It was further stated that:

1. he often left church and went to the alehouse rather than hear a sermon;
2. he had spoken against the priest while he was in the pulpit, saying "Now the priest standeth in the pulpit and he doth nothing but chide and travail for I look more on his deeds than of his words whatsoever he saith";
3. he despised the authority of the Church saying that the Church's sentence had no effect, only that of God who was not in the power of priests and bishops;
4. after being accursed by the Archbishop of Canterbury and so openly by my curate

---

[16] *Register*, f. 47r.

demanded now of late in the church of Westerham", he replied, in the presence of divers persons, "Sirs, though my lord of Canterbury has accursed me, I am, I trust, not yet accursed of God, and pray, sirs, fear ye not to company or eat and drink with me for all that.";

5. he had a bad reputation for heresy.

The usual penance of going in procession was imposed; he was not to leave the diocese for four years, and during those years, he was to present himself annually to the bishop. Richard Gavell made his mark. The penance was to be carried out at Bromley and at Rochester, but he was dispensed by the bishop from appearing in the cathedral.

The problem of heresy must be dealt with more fully later in these pages; here it may be noted that the penances imposed by the bishop were of the customary character.

Some further examples from the Register will indicate the scope of the bishop's activities.

On 17th July 1508 in the chapel of St. Blaise at Bromley, the bishop received the profession of William Temple, "singleman", as a hermit.[17] He gave him the eremetical habit with his blessing. The hermit promised before God and the Saints to direct his conduct and conversation according to the rule of St. Paul the first hermit; he was to live in the hermitage built in honour of St. Catherine at Dartford. All this was written down and the hermit made his cross.

There is one example of the bishop's desire to have a better instructed clergy. On 29th November 1508, Hugh

---

[17] *Register*, f. 50v.

Taylor of Foot's Cray came before the bishop with letters of presentation from the canons of St. Mary Overy, Southwark, to that benefice.[18] The bishop examined him but was not satisfied with his attainments. Hugh Taylor was therefore told that he must spend a year in a grammar school, and if, after that, he had made sufficient progress, he would be admitted. Meanwhile a curate would be put in charge. Hugh Taylor made good use of his twelve months and was then able to satisfy the bishop.

On 21st April 1511, the bishop received the vow of chastity of Elizabeth Fitzwaren, a widow of Beckenham.[19] She undertook "to be chaste of my body and truly and devoutly shall keep me chaste from this time forward as long as my life lasteth after the rule of St. Paul [the hermit]."

The bishop presided at a synod of his clergy on 6th October 1518.[20] After a Mass of the Holy Ghost had been sung, he preached a sermon; this was followed by the reading of the constitutions, provincial and legatine, against concubinage.

The Acts of the Consistory Court do not add much to out knowledge of the bishop's work. The court was held in the churches of parishes conveniently situated for the cases to be heard. Thus in December 1511 the itinerary was West Mailing, Strood, Gravesend, Dartford, Trottescliffe and Swanscombe, dealing with over a hundred cases in all. The bishop himself rarely presided, but from time to time he was present for more serious cases; thus on 17th March 1511 at Lambeth he absolved a priest from his contumacy (the nature of which is not

---

[18] *Register*, f. 51ir.

[19] *Register*, f 54r.

[20] *Register*, f. 77v.

stated), but suspended him from saying Mass in his parish or elsewhere in the diocese.

The Register records one royal intervention in the work of the court.[21] A letter from the king, 13th February 1520, ordered the bishop not to proceed with the action brought by William Rogers, vicar of Plumstead, for tithes against William Goldwyn, gent. The vicar had denounced Goldwyn in the church at Woolwich and declared him excommunicate in defiance of the decision of the civil courts.

The Acts of the Consistory Court and the Register do little more than tell us of the normal duties of a bishop; the unusual feature for the times was that John Fisher carried out these duties himself as far as other responsibilities would allow.

The early biographer adds life to the bare facts of these records.

> Wheresoever he lay, either at Rochester or elsewhere, his order was to inquire where any poor sick folks lay near him, which, after he once knew, he would diligently visit them. And where he saw any of them likely to die, he would preach to them, teaching them the way to die, with such good persuasions, that for the most part he never departed till the sick persons were well satisfied and contented with death. Many times it was his chance to come to such poor houses as for want of chimneys were very smoky and thereby so noisome that scant any man could abide in them. Nevertheless himself would there sit by the sick patient many times the space of three or four hours together in the smoke, when none of his servants were able to abide in the house, but were fain to tarry

---

[21] *Register*, f. 102v.

without till his coming abroad. And in some other poor houses where stairs were wanting, he would never disdain to climb up by a ladder for such a good purpose. And when he had given them such ghostly comfort as he thought expedient for their souls, he would at his departure leave behind him his charitable alms, giving charge to his steward or other officers daily to prepare meat convenient for them (if they were poor) and send it unto them. Besides he gave at his gate to divers poor people (which were commonly no small number) a daily alms of money, to some 2d., to some 4d., some 6d., and some more after the rate of their necessity. That being done, every one of them was rewarded likewise with meat, which was daily brought to the gate. And lest any fraud, partiality, or other disorder might rise in the distribution of the same, he provided himself a place whereunto immediately after dinner he would resort and there stand to see the division with his own eyes.[22]

To this may be added William Rastell's testimony:

> He, like a good shepherd, would not go from his flock, but continually fed them with preaching of God's word and example of good life. He, like a good shepherd, did what he could to reform his flock both of the spirituality and temporality, when he perceived any of them to range out of the right way, either in manners or doctrine.[23]

---

[22] *Ortroy*, p. 101

[23] *Harpsfield*, p. 251.

The first half of John Fisher's episcopate was a period of steady work and quiet achievement. He had regulated his diocese and had gathered round him like-minded men such as Nicholas Metcalfe. He knew his small diocese as only a diligent bishop could know it. By 1520 the priests must have known him as a person and as a pastor to whom they could turn in times of difficulty. The example of his austere and devout life would be a reproach to the easy-going and an inspiration to the faithful. "All pastors and curates used him for their lantern, as one of whom they might perfectly learn when to use action and when contemplation; for in these two things did he so far excel that hard it were to find one so well practised and expert in any one of them, apart, as he was in both of them together."[24]

His work for his university had prospered; Christ's College was established, and, in spite of all the obstacles, St. John's had been well founded. His encouragement of sound learning and preaching, and of the study of Greek and Hebrew had helped to lead Cambridge out of the lethargy of the past into the more vigorous world of the new scholarship.

The second half of his episcopate was to prove more and more discordant; the rapid spread of heresy, not least in his own beloved university, and the increasing bitterness of anti-clericism, of themselves would have brought sorrow enough, but to these was to be added "the king's great matter" and his subsequent claim" to be "the only supreme head in earth of the Church of England."

---

[24] *Ortroy*, p. 98.

CHAPTER IX
FROM WYCLIFF TO LUTHER

ON 6th February 1512 the Convocation of Canterbury met in St. Paul's Cathedral. The preacher was the dean, John Colet. His congregation included the archbishop, William Warham, the Bishop of Rochester, John Fisher, and the Dean of Lincoln, Thomas Wolsey who was also a canon of Windsor, a prebendary of Hereford, and parish priest of Torrington, Devon.

The sermon[1] was a bold denunciation of the "secular and worldly living in clerks and priests" and had those present taken the preacher's words to heart, many of the evils of the coming years would have been avoided.

John Colet took as his text, "Be ye not conformed to this world, but be you reformed in the newness of your understanding, that ye may prove what is the good will of God, well pleasing and perfect." (Rom. xii. 2). The preacher's argument was that "if priests and bishops, that should be as lights, run in the dark way of the world, how dark then shall the secular people be?"

He named four particular evils that beset the clergy. First there was pride of life. "How much greediness and appetite of honour and dignity is nowadays in men of the church? How run they, yea, almost out of breath, from one benefice to another, from the less to the more, from the lower to the higher?" Second was "carnal concupiscence." "They give themselves to feasts and banqueting; they spend themselves in vain babbling; they give themselves to sports and plays; they apply themselves to hunting and hawking; they drown

---

[1] Printed in the Appendix to *A Life of John Colet* by J. H. Lupton (1909).

themselves in the delights of this world." The third evil was covetousness. "For what other thing seek we nowadays in the church than fat benefices and high promotions? Yea, and in the same promotions, of what other thing do we pass upon than our tithes and rents?" The fourth charge was "the continual secular occupation wherein priests and bishops nowadays doth busy themselves, the servants rather of men than of God; the warriors rather of this world than of Christ."

The preacher pointed out that as a result the priesthood was dishonoured and despised, and "we are also nowadays grieved with heretics, men mad with marvellous foolishness. But the heresies of them are not so pestilent and pernicious unto us and the people, as the evil and wicked life of priests."

Having fearlessly condemned the shortcomings of the times, John Colet, with equal daring, went on to point out the remedies. The main need was put bluntly. "If you will ponder and look upon our motes, first take away the blocks out of your eyes. It is an old proverb, Physician, heal thyself. You spiritual physicians, first taste you this medicine of purgation of manners, and then after offer us the same to taste." There was no need, he said, to add to the canon law; let them enforce what was already required; he referred to the obligations to admit only worthy men to holy orders, to avoid simony, and to enforce residence both on themselves and on parish priests. They should remind monks of the duty of living according to their rule, and they should see that the "goods of the church be spent, not in costly building, not in sumptuous apparel and pomps, not in feasting and banqueting, not in excess and wantonness, not in enriching of kinsfolk, not in keeping dogs, but in things profitable and necessary to the Church." The Church courts should be purged of "those daily new found crafts for lucre." He summed up his message in the sentence, "if you will have the lay people to live after your wish and will, first live you yourselves after the will of God."

This was a heavy indictment, and many of his listeners must have felt uncomfortable at his words. He had seen where the true solution was to be found, but time was needed, and time was to prove short. John Colet was preaching against a background of darkening discontents—some religious, some political, and some social. No simple statement can give a true picture of the times, for so many factors contributed to that confusion of men's minds out of which came the upheaval of the Reformation. Yet, even so, had all the bishops resolved to live "after the will of God" a true reformation could have been effected. Unhappily the man who so soon was to dominate Church and State, Thomas Wolsey, proved to be in an exaggerated form a living example of the very evils against which Colet had warned Convocation. The cardinal —archbishop—chancellor brought to a head in his own person the discontents that he should have been the first to assuage.

Rome itself did little to ease the path of the true reformer, though there were some, then and later, such as Contarini and Caraffa, who earnestly strove for a purification of the Church. The Great Schism from 1378 to 1418 after more than seventy years of the Babylonish (Avignon) Captivity had shaken men's faith in the papacy. Such events may have seemed far removed from the year 1500, but folk memory is long memory, and the wound had not been completely healed. The man of 1500 had immediate cause for inquietude. The Borgia pope, Alexander VI, ruled in Rome, and the tales of his greed and nepotism and concupiscence lost nothing in the telling. He was followed in 1503 by Julius II whose warlike activities shocked Erasmus.

The ordinary man or woman may not have known much of these matters, though tales of the shortcomings of the mighty are always popular. Rumours can shape popular opinion more definitely than truth. Many had their own local grievances. Colet could have illustrated his general indictment by giving actual examples of the evils he named. There were justified complaints of priests who neglected their duties or lived in open sin; the delays and costliness of going to the ecclesiastical courts were a source of bitterness; there were murmurs at the pride and wealth of some churchmen; there was resentment at exactions for fees and dues. Envy, greed and malice played their parts, but there were serious defects that should have been put right, but were not put right.

It is easy to paint too dark a picture, and that has been so frequently done that the patches of sunshine are often overshadowed. There were holy and saintly priests utterly devoted to the care of their flocks who were a reproach to the worldly and the self-seekers. Chaucer drew the portraits of the worldly monk and friar, but he did not forget the clerk of Oxford nor the poor parson,

That Christes gospel trewely wolde preche;
His parisshens devoutly wolde he teche.

Nor must we forget him, nor his brother, the plowman,

Livinge in pees and pa fit charitee.

John Colet had little to say of heretics in his sermon; his brief reference to these men who were "mad with marvellous foolishness" recalls the strange opinions recorded in John Fisher's register.[2]

Heresy had not been a serious problem in England before the coming of John Wycliff (d. 1382). The ideas he put forward, or, the vulgarized version of them, were the basis of Lollardism which, for half a century after his death, had considerable strength in some parts of the country.

This is not the place to attempt an exposition of Wycliff's philosophy or teaching except in so far as it affected popular opinion. He taught that power, possession, and property are held on condition of service to God, and that abuse of these justified deprivation and dispossession. As all are equal in the sight of God, there is no necessity for the mediation of a priest; least of all can an ill-living or neglectful priest claim authority over us. The organized Church is a convenience, but if its bishops, from the pope downwards, fail to serve God, they forfeit all regard and their injunctions can be ignored. This teaching led Wycliff to attack the pope, the hierarchy and the priesthood in the most bitter terms. He would have had the Church deprived of its possessions and reduced to that poverty which he regarded as an essential for effective ministry. The accretions during the centuries of ritual and ceremony should be swept away, and men should return to the plain teaching of the Gospels. Out of this grew his desire for a vernacular translation of the Bible, and this was at length done by him and his followers. His ideas were spread by his poor preachers, some of them laymen, who preached and taught as they moved about the country, and read the new translation to those who were drawn to listen. The Lollards were not an organization, and by 1430 they had ceased to be of

---

[2] See above, p. 92.

influence except in particular areas. A few tracts were in circulation; such was *The Wicket*[3] which taught that "a sacrament is no more to say but a sign or mind of a thing passed, or a thing to come."

The early copies of the Lollard Bible were condemned by the bishops not because the language was English but on account of the heretical tendencies of its preface or prologue. When that was removed, there was no hindrance put to its use. These manuscript copies were expensive and few could afford to possess one, so a reader would gather round him those who could not read for themselves. This in itself was unobjectionable, but the reading was sometimes combined with an exposition that was heretical, and linked up with an attack on the clergy, the bishops and the pope. It was inevitable that this last part of the Lollard message proved the most popular. There are always those who listen eagerly to vilification and are ready to add their portion of scandal. Wycliff himself set the example; in his tract on the office of curates he listed thirty-three accusations against them and had nothing to say in their favour; to him the pope was "head vicar of the fiend", and monasticism was "the religion of fat cows."

Much of this propaganda, as it may be called, was by word of mouth, and as the message passed from man to man, so it became distorted and even meaningless as we have seen in the records from John Fisher's Register.

The generally accepted picture of Lollardism is not true to the facts. From some statements that appear in history textbooks, it might be imagined that the people were clamouring for an English translation of the Bible and were only prevented from having it by the wicked machinations of the bishops who were afraid that they

---

[3] Sometimes called Wyclif's Wicket, but doubtfully ascribed to him.

might be found out if the truth were made public! The comparatively small number of people who could read, and the expense of a manuscript copy of a Bible in Latin or English before the age of printing, made it impossible for any book to be widely used or bought. Nor had people been deprived of a knowledge of the Scriptures; John Fisher's sermons are typical in this respect; the many Scripture quotations seem to us to be over lavish, but this was but one way in which people learned the words of the Gospels, and Epistles. Necessity had developed a quick verbal memory; this we have lost as we can so easily refer to the printed book, Indeed it would be probably true to say that ordinary folk in the fifteenth century had a better knowledge of the words of the Scriptures than many in the twentieth century; this would not be true, perhaps, of the nineteenth century, but it is certainly a fact of today.

The attitude of the Church was clearly stated by St. Thomas More in the twenty-second chapter of the first book of his Dialogue Concerning Heresies. The summary at the head of the chapter states his argument.

> Because the Messenger had in the beginning shewed himself desirous and greedy upon the text of scripture, with little force of the old fathers' glosses, and with dispraise of philosophy and almost all the seven liberal sciences, the author therefore incidentally sheweth what harm hath happed sometime to fall to divers of those young men who he hath known to give their study to the scripture only, with contempt of logic and other secular science, and little regard of the old interpreters. Wherefore the author sheweth that in the study of scripture the sure way is, with virtue and prayer, first, to use the judgment of natural reason, whereunto secular

literature helpeth much. And, secondly, the comments of holy doctors. And, thirdly, above all things, the articles of the Catholic faith received and believed through the church of Christ.[4]

The three cases of heresy given in the last chapter may be regarded as in the Lollard tradition. They are typical of the crude thinking and anti-clericism that were the outcome of the vulgarization of Wycliff's teaching. A new and more dangerous situation was created in 1517 when Martin Luther made his attack on the system of indulgences. Even as late as 1519 he wrote, "If unfortunately there are such things in Rome as might be improved, there neither is, nor can be, any reason that one should tear oneself away from the Church in schism. Rather, the worse things become, the more a man should help and cling to her, for by schism and contempt nothing can be mended."[5] That opinion could have been expressed by John Fisher, John Colet, or Thomas More. But within a year, Luther had swung far away from that reasonable position. In 1520 he published three books which made nonsense of his professed desire to avoid severance from the Church; *To the Christian Nobility of Germany*, *The Babylonish Captivity of the Church*, and *The Liberty of a Christian Man*, were challenges to authority that could not be ignored. At the end of that year, Luther publicly burned the Papal Bull,[6] *Exsurge, Domine*, which had condemned his teaching.

Lutheran books were soon brought into England; the merchants of the Steelyard were at first the chief

---

[4] *English Works* (ed. Campbell), II, p. 79.

[5] Quoted by Gordon Rupp in *The Righteousness of God* (1953), p. 9.

[6] 15th June 1520.

importers, and found it a profitable trade. These books and tracts were in Latin or German so their first market was amongst scholars; but the ideas also disseminated by word of mouth and were readily accepted by the inheritors of the Lollard opinions. They had come to be called the "known men," but how far they were linked with the Lutherans cannot now be determined; there was certainly no direct contact between the latter-day Lollards and the German Reformers at this early stage. The "known men" were fertile soil for this new crop of heresies, and they were amongst those who helped to distribute the Lutheran books. They became merged in the "Christian Brethren" who were the early advocates of the continental teaching.[7]

One group of scholars at Cambridge met at the White Horse tavern which was soon nicknamed "Little Germany"; some of their names are known; these included John Frith, Thomas Bilney, Matthew Parker, Thomas Cranmer, Hugh Latimer and Nicholas Ridley. How far John Fisher was aware of this Cambridge Movement, as it may be termed, is not known; rumours of it must have reached him as chancellor, and his spirit must have been deeply distressed at what was happening in his own beloved university.

This resurgence of heretical ideas alarmed the hierarchy, so we read in John Fisher's Register under the date 4th June 1521 of the reception of letters from Cardinal Wolsey as papal legate *a latere*, according to the instructions of Leo X, condemning the Lutheran heresy;

---

[7] On this subject, see, E. G. Rupp, *The English Protestant Tradition* (1949), chap. 1.

this was to be published by the clergy throughout the diocese.[8]

The change in emphasis from the Lollard to the Lutheran teachings is well illustrated in John Fisher's Register. A case of abjuration in 1513 has been given; the next is dated February 1525.[9] Thomas Bateman, hermit, and late keeper of St. William's Chapel in the parish of St. Margaret, Rochester, was accused of saying that beyond the sea people communicated under both kinds as they should here; also that over there religious persons were leaving their religion and taking wives; he had advised the hermit who succeeded him at St. William's not to be hasty in making his profession as "a new world was to come and his straight [strict] religion shall not be accepted."

He signed the abjuration with his mark.

His penance was imprisonment at the bishop's will, but he was allowed out on occasions as provision was made for him to wear the outward signs of a penitent. As he had been a professed hermit, his penance was more severe than was usual.

Early in the following year, 1526, the first copies of William Tyndale's translation of the New Testament arrived in England. His influence was to prove far more powerful in this country than that of Luther. Tyndale's controversial works were written in a style that all could understand without that prolixity that must have weakened the effect of the answers of some of his opponents. His entry into the arena marked the beginning of another act in this tragedy.

---

[8] It should be noted that in spite of Wolsey's great powers, the Bull (dated 2nd January 1521) could not be promulgated until Henry had given permission; the delay was due to him. *L.P.*, III, nos. 1220, 1233.

[9] f. 107v.

It is against this background that the second half of John Fisher's episcopate must be seen; the contention with heresy alone would have demanded all his powers, but there were to be other problems to add to his anguish of mind and spirit.

CHAPTER X
FIRST CONTROVERSIES

BOTH St. John Fisher and St. Thomas More had passed their fiftieth birthdays when they wrote their first controversial books, and both did so at the request of others. In 1528 Bishop Cuthbert Tunstal of London asked Sir Thomas More to reply to the heretical books that were all too easily obtainable in London; the result was the liveliest of More's controversial writings, his Dialogue Concerning Heresies. Ten years earlier, Bishop Stephen Poncher of Paris, drew John Fisher's attention to a book by a learned Dominican, Jacques Lefèvre d'Etaples, on the problem of the identification of Mary Magdalen.

It may be noted that, although he had not published any theological work, John Fisher's reputation as a scholar was such that his opinion was sought by the bishop of another country.

Both Stephen Poncher and Jacques Lefèvre were admirers of Erasmus who wrote that he "liked the little book on The Three Magdalens";[10] Erasmus and Lefèvre were to quarrel later, but at this period they were on friendly terms.

Lefèvre discussed the question of whether Mary Magdalen, out of whom Jesus cast seven devils (Luke viii. 2), was the sinful woman who anointed Jesus (Luke vii. 37). Could she also be the Mary, sister of Martha and Lazarus, who anointed Jesus before the Pasch (John xii. 3)?

---

[10] Allen, III, no. 766.

Latin tradition identified the three as one, but Lefèvre distinguished three separate women, Mary Magdalen, the sinful woman, and Mary the sister of Martha.

John Fisher had already read Lefèvre's book before Stephen Poncher had asked for his opinion; on second reading, Fisher carefully examined the argument in the light of the Gospel texts and came to the conclusion that Lefèvre's opinions were not based on a thorough study of the evidence. More distressing was the fact that the teaching of the early Fathers had been rather hastily rejected; this, he felt, might encourage a sceptical spirit and lead to a lessening of the authority of the Church. So he decided to write a book in support of the traditional view.

It is not necessary here to go over the arguments put forward by the two opponents; the problem is still an open one.[11]

John Fisher sent his manuscript to Erasmus and asked him to get it printed. There was some difficulty at first, but no sooner was the book published in Paris (March 1519) than it was eagerly bought and a reprint was needed within a few months. Meantime another scholar had entered the field on behalf of Lefèvre; this was Josse Clichtove of Nieuport in Flanders, another friend of Erasmus and an opponent of Luther. John Fisher at once replied to him, and in September of that same year he published yet a third book on the same subject. Erasmus thought that John Fisher had been too severe on Lefèvre in the first book, but considered that the final contribution to

---

[11] *Mary Magdalene* by R. L. Bruckberger, O.P. (1954), is such a mixture of fact and fancy that it cannot be regarded as a serious contribution to scholarship, but it is evidence of the conflicting opinions that may be held.

the argument showed an improvement in style and temper.

A fragment of a letter from Sir Thomas More seems to refer to this book.

> I cannot express in words my delight, both for your own sake and for the sake of our country, that your lordship writes in a style that might well be that of Erasmus. As for the subject matter, ten Erasmuses could not be more convincing . . . . Farewell, my lord bishop, most highly esteemed for virtue and learning.[12]

The year following this small paper war, saw John Fisher in the most inconsonant surroundings; he was in the entourage of the king at the Field of Cloth of Gold (June 1520). Thomas More was also there but he left no record of his impressions. Every detail of that glittering display of magnificence was recorded by the chroniclers. Its occasion was a meeting near Calais of Henry VIII and Francis I of France. The two kings swore friendship to each other. A few days later, Henry met the Emperor Charles V nearby at Gravelines. John Fisher still accompanied the king. The two princes decided not to conclude an alliance of friendship with Francis. Rightly has an historian described the Field of Cloth of Gold as "the most portentous deception on record."[13]

---

[12] *Rogers*, no. 78

[13] A. F. Pollard, *Henry VIII*, p. 114.

John Fisher's reflections on this experience are given in the first of two sermons he preached on the Feast of All Saints in 1520.[14]

There is no indication that these sermons were preached on official occasions; they may be regarded as examples of what may be termed John Fisher's parish preaching, and are all the more precious for that reason. The language is of a kind that all could understand; there is no display of learning or of authorities, nor is there anything controversial; the pastor is speaking to his flock.

The text was Matthew v. 20. "Unless your rightwise life be more abundant than was the living of the Scribes and Pharisees, ye shall not enter into the kingdom of heaven." The preacher began by outlining the scheme of his sermon; first he would consider "the sovereign joys and pleasures which be above in the kingdom of heaven where these Saints be present now with our saviour Christ;" secondly, he would remind his hearers of the "grievous pains of Purgatory," and thirdly, he would show how these matters concerned their own souls.

After all had said a Paternoster, the preacher turned to the first part of his subject, and here used his memories of the meetings of the princes to illustrate his theme. It is not difficult to imagine with what attention his description would be followed. The Field of Cloth of Gold was already entering the world of fable; the preacher gave them his impressions of a great occasion at which all would have liked to be present, but the moral he drew must have been unexpected, and would certainly not have pleased King Henry had he been in the congregation. We can take delight in the preacher's skill; he made no direct attack on

---

[14] Printed by William Rastell in 1532. Only four copies are known; three are in the U.S.A., and one in the Bodleian Library. They have not been reprinted since 1532.

the princes nor on the purposes of the meeting, but his listeners must have concluded with him that all was vanity.

Our eyen hath seen many pleasures, many gay sights, many wonderful things that bath appeared and seemed unto us joyous and comfortable. But yet all these were but counterfeits of the true joys, all these were but dull and dark images of the perfect comfort which the blessed saints have now above in the kingdom of heaven. I doubt not but ye have heard of many goodly sights which were showed of late beyond the sea, with much joy and pleasure worldly. Was it not a great thing within so short a space to see three great Princes of this world? I mean the Emperor, and the king our master, and the French king. And each of these three in so great honour, showing their royalty, showing their riches, showing their power with each of their noblesse appointed and apparelled in rich clothes, in silks, in velvets, cloths of gold, and such other precious arrayments. To see three right excellent Queens at once together, and of three great realms. That one, the noble Queen our mistress, the very exemplar of virtue and nobleness to all women. And the French Queen. And the third Queen Mary,[15] sometime wife unto Lewis French king, sister to our sovereign lord, a right excellent and fair Lady. And every of them accompanied with so many other fair ladies in sumptuous and gorgeous apparel, such dancings, such harmonies [music], such dalliance, and so many pleasant pastimes, so curious houses and buildings, so preciously apparelled, such costly welfare of dinners, suppers and banquets, so delicate wines, so

---

[15] Mary Tudor, Duchess of Suffolk, grandmother of Lady Jane Grey.

precious meats, such and so many noble men of arms, so rich and goodly tents, such joustings, such tourneys, and such feats of war. These were assuredly wonderful sights as for this world, and as much as hath been read of in years done, or in any Chronicles or Histories heretofore written, and as great as men's wits and studies could devise and imagine for that season. Nevertheless, these great sights have a far difference from the joys of heaven, and that in five points.

First, the joys and pleasures of this life, be they never so great, yet they have a weariness and fastidiousness[16] with them adjoined, whereby men at length of time be weary of them, as thus: there is no meat nor drink so delicate, so pleasant, so delectable, but if a man or a woman be long accustomed therewith he shall have at the length a loathesomeness thereof. Take the most delicate and pleasant fish or flesh that the heart standeth unto, and use it customably and none other, and thou shalt be full soon weary thereof. And in like manner it was of those goodly sights which were had and done beyond the sea. I say not the contrary but that they were pleasant sights. But yet doubtless many were full weary of them at length, and had a loathesomeness and a fastidiousness of them, and some of them had much liever be at home.

Does that last sentence express the feelings John Fisher had himself experienced in Picardy?

In his sermon he then elaborated the contrast between earthly and heavenly joys; he continued:

---

[16] Used here in the older sense of causing disgust.

> ... and verily of such pleasures ariseth their own destruction at the end which did right well appear in the pleasant sights whereof I spake before. For by the reason of them, great money was spent, many great men's coffers were emptied and many were brought to a great ebb and poverty. This ebb caused a greater flow of covetise [covetousness] afterwards in many men's hearts. Some of them were the sicker and weaker in their bodies, and divers took their death thereby. Some by reason of their sumptuous apparellment learned so great pride that hitherto they could not shift it from them. Never was seen in England such excess of apparellment before as hath been used ever since. And therefore also must needs arise much heart burning and secret envy amongst many for the apparel. They which had the least, did envy the other which had richer apparel than they had or might reach unto. Thus, many for these pleasures were the worse, both in their bodies and in their souls ...

Again the preacher made the contrast with the true joys of the saints.

> ... For that little while that we were there, sometime there was such dust, and therewithal so great winds, that all the air was full of dust. The gowns of velvet, and cloth of gold were full of dust, the rich trappers of horses were full of dust, hats, caps, gowns were full of dust and briefly to speak, horse and men were so encumbered with dust that scantly one might see another. The winds blew down many tents, shaked sore the houses that were builded for pleasure, and let divers of them to be builded. Sometimes again

we had rains and thunders so immeasurably that no man might stir forth to see no pleasures. Sometime when men would longer have disported them at the jousts, came the night and darkness upon them .and interrupted their pleasure.

In Heaven is no such interruptions . . . .

. . . Kings and Emperors all be but men, all be but mortal. All the gold and all the precious stones of this world, can not make them but mortal men. All the rich apparel that can be devised, can not take from them the condition of mortality. They be in themself but earth and ashes, and to earth they must return, and all their glory well considered and beholden with right eyen is but very miserable.

So he passed on to consider the pains of purgatory, and besought his hearers to pray for the souls there since even the beasts of the field come to the help of their own kind.

We may see the unreasonable creatures how soon they be moved to have ruth, pity, and compassion of their resemblance, of such as be like unto them in nature only. The hog, which is but a very churlish beast, yet when one of their kind crieth, all the residue nigh thereabout, gather to the relief of the same. When one sparrow or other bird is taken in a gylder [snare] or with a lime twig all the other near about gathereth about her to save or succour her life.

The third part, directed to the salvation of the souls of his listeners, leads to the conclusion.

Now therefore Christian man whiles thou art in this life, and while thou hast time and space, study to make amends for thy sins. Study to store thy soul by true contrition and sorrow for thy sins. Study here for to wash the same often with the gracious water of tears. Study to cleanse thy soul with often renewing of thy confession. Study here by thy good and gracious works to pay thy own debts before thy departure hence. Study to keep the commandments of God without the which thou can not enter into the kingdom of heaven. Be now ready to forgive all injuries and wrongs done unto thee, that thereby almighty God may the rather forgive thee such trespasses or injuries as thou hast beforetime committed unto him. Pray for thyself fast. For thyself give alms. For thyself pray, and procure other to pray for thee likewise. Better is now one penny spent for the wealth and salvation of thy soul when thou mayst keep it unto thyself than thousands after thy death when thou mayst no longer have the use thereof.

Do thus, and by the grace of God thou shall eschew that painful prison.

Do thus and thy soul shall be cleansed and stored against thy departure out of this world, that thou shalt without any long delays or tarrying by the way, be received into the joyous kingdom where thou shalt see the glorious sights of that most wonderful country, and be made partner of the most excellent joys and pleasures which there everywhere doth abound, and ever shall endure to the which he bring us that for us all died upon the cross, our saviour Christ Jesu. Amen.

It has seemed well to quote extensively from this sermon not only because of its intrinsic value, but to give

FIRST CONTROVERSIES

the reader some idea of the style of John Fisher's everyday preaching.

The second of these two sermons may be more briefly considered. There is no indication of the interval between the two, but the second may have been preached on All Souls' Day. It opens with a recapitulation of the previous sermon.

> ... the joys of this world be like midsummer games and Christmas games or plays. The Court of King Edward, the court of King Richard and the court of the King that now is dead, where be they now? All they were but counterfeit images and disguising for a time, it was but a play for a time. But the court of heaven is alway stable in one point where the officers change never. There is the true nobleness, the sure honour, the very glory. This glory, this honour, this nobleness we shall never see, we shall never come into it, unless our life be more righteous than the lives of the Jews. A sore word, a sore threat, nevertheless it is true.

He took as his theme the fall of Adam. His treatment of the relative positions of Adam and Eve was in keeping with medieval notions, but would not be acceptable today.

> Every man and woman that liveth in this world hath in them a manner of representation, these two persons, Adam and Eve, for they have a soul and a body, and the soul representeth Adam, and the body Eve. For as the man should order his wife, so should the soul rule and govern the body.... Where the soul governeth, there wisdom governeth, there reason governeth, there Adam is master, and there is all well. Where the body governeth, there folly governeth,

there beastliness governeth, there Eve is mistress and all is amiss.

The sermon then treats of first "what these fruits do mean;" secondly, "when we sin by tasting of this fruit," and thirdly, "the folly of Adam and all sinners." Finally the preacher considered stops that be in the way' of Paradise—the double-edged sword, "the brenning flame," and "the angels of the order of the Cherubim."

John Fisher's first controversial publication against the Lutherans was on one specific question: was St. Peter ever at Rome? Ulrich Velene [Velenus] of Minden published a book claiming to prove that St. Peter could not have been at Rome and that therefore the claims of the popes to be his successors was an idle boast. The argument is set out in eighteen theses, and followed by refutations of seven claims put forward by the supporters of the popes. Cuthbert Tunstal, the new Bishop of London, had brought the book to the notice of John Fisher who said he had never read anything more impudent; he at once set to work to answer it. His reply was published in 1522.[17]

One by one he examined and rejected the eighteen theses and refuted the refutations. It would be wearying to go over the same ground here. One of John Fisher's answers has a special interest. Velene had argued that as there is no mention of St. Peter in the letters St. Paul wrote to Seneca, St. Peter could not have been at Rome. To this John Fisher replied that the letters were not genuine, and on this matter he was content to accept the opinion of Erasmus whose judgment was more to be relied on than that of a thousand other scholars.

---

[17] *Convulsio calumniarum Ulrichi Minhoniensis quibus petrum numquam Romae. . . .*, Paris and Antwerp.

FIRST CONTROVERSIES

One passage in John Fisher's book shows how acutely aware he was of the scandal caused by the luxury and venality of the Curia.

> Perhaps some may say, "Nowhere else is the life of Christians more contrary to Christ than in Rome, and that, too, even among the prelates of the Church, whose conversation is diametrically opposed to the life of Christ. Christ lived poverty; they fly from poverty so far that their only study is to keep up riches. Christ shunned the glory of this world; they will do and suffer everything for glory. Christ afflicted himself by frequent fasts and continual prayers; they neither fast nor pray, but give themselves up to luxury and lust. They are the greatest scandal to all who live sincere Christian lives, since their morals are so contrary to the doctrine of Christ, that through them the name of Christ is blasphemed throughout the world." This is perhaps what an adversary might object. But all this merely confirms what I am proving. For since the Sees of other Apostles are everywhere occupied by infidels, and this one only, which belonged to Peter, yet remains under Christian rule, though for so many crimes and such unspeakable wickedness, it has deserved like the rest to be destroyed, what must we conclude but that Christ is most faithful to his promises since he keeps them in favour of his greatest enemies, however grievous and many may be their insults to him?

Such outspoken words from a bishop must have been noted in Rome, and it may be that knowledge of them prompted Clement VII in 1524 to write to Wolsey to suggest that the Bishop of London (Tunstal) and the

122   THE LIFE OF ST. JOHN FISHER

Bishop of Rochester should go to Rome to discuss how to remove abuses in the Church.[18] The project came to nothing, for Clement was soon entangled in the meshes of his own diplomacy and forgot the good intentions formed in the first year of his pontificate.

---

[18] *L.P.*, IV, I, no. 435.

VIII - Thomas Wolsey, Cardinal and Lord Chancellor
Unknown Artist

IX The Field of the Cloth of Gold

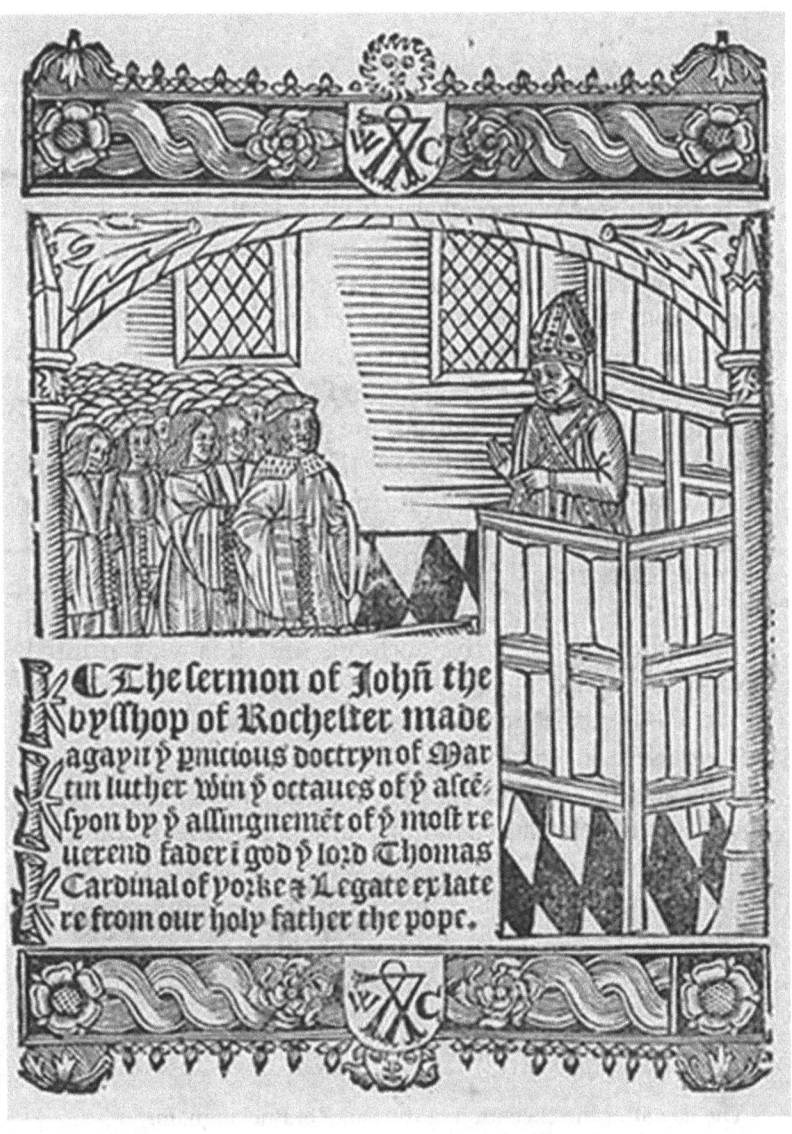

X. John Fisher Preaching against Luther

CHAPTER XI
LUTHER

THE greatly increased influx of Lutheran books and tracts from about 1520 was a problem of grave concern to the bishops. Those who were found with such books in their possession could be brought before the ecclesiastical authorities, but comparatively few were taken in this way. The pope's Bull[1] condemning forty-one heretical opinions of Luther must have been known to Wolsey early in 1521 although the king did not allow its promulgation until June. It may have been with this knowledge in mind that the cardinal decreed the public burning of heretical books at Paul's Cross on 12th May, the Octave of the Ascension.[2] Bishop John Fisher was appointed to preach the sermon, and this was printed shortly afterwards.[3]

It was a distinguished congregation with the cardinal on a dais, the Archbishop of Canterbury (Warham) and the Bishop of London (Tunstal) sitting at his feet. Other bishops with the ambassadors and high officers of state were assembled. One foreign observer said that 30,000 were present, but that figure (half the population of

---

[1] See above, p. 107.

[2] The day after the execution of the Duke of Buckingham.

[3] The sermon was scarified in Tyndale's *Obedience of a Christian Man* (1528), where he wrote of John Fisher's "juggling, his conveying, his foxy wiliness," etc. (See Parker edition, pp. 189, 208, 213, 341.) This sermon was translated into Latin by Richard Pace; at the suggestion of Nicholas Wilson it was printed by Siberch of Cambridge in 1522.

London) should be read "tropically". The sermon must have taken two hours to deliver.[4]

The text was from the gospel of the day. "When the comforter shall come whom I shall send unto you, the spirit of truth that issueth from my father, he shall bear witness of me." (John xv. 26).

The preacher began by describing a clear, sunny day on which "riseth in some quarter of the heaven a thick black cloud that darketh all the face of the heaven and shadoweth from us the clear light of the sun." This picture he used as a figure of the "black cloud of heresy" raised by "one, Martin Luther, a friar." Having given the heads of his argument, the preacher made the bidding prayer, "unto this Holy Spirit of truth."

> That in this dangerous storm and perilous tempest he will stay our hearts with the testimony of his truth; that we waver not in the catholic doctrine of our mother Holy Church, but fastly believe such eruditions as hath been delivered unto us from our saviour Christ Jesu by his apostles and their successors, the holy bishops and fathers and doctors of the church; for the which and for grace necessary for you and for me every person say their devotion.

The main argument of the sermon was that the promise of the spirit of truth safeguards the universal Church of Christ from false teaching. The preacher's summary at the end shows how his argument was developed.

> I have remembered unto you according to my promise four instructions that be offered unto us of

---

[4] *E. W.*, pp. 311-48.

this gospel graciously. First that the Holy Spirit which is the third person in the divinity was sent from the father Almighty God and from his son our saviour Christ Jesu, to be the spirit of truth residing for ever in the church of Christ, and to be as a comforter from time to time against all storms and tempests of heresies ascertaining us in the time of every doubtfulness the very truth whereunto we shall hold and keep us. By the occasion of this instruction I showed three things. First that this instruction and all the whole gospel pertaineth to the universal church of Christ, which thing I proved by Luther's own words. Second that the head of this universal church was the Pope under Christ, which one point taketh away one great ground of Martin Luther and shaketh sore many of his erroneous articles. Third that Martin Luther dividing himself from the head of this body cannot have in him this spirit of truth.

For the second instruction I showed that the heat of charity spread in our hearts by the Holy Spirit of God giveth evidence of the lively light of faith shining upon our souls from our saviour Christ, by the which instruction was undermined another great ground of Martin Luther's, which is that only faith doth justify a sinner without works.

For the third instruction I showed that the eruditions left unto the church by the holy apostles beareth unto us testimony of the faith of Christ and what thing we shall believe in his church; where also was lost another ground of Martin Luther which will not admit any other testimony but only that that is written in scripture. Against whom I proved that he must besides the scriptures written receive also the traditions of the apostles not written, over this the

Councils general in whom the Holy Ghost did speak, and the interpretations made by the holy bishops and doctors of the church by whose mouths the third person in the godhead, the spirit of truth, spake and speaketh, informing the church for this time like as did the father Almighty God by his prophets before, and as did his son the second person by his apostles.

For the fourth instruction I showed you that the defence which is made for Martin Luther by his adherents whereby many weak souls be overthrown is clearly taken away by the most loving and most gracious forewarning of our saviour Christ as we have heard in the end of the gospel.

The preacher supported his arguments by quotations from the Scriptures and the Fathers, but the sermon was not overloaded with scholarship; it was not John Fisher's custom to parade his learning; it was the solid foundation on which he based his preaching.

One passage has a special interest.

But touching these sacraments, the king's grace our sovereign lord in his own person hath with his pen so substantially foughten against Martin Luther that I doubt not but every true Christian man that shall read this book shall see those blessed sacraments cleared and delivered from the slanderous mouth and cruel teeth that Martin Luther hath set upon them, wherein all England may take great comfort and specially all those that love learning.[5]

---

[5] Bridgett criticizes this sermon as unsuited as a discourse to the people. The chief part of the congregation was made up of leaders of the church and state, and it is to them that the preacher directed his words. However many of the populace may have been present, they would have been kept apart from the dignitaries. Probably few could have heard the

It is recorded that during the sermon, the cardinal held a copy of the King's Book in his hand.⁶ This was Henry's *Assertio Septem Sacramentorum* which was his reply to Luther's tract *De Captivitate Babylonica* published in 1520. Luther maintained that there were not seven sacraments—Baptism, Confirmation, the Eucharist, Penance, Extreme Unction, Holy Orders, and Matrimony—but only three, Baptism, Penance, and "of Bread." This he regarded as a provisional opinion as he thought, in fact, that there was only one sacrament and three "sacramental signs."

The king's reply was not a deep theological treatise, but the kind of exposition that an intelligent and well-instructed layman might write. The manuscript was submitted to some theologians of whom John Fisher was one, and given its final form by Sir Thomas More.⁷ The book was printed by Richard Pynson in July 1521. Special copies were printed on vellum and sent to the princes of Europe who were no doubt surprised to receive such a gift; one copy, bound in cloth of gold, was presented to Pope Leo X in September, and a month later Henry was granted the title of *Fidei Defensor*.

---

preacher's words. We may suspect that the ordinary folk were attracted to the spectacle that Wolsey knew so well how to stage, and, no doubt, the bonfire was an added attraction!

⁶ C.S.P. Venetian, III, no. 210. Is this an early example of pre-publication publicity?

⁷ This is how I interpret More's statement that he was "only a sorter out and placer of the principal matters." (See my *St. Thomas More*, pp. 158-9, and A. F. Pollard, *Henry VIII*, pp. 98-100). It has been maintained that John Fisher was the true author (e.g. *Lewis*, pp. 109-10), and this may explain the inclusion of the book in the 1597 folio of his Latin works. His eulogy of the book (apart from other considerations) rules this out; it would have been contrary to his known probity to have praised what was his own work, even to satisfy the exigences of courtliness.

It may have been praise of the King's Book that led to attempts in later years by Henry and Thomas Cromwell to call in all copies;[8] the king had changed his views on the authority of the pope since the day he defended him against Luther.

Meanwhile John Fisher was at work on his own refutation of Luther. In reply to the pope's condemnation of forty-two heretical propositions, Luther wrote his *Assertion*; this was published at the end of 1520. John Fisher's *Confutatio* was published in Antwerp in January 1523 but there seem to have been earlier and unauthorized printings.[9] The preface includes another tribute to Henry "*qui dudum gladio Romanam protexit ecclesiam.*"[10]

On the back of the title page are some verses contributed by George Daye[11] who was one of John Fisher's chaplains at Cambridge. Four of the lines read:

Hic pugil est Christi, vitæ probitate refulgens, Ingenio clarus, clarus et eloquio, Anglia quem genuit, Docuit schola Cantabriana, Rolla tenet, tanto nobilitata viro.	"This is the pugilist of Christ, shining with uprightness of life, renowed in genius and eloquence, whom England nourished and Cambridge taught, Rochester holds, ennobled by such a man."

---

[8] *L.P.*, VIII, no .55; IX, no. 963.

[9] A list of Henry Bullock's books includes *Roffensis contra Lutherum*, 25. 4d.

[10] Henry who for so long has protected the Roman Church with the sword. - Editor.

[11] Later Master of St. John's College and Bishop of Chichester. He went part of the way with the Reformers; he was deprived and imprisoned in 1551; he was released from the Tower on Mary's accession and preached at her coronation.

John Fisher's Rochester chaplain, John Addison (or Adeson), was granted the privilege by the king of printing the book for three years.

Twenty pages of the main text are devoted to an exposition of ten truths on which the author proposed to base his refutation of Luther's opinions. As these form the heart of his argument, they deserve quotation.

1. Those who have trusted to their own wits in the interpretation of the scriptures have generally erred grievously.
2. Anyone who relies on his own inspiration alone in the interpretation of the scriptures easily falls into error.
3. When any dispute arises concerning the scriptures or indeed concerning any truth affecting the church, there is need for some authority to whom appeal can be made.
4. An appeal to the scriptures alone cannot always settle a dispute.
5. It was for this reason that the Holy Spirit was sent, and has remained with the church, so that when errors arise they can be corrected.
6. The Holy Spirit has spoken, and will always speak, by the tongues of the fathers as well as by the full teaching of the church, to root out heresy.
7. It is clear that anyone who does not accept the teaching of the fathers despises the work of the Holy Spirit, and shows that he has not that Spirit himself.
8. If the Holy Spirit has spoken by the mouths of individual fathers for the instruction of the church, how much greater credit must be given to the fathers assembled in council.

9. Those apostolic traditions which are not recorded in the scriptures must none the less be observed.
10. In addition to these traditions, the customs received by the universal church must not be rejected by any Christian.

Having established this basis for his confutation, John Fisher proceeded to examine one by one Luther's defence of the forty-one propositions condemned by the pope. We need not here follow the chain of argument link by link. The text has the appearance of a dialogue between "LUTHE" and "EPISCO." Each quotation from Luther is followed by a refutation from the bishop. Luther's words take up perhaps a quarter of the 200,000 words of the book. The effect, however, is not comparable with, for example, Sir Thomas More's *Dialogue against Heresies* (1529); here are none of those lighter touches that make the younger scholar's book still so readable. John Fisher was solely intent on demolishing the teaching of his opponent and he made use of his vast knowledge of the Fathers to support his arguments. The book was written in Latin, as were all his controversial writings, and it was the world of learning that he had as his audience. Thomas More wrote in the vernacular in order to reach a literate but untrained public. It may be noted that both writers shared a devotion to St. Augustine.

The younger man owed much to the erudition of the older theologian. *The Dialogue against Heresies* contains one direct reference to this Confutatio: . . . "as an honourable prelate of this realm in his most erudite book answereth Luther . . ."[12]

---

[12] *E.W.*, II, p. 319.

In his letter to a monk[13] (1520) Thomas More spoke of John Fisher as "noble not more in learning than in virtue, than whom no one living to-day is more illustrious."

Not much is known of the personal association of these two saints. The difference in age, ten years, and the episcopal and academic dignities of the elder would preclude easy familiarity; moreover, as has been noted with Erasmus, the younger man had such a Veneration for the bishop that their dealings could not have been of such a lively character as that between More and his intimate friends. There is no record of John Fisher having visited Thomas More either in Bucklersbury or at Chelsea, and the only known occasion when Thomas More went down to Rochester has already been mentioned.[14]

Thomas Stapleton in his Tres Thomae has preserved for us a few fragments of their correspondence of which the originals have perished. One passage has already been quoted.

Soon after Thomas More was knighted (1524), John Fisher wrote to him:

> I beg that, through your good offices with our most gracious king, we at Cambridge may have some hope that our young men may receive encouragement to learning from the bounty of so noble a prince. We have very few friends at court who have the will and the power to commend our interests to the king's majesty, and among them we reckon you the chief; for hitherto, even when you were of lower rank, you have always shown favour to us. We rejoice that now you are raised to the dignity of knighthood and become so intimate with the king, and we offer you our heartiest

---

[13] *Rogers*, No. 83.

[14] See above, p. 44.

congratulations, for we know that you will continue to show us the same favour. Please now give your help to this young man, who is well versed in theology and a zealous preacher to the people. He puts his hopes in your influence with our noble King and in your willingness to accept my recommendation.[15]

It may seem curious that a bishop who had been such a close associate of the king's father and grandmother and was himself a member of the council should have found it necessary to appeal for the king's patronage in this indirect way; this suggests—and there are other slight indications—that the king did not regard John Fisher with favour.

Thomas More replied:

> As to this priest, Reverend Father, of whom you write that he will soon obtain a prebend if he can obtain a powerful advocate with the king, I think I have so wrought that our prince will raise no obstacle. Whatever influence I have with the king—it is very little, but such as it is—is as freely at your disposal, for yourself or your scholar, as a house is to its owner. I owe your students constant gratitude for the heart-felt affection of which their letters to me are a token. Farewell, best and most courteous of bishops, and continue your affection for me.

Who were the students who wrote to Thomas More? Why did they write? These questions cannot be answered but they suggest a link with Cambridge of which no record remains. The next recorded correspondence between the two saints was when both were in the Tower.

---

[15] *Rogers*, Nos. 104, 105; *Stapleton* (tr. Hallett), pp. 47-48.

> Brother for I pray you to delyver unto the bryng herof Roger
> Nott for my ladyes power ffolys at layefeld. And this
> byll assigned with my hande shalbe your discharge from Lamberth
> this the xxviij day of June. Jo. Roffs
>
> & I pray you do so moch to se peters work for my ladyes
> tomb & whan ye have ony leyser I woll com my self togeder

XI. [manuscript] Bishop John Fisher to the prior of St. Bartholomew's.

XII. A Late Manuscript

CHAPTER XII
FURTHER CONTROVERSIES

THE early biographer records an episode that took place at Cambridge about 1521.[1] As Chancellor, John Fisher had copies of the papal condemnation of Luther's opinions posted on the gates of the colleges and at other suitable places. Some sympathizer of Luther wrote on one copy, "Beatus vir cuius est nomen Domini spes eius, et non respexit vanitates et insanias falsas *istas*"—the last word being a gloss upon the text, thus applying the meaning to the words of the condemnation itself: "Blessed is the man whose hope is in the name of the Lord, and who has not regarded *these* vanities and lying follies." This act of defiance created a stir in the university, but the authorities were unable to discover the culprit. John Fisher therefore called the students together, and, expressing his great sorrow, urged the offender to confess his fault by a given date.

When the day was come, and the assembly ready, which was no small number at so rare a case, the Chancellor there moved the malefactor the second time to repentance and confession of his offence; but

---

[1] There are difficulties in dating this episode. The biographer stated that it happened at a time when Leo X granted an indulgence to all who repudiated Luther's teaching. There is no record of such an indulgence. Leo X died in 1521. There may be confusion here with the Bull of 1520 (promulgated in England in 1521) which threatened Luther and those who protected him with excommunication. The "istas" added by the malefactor would refer to the forty-one condemned opinions. Ortroy suggests 1525-30 when Lutheranism was growing in Cambridge. Bridgett more reasonably, I think, suggests 1521.

the spirit that before suggested this wicked attempt into his heart, would by no means suffer him to hearken to any admendment. Wherefore the Chancellor, seeing the sickness desperate and not likely to be cured in so obstinate and stubborn a patient, feared most the infection of others and therefore fell to his last and extreme remedy. And so causing a bill of excommunication to be written, took the same in his hands and began to read it, but after that he had proceeded a space in the reading thereof, he stayed and began again to consider in his mind the great weight of his grievous sentence, which so much pierced his heart, that even before them all he could not refrain weeping. The auditory seeing that lamentable sight, fell likewise to such a compassion that as well the ancient reverend doctors and masters as other students of the younger sort, perceiving the mild nature of that holy man, fell eftsoons into great weeping and lamentation, and so left off without further proceeding in the excommunication for that time. Nevertheless appointing a third day for their purpose, against which time if he came not in, then to proceed to the end without any further delay.[2]

The third day came but the culprit did not confess, so the penalty was pronounced.

The early biographer added that the unknown student was Peter de Valence, a renegade priest from Normandy.[3]

---

[2] *Ortroy*, p. 112.

[3] He became chaplain to Bishop Goodrich of Ely who recommended him as tutor to Gregory, the son of Thomas Cromwell. (*L.P.*, VII, no. 1583; *L.P.*, VIII, no. 618.) Valence later returned to Ely as almoner (Strype, *Mem.*, vol. II p. 294).

Public affairs under the guidance of Wolsey were at this period nearing a critical stage. The senseless war with France had emptied the treasury. A loan from London and forced loans of doubtful legality were insufficient to meet the costs, and, reluctantly, Wolsey had to recognize that a Parliament was unavoidable; the last had met in 1515. John Fisher's register records the procedure.[4] The summons to Parliament was dated 23rd January 1523 for the meeting on 15th April. A month later came the summons to Convocation of Canterbury to meet at St. Paul's on 20th April for the purpose of discussing the defence of the Church. By a writ dated 7th May, Cardinal Wolsey convoked the clergy to a combined meeting of Canterbury and York at Westminster Abbey on and June; the reason for this Convocation was stated to be the reform of clerical life and the need for a visitation of both secular and regular clergy exempt and nonexempt. This arrogant supersession of the normal Convocations was an extreme use of Wolsey's powers as legate *a latere*; he brushed aside the authority of Archbishop Warham. As the poet Skelton put it,

> Gentle Paul, lay down thy sword,
> For Peter of Westminster hath shaven thy beard.

The talk of the defence of the Church concealed the real purpose of the Convocation. Wolsey's demand for a high tax on clerical incomes was resisted at St. Paul's. Polydore Virgil, who was probably present, wrote, "Wolsey dealt much more harshly with those who opposed him. For many opposed him, and especially Richard [Fox] bishop of Winchester, John bishop of Rochester, and above all, Rowland Phillips, vicar of

---

[4] *Register*, 109r. and v., 110r. See Pollard, *Wolsey*, pp. 189-90.

Croydon, and canon of St. Paul's, who was a splendid preacher. This last speaker Wolsey summoned while the discussion was going on and so frightened him that he afterwards appeared no more in Convocation, thereby very gravely impairing his integrity."[5]

The clergy at length consented to a tax of half of incomes over £8 a year and one third of those below £8, the payment being spread over five years. John Fisher's Register[6] gives us some indication of how this affected his diocese. He received a letter from Bishop Tunstal, acting for Archbishop Warham, stating that they were appointed collectors for the subsidy which must be paid. The prolongation of the payments over five years did not meet the urgent need for money, so a letter was issued (and November) under the king's authority, demanding that holders of benefices worth over £20 a year should pay up by the end of the month. A list in the Register shows that only a dozen priests had that income in addition to seven religious houses.

This harsh demand was followed a few weeks later by a letter addressed to the bishop, the mayor and bailiffs of Rochester asking them "to practise with" all citizens worth £40 or more to get them also to anticipate payment of the subsidy.

The collection from the clergy did not go smoothly for on 22nd April 1524 a letter from Tunstal complained that the returns made to the collectors were incorrect. A certificate stating that all was in order had to be sent to them by the end of June.

To our picture of the bishop's life we must add these financial responsibilities; his officials would carry out the

---

[5] *Anglica Historia* (Camden Society, 1950), p. 307. For Rowland Phillips see my *St. Thomas More*, p. 292.

[6] Register, 117v., 118r., 119v.

FURTHER CONTROVERSIES

actual collection but there must have been many hard cases amongst the poorly paid priests. These facts may be contrasted with the complaints made at that period of the easy conditions in which priests, lived.

John Fisher's opposition to Wolsey's original demands must have put him out of favour; the cardinal did not tolerate opposition. He was later to take advantage of his exceptional powers to ignore John Fisher's prerogative as diocesan.

In 1524 Wolsey obtained from the pope, Clement VII, powers to suppress monasteries he considered were no longer fulfilling their purpose; the funds he could use for other purposes. Amongst the earliest he dissolved was the Augustinian Abbey of Lesnes, Kent, in 1525. The entry in John Fisher's Register[7] has the note "*inconsulto Reverendo patre Johanne Roffensi episcopo*"[8]—that: it was done without the bishop of the diocese being consulted. Wolsey had the power to act in this high-handed fashion, but, as a matter of courtesy, the advice of bishop of the diocese should have been sought. In 1526 the Priory of Tonbridge was also suppressed.

The name of Polydore Virgil has been mentioned. His tributes to John Fisher must be recorded. In one place the historian wrote of the bishop as "most learned, most kindly, and most virtuous," and elsewhere as "a man of great learning and of the highest honour and piety."[9] When Virgil published his commentary on the Lord's Prayer, he prefaced it with an epistle to John Fisher.

---

[7] Register, 129v.

[8] A. W. Clapham in his Lesnes *Abbey* (1915) mistranslates this entry to mean, the bishop consenting'. This error was pointed out by A. Wood in the *History of the Catholic Church in Plumstead*.

[9] *Anglica Historia*, p. 145 and p. 335.

The labour of combating Luther continued. Two books by John Fisher were published in 1525 at Cologne. The first was *Sacri Sacerdotii Defensio*[10] (Defence of the Priesthood) which was dedicated to Cuthbert Tunstal, Bishop of London; the second book was the *Defensio Regie Assertionis*, a defence of the King's Book on the seven sacraments.

The author seems to have been working on both books during the same period. The first was a reply to Luther's *De abroganda missa privata* (1522) in which he rejected the sacrifice of the Mass and declared that all Christians were priests though for the sake of order and decency it was necessary to appoint some as elders. John Fisher described the book as pestilential, unsound and impudent. His method of refutation was similar to that used in his *Confutatio*; he enunciated ten principles or axioms and then he proceeded to examine Luther's arguments one by one. The ten axioms are the basis of the book.

1. It is reasonable, in matters concerning the salvation of souls, that some men be set apart to act in the name of, and bear responsibility for, the whole multitude.
2. Christ himself, whilst he was on earth, put certain pastors in charge of his flock, to watch over, rule, and teach it.
3. It is fitting that those who are thus appointed pastors of the Christian flock should receive more abundant gifts of grace than others.
4. Not only was it fitting that Christ should do so, but in fact he did bestow upon such pastors of his

---

[10] English translation by Mgr. P. E. Hallett, *The Defence of the Priesthood* (1935). The original Latin text was reprinted in Germany in 1925.

Church grace and power suitably to discharge their duties.
5. The institution of pastors not only was necessary in the early days of the Church's life but needs to last for ever, until the building-up of the Church is fully completed.
6. No one rightly exercises the pastoral office unless he be called, and duly receive from the prelates of the Church both ordination and mission.
7. Those who are lawfully appointed by the pastors of the Church to the pastoral office are undoubtedly called also by the Holy Ghost.
8. All those lawfully ordained receive from the Holy Ghost gifts of grace by which they are made more fit worthily to carry out the duties of their ministry.
9. The Holy Spirit willed that grace should be attached to an outward sensible sign so that when the sign is duly performed we know by faith that grace is at the same moment bestowed.
10. Those who are lawfully ordained pastors and priests of the Church are called, and truly are, priests of God.

Two passages, in translation, will show John Fisher's style of argument. The first comes early in the book.

> Now when we follow the early fathers, unanimous in their witness to the priesthood, we are following the Church, for what else was the Church, but a congregation composed entirely of prelates and subjects? And clearly, all these prelates from the beginning taught this doctrine, and all subjects accepted it. Therefore there cannot be the slightest

doubt that he who has believed this teaching has followed the Church. Undoubtedly, then, it must be considered the more secure way to follow the teaching of the fathers against which no orthodox. Catholic throughout the ages has protested, than to follow so notorious a heresiarch as Luther. For who can doubt that the early fathers who received the command to teach, and who were appointed to that office by the Holy Ghost, were in fact taught infallibly by that same Spirit? This we may conclude especially in regard to those doctrines about which there was never any controversy among them. Wherefore, he who shall take his stand with Luther against the fathers especially when Luther can quote for his side neither any clear text of scripture, as we shall soon prove, nor the witness of any orthodox writer, he is clearly casting himself into a peril not doubtful but most evident.[11]

The second passage comes towards the end of the book.

> The people are like a flock over which the priests are placed as shepherds and rulers. Therefore did Christ thrice say to St. Peter "Feed my sheep." And just like sheep when their shepherds are absent they suffer from many evils. For some wander away and become separated from the rest of the flock, some fall sick and, unless a remedy be at once applied, become incurable. Others are devoured by wolves or other wild beasts. Others, because they are not fed and watered at proper times, perish of hunger and thirst. So, too, of the people, unless protected by the diligent care of their

---

[11] Hallett's translation, p. 21.

pastors, some contract diseases of the soul and give way to every kind of crime, some are pitifully harried and destroyed by heretics and schismatics. Many perish of hunger and thirst because they are deprived of the word of God. Multitudes wander in the desert, and stray far from the straight path, according to the proverb of Solomon, "Where there is no governor the people shall fall".

Men might be bold enough to deny the truth of this picture were it not that we see it daily enacted before our eyes. Where the priests feed the flock committed to them both by their word and by their example the people are preserved from many errors. But on the other hand when the priests are negligent in the performance of their duties the people fall headlong into the abyss of all evils. For this reason did Christ, even when his flock was still quite small, appoint twelve apostles and add to them seventy disciples, commanding them all to teach the people. Upon St. Peter, indeed, whom he made the chief pastor of his flock, he especially enjoined this duty, that if he loved him he should diligently feed his flock. In addition, power was given to the apostles, either through Christ or through the Spirit of Christ, to consecrate priests as they judged fit and to place them in authority over the churches. Nor was there ever lacking the promise of grace as often as the should for this purpose impose hands on anyone.[12]

The argument throughout was supported by a wealth of quotations from the Scriptures and from the Fathers;

---

[12] Hallett's translation, p. 137. For readers who would like a specimen of John Fisher's Latin, the original text of this passage is given at the end of the chapter.

there are some two hundred and fifty references to the Bible in this short book. Such was John Fisher's method. The Lutherans appealed to the Scriptures to justify their contentions; their opponent used the same source but in conjunction with the writings of the Fathers and the traditions of the Church. In all his controversial works, John Fisher again and again emphasized that the Scriptures alone are not sufficient; they must be read in the light of the interpretations of the Fathers and of the teaching of the Church; to do otherwise would inevitably lead to error and heresy and schism.

Luther replied to the King's Book in 1522 in a scurrilous fashion calling Henry, for instance, a frothy buffoon and a senseless monster. Sir Thomas More, under the pseudonym of Gulielmus Rosseus, answered Luther in a vindication published in 1523, and it must be admitted that he was not sparing in vituperation.[13]

One passage links him with John Fisher:

> The Reverend Father John Fisher, Bishop of Rochester, a man illustrious not only by the vastness of his erudition, but much more so by the purity of his life, has so opened and overthrown the assertions of Luther, that if he has any shame he would give a great deal to have burnt his assertions . . . . As regards the primacy of the Roman Pontiff, the Bishop of Rochester has made the matter so clear from the Gospels, the Acts of the Apostles and from the whole of the Old Testament, and from the consent of all the holy fathers, not of the Latins only, but of the Greeks also (of whose opposition Luther is wont to boast), and from the definition of a General Council, M which the Armenians and Greeks, who at that time had been

---

[13] See my *St. Thomas More*, pp. 163-5.

most obstinately resisting, were overcome, that it would be utterly superfluous for me to write again on the subject.[14]

Sir Thomas More must have seen John Fisher's *Confutatio* in manuscript, and he may have also read the bishop's *Defensio* which was published in 1525. This was dedicated to Dr. Nicholas West, Bishop of Ely, and a Cambridge contemporary. In the course of the introductory epistle John Fisher mentioned that West had read part of the book two years earlier. Publication had been delayed, he said, because there had been some hope that Luther might yet submit to the pope, but as this had proved illusory, he had sent the manuscript to the printer.

It was a short book and concentrated on Luther's denial of the Church's doctrine of the Eucharist. The attack on Luther as a person was more bitter than in John Fisher's other writings; this "calling bad names in good Latin" was in the manner of the times, and much as it would offend our modern taste, it would be foolish not to realize that Luther as the leader of the revolt against the Church was an evil monster in the sight of his contemporary opponents. To them he was not an historic figure of the past, but a living threat to the unity of the Church. To them this was not a polite academic disputation but a war for the faith itself.

John Fisher wrote one more book, *De Veritate corporis*, against the Lutherans. Joannes Oecolampadius (Johann Mussgen) professor of theology at Basle, published a short book in 1525 on the Eucharist, in which he argued that the words "This is my body" are to be taken figuratively. The book revealed a division of opinion amongst the

---

[14] Bridgett's translation, *Fisher*, p. 138.

Reformers themselves. On this splitting of the ranks, John Fisher wrote:

> It is related in the Book of Genesis of certain men that they resolved to build a tower, whose top should reach to heaven, so as to leave their names famous to posterity. The world was then of one tongue, but God so punished their pride as to confound their speech, so that one understood not the other. The same punishment has befallen these factious followers of Luther. They also had conceived in their minds that they would build a new church and get fame throughout the world. And in this endeavour it is wonderful how united they were and banded together, so that they seemed to be like one man, with one heart and mind. Nor would they have ceased from this work had not God, pitying his church, looked down from on high, and bridled their madness by the strife of tongues. He has brought it about that those who seemed leaders amongst them understand not each other's voice. They strive with one another, and no one deigns to listen to his neighbour. The followers of Carlstadt have separated from the Lutherans, and they are pouring out insults one against the other. It may be seen from letters just printed in the name of Luther, how great a controversy rages. Even Melancthon, as I have heard from trustworthy men, is not well agreed with Luther. And now at length another of these leaders comes to the front, named John Oecolampadius, who formerly followed Luther in everything, and now he most vehemently differs from him in many points.[15]

---

[15] *Bridgett*, p.135.

The whole of Oecolampadius's book is quoted passage by passage each followed by John Fisher's much lengthier rejoinder. He made the same mistake that Sir Thomas More was to make in his unfinished Confutation of Tyndale; a long drawn-out argument becomes tedious and defeats its purpose. This seems to be a fate that few controversialists can avoid; their earlier works are often the more effective because they are of reasonable length, but as time goes on they get wordier and wordier. It is impossible to say how far such controversies have had effect on opinion; few have changed their views as a result of paper arguments; controversy indeed is an ephemeral form of writing and rarely produces books of permanent influence. Truth, however, must be defended, and the Church has had few more learned or more devoted champions than John Fisher. Our regret must be that he did not write in the vernacular for his few sermons show that he commanded a style that only Sir Thomas More rivalled in their days. If only side by side with the Dialogue against Heresies we could put a book by John Fisher!

Oecolampadius seems to have taken no notice of this attack on his opinions.[16] Erasmus, who had been his friend and now lived in the same city, rejected this new teaching by one who was gaining more and more influence in Basle. When Oecolampadius at length secured a dominating influence in Basle, Erasmus decided that he could no longer live there, and he took refuge in Freiburg.

Within five years, John Fisher had produced five books combating the Lutheran heresies. While he was so engaged, those very heresies were spreading amongst the younger men at Cambridge; it must have been with a sore heart that their chancellor witnessed this development in

---

[16] John Fisher's book was translated into German by John Cochlæus.

the University he had believed would be a nursery of good priests.

JOHN FISHER'S LATIN

Plebs enim formam gregis tenet, cui regendo sacerdotes velut pastores preficiuntur. Propter quod et Christus Petro iam tertio dixit: "Paste oves meas." Et profecto, quemadmodum oves, ubi pastores abfuerint, pluribus malis afficiuntur. Quedam enim aberrant et disperguntur a reliquo grege, quedam in morbos incidunt, quibus nisi medela protinus adhibeatur, evadunt incurabiles. Alie a lapis atque ceteris id genus crudelibus feris devorantur. Nonnulle, quod non satis ad aquas et pascua ducantur temporibus, siti fameque sepius intermoriuntur. Sic nimirum et populus, nisi maxima sollicitudine pastores evigilent, quidam in morbos animi dilabuntur et in omne scelus ruunt, quidam per hereticos et schismaticos deperiuntur et laniantur misere. Multi fame sitique pereunt ob divini verbi penuriam. Innumeri denique per invia discurrunt et a recto tramite longius divagantur, ut, quemadmodum in proverbis Salomon ait: "Ubi non est gubernator, dissipabitur populus." Ista, nisi cotidie fieri nostris oculis conspicaremur, auderet forte quisquam impudentior ea penitus inficiari. At compertissimum habemus, ubi sacerdotes gregem sibi commissum pascunt verbo pariter et exemplo, populus a multis erroribus cohibetur. Et contra, quum sacerdotes officia sua negligentius agunt, populus in malorum omnium barathrum preceps corruit. Eapropter haud dubie Christus, quum pusillum admodum haberet gregem, duodecim apostolos instituit, quibus et septuaginta discipulos adiecit, utrisque mandans, ut docerent plebem. Petro tamen, quem suo gregi primarium reliquit pastorem, id officii peculiarius iniunxit, nimirum ut, si se amaret, gregem suum studiose pasceret. Preter hec et apostolis sive per Christum seu per Christi Spiritum facta est potestas, ut illi pro suo iudicio presbyteros consecrarent consecratosque preficerent ecclesiis. Neque defuit sponsio future gratie, quoties illi cuipiam ad hunc finem suas essent imposituri manus. (Pages 82-3 of the 1925 reprint).

CHAPTER XIII
ROBERT BARNES

SIR THOMAS MORE was appointed High Steward of the University of Cambridge in 1525; he already held the same position at his own University of Oxford. The steward was not an academic officer, but was concerned with the legal problems of the university. Roper tells us that this connexion with the two universities brought many scholars to More's house and he took delight in conversing with them. He accompanied the king on visits to the universities "where he was received with very eloquent orations, his Grace would always assign him [More] as one that was prompt and ready therein, ex tempore to make answer thereunto."[1] This appointment must have given pleasure to John Fisher who was probably responsible for the request in 1524 that Sir Thomas More should be appointed on the death of Sir Thomas Lovell, but the king preferred Sir Robert Wingfield who died a year later. Cambridge had now a scholar as its steward and not a courtier. The new steward and the chancellor had much to unite them, not least their unremitting opposition to heresy.

During that same year John Fisher had amongst his visitors John Eck, professor of theology at Ingolstadt, the most redoubtable of Luther's opponents. He recorded that "when last summer I passed over to England to visit the king and the Bishop of Rochester, though tumults and seditions were raging in Germany, I never once heard the name of Luther mentioned except in malediction." John

---
[1] *Roper*, p. 22.

Fisher referred in his book against Oecolampadius to the pleasure Eck's visit had given him. On his return to Germany the theologian took with him a letter from John Fisher to Duke William IV of Bavaria:

> You will wonder, excellent prince, at receiving a letter from me, a man unknown to you. I write not so much for myself as for the learned man who is the bearer of this letter. It chanced that he passed over into England, and when I heard who had come, not only was I delighted, but by my persuasion he visited our most illustrious king, and thus it happened that he stayed longer than he had intended. So if he has too long interrupted his lectures in your university, the loss is more than compensated, for your name, which was hitherto not known to us, has now become famous. We have learned from him and greatly congratulate him on the fact, that you are a prince entirely Catholic, and that you oppose these Lutheran factions, as a true Christian should do, with all your strength. May God preserve you, and all the princes of Germany who are still orthodox, in the same mind. Wishing your highness health and long life, and eagerly desiring to see you.
>
> JOHN OF ROCHESTER.[2]

Eck may not have noticed many overt signs of Lutheranism, but beneath the surface the ferment was at work.

On the Christmas Eve of 1525, Robert Barnes, an Augustinian friar, preached a sermon at Cambridge that created a considerable stir. He was one of the circle of

---

[2] Bridgett's translation, p. 115.

younger scholars who met at the White Horse Tavern to discuss the new doctrines; indeed he seems to have been accepted as the leader of the group. Stephen Gardiner recalled that "Barnes, whom I first knew at Cambridge, was a trim minion friar Augustine, one of a merry scoffing wit, friar-like, and as a good fellow in company was beloved of many." It was inevitable that sooner or later Barnes would exceed the limits of prudence. On this occasion he was provoked by seeing in the congregation an official who had been responsible for a petty act of tyranny over the property of a poor man who had died and left the Church a kettle worth 2s. 4d. The presence of this person excited Barnes to a denunciation that in itself could be justified, but in his enthusiasm he went far beyond the needs of the moment and expressed opinions that could not be ignored by the authorities. A list of twenty-five offensive opinions was drawn up, and Barnes was inhibited from preaching by the vice-chancellor, Dr. Edmund Natares. The chancellor does not seem to have been troubled with the matter. Barnes had many friends who thought he had been unjustly treated, and eventually the case was remitted to Wolsey. The cardinal was not disposed to deal hardly with Barnes in spite of some caustic remarks made by the friar about Wolsey's pomp and affluence. Barnes could not be persuaded to withdraw his offending opinions so the cardinal decided that he must be further examined. The friar was brought before the Bishops of London (Tunstal), Rochester (Fisher), Bath (Clerk), and St. Asaph's (Standish).

The only account we have of the proceedings was written by Barnes himself[3] so it is impossible to test its accuracy. He makes two references to John Fisher; both concern the friar's contention that all days should be

---

[3] *Supplication .. to Henry VIII* (1534).

regarded as equally holy. On the first day "my lord of Rochester allowed this article saying he would not condemn it for a hundred pounds, but it was foolishly said, quoth he, to preach this before the butchers of Cambridge." This remark annoyed Barnes who pointed out that it was not a congregation of butchers but "the most part of the university." At a later session he was asked "if we should keep any holy days? I said, Yes. And in this matter we had a great disputation till at last my lord of Rochester came. And he asked me if this commandment *Sabatum sanctifices* were a ceremonial or a moral precept. I answered that it was a ceremonial alleging for me St. Augustine. Then said he that I was not learned."

The charges brought against Barnes suggest that his offence was not one of unsound theology but of advancing criticisms of the Church and the hierarchy in a way that was likely to predispose his listeners to sympathize with the Germany teachings. For instance he said that the bishops were the successors of Judas Iscariot and that their prophet was Balaam. His own account is a mixture of naivety and self-assurance. Eventually he was persuaded to abjure his eccentric opinions.[4]

The public ceremony of abjuration took place on 11th February 1526 in St. Paul's Cathedral, beginning with a two hours' sermon preached, at the king's suggestion, by Bishop John Fisher. The cardinal was seated in state and there were present thirty-six bishops and abbots in their mitres. Four merchants from the Steelyard were also there with Barnes as penitents; the friar was annoyed at being

---

[4] The later history of Barnes reveals a man of unstable character and muddled ideas. After his imprisonment he went to Luther's city of Wittenberg. Later he worked for Henry and Cromwell, but as soon as his usefulness ended, he was discarded and burned as a heretic (1540). See E. G. Rupp, *English Protestant Tradition*, pp. 31-46.

classed with these Lutherans. After hearing the sermon, the five men, on their knees abjured their heresies and were absolved. Then, carrying their symbolic faggots, they went out into the pouring rain to the churchyard where a bonfire was burning. They added their faggots to the flames.

Hall gives a perverse account of John Fisher's sermon: "he spoke so much in honour of the pope and his cardinals, and of their dignity and pre-eminence, that he forgot to speak anything of the Gospel, which he took in hand to declare, which sermon was much praised by the cardinal and the bishops, wherefore the cardinal gave to all the people his benediction, and then departed."[5]

The sermon was immediately printed by Thomas Berthelet who thereby got himself into trouble for he had omitted to get the necessary imprimatur of the Bishop of London who had recently tightened his censorship in his campaign against Lutheran books. When the printer appeared before the vicar-general he explained that he had published the sermon at the suggestion of one of the Bishop of Rochester's chaplains. Berthelet was ordered to bring either the bishop's manuscript, or a copy signed by him.[6] Presumably there was no further trouble; only six copies are now known to exist, but as these represent three distinct printings, there must have been a big demand.[7]

The introductory epistle to the reader does not support Berthelet's story of the chaplain; it reads as if John Fisher

---

[5] *Hall* (ed. Whibley), II, p. 58.

[6] A. W. Reed, *Early Tudor Drama*, pp. 269-70.

[7] J. E. B. Mayor did not know of this sermon when he edited *The English Works of John Fisher* (1876), but in the 1935 reprint it has been added from an imperfect copy. The extracts given here are from pp. 431-76 checked by a perfect copy.

himself had arranged the printing. A passage from this epistle has a reference to the conditions under which the sermon was delivered:

> I have put forth this sermon to be read which for the great noise of the people within the church of St. Paul's when it was said might not be heard. And if peradventure any disciple of Luther shall think that mine arguments and reasons against his master be not sufficient: first let him consider that I did shape them to be spoken until a multitude of people which were not brought up in the subtle disputations of the school. Second, if it may like the same disciple to come unto me secretly and break his mind at more length I bind me by these presents both to keep his secrecy and also to spare a leisure for him to hear the bottom of his mind and he shall hear mine again if it so please him, and I trust Our Lord that finally we shall so agree that either he shall make me a Lutheran or else I shall enduce him to be a catholic and to follow the doctrine of Christ's church.

The first half of the sermon was, in spite of Hall's criticism, based on the Gospel of the day but skilfully—perhaps, at times, too ingeniously for our ears—applied to the purpose of the occasion. It was Quinquagesima Sunday so the Gospel was St. Luke xviii 31-43, the story of giving sight to the blind man near Jericho. The text chosen was *"Respice, fides tua te salvum fecit."*—"Open thine eyes, thy faith hath made thee safe." The preacher drew a parallel between the blind man and the heretic.

First, here I say that this man was singular by himself; and so the heretics study to be singular in their opinions . . . .

Second, this man was blind, and had lost his sight. And the heretics by the error of false doctrines and of perversed heresies, be blinded in their hearts, and have not the clear light of faith.

Third, this man sat out of the right way and walked not: and so likewise these heretics sit out of the right way and walk not in the journey toward heaven.

Fourth, this man was divided from this people among whom Christ Jesus was; and so be the heretics likewise: they be divided from the church of Christ, with whom our saviour Christ continueth unto the world's end.

Later the preacher considered how the blind man was restored to sight; the heretic must follow the same way; "by hearing and inquiring the very truth;" by crying for mercy; by being brought to Christ. This third point is developed in these words:

Our saviour did command that this blind man should be brought unto him; and so must the heretics be reduced unto the ways of the church. But by whom commandeth our saviour that thus they shall be reduced? Truly by them that be set in spiritual authority; as now the most reverend father in God my lord legate, having this most sovereign authority, hath endeavoured himself for these men here present, and other, which were out of the way, to reduce them in to the ways of the church. The heretics contend that it shall not be lawful thus to do, but they would have every man left unto their liberty. But doubtless it may not be so, for the nature of man is more prone to all naughtiness rather than to any goodness. And therefore many must be compelled, according as the Gospel saith in another place, *Compellite eos intrare.* If every man should have liberty to say what he would, we should have a marvellous world. No man should stir anywhere for heresies.

The preacher saw the limitations of such compulsion; he added:

> He may be compelled to come bodily, but if he come not also with the feet of his soul, and fully assent unto the church, he can not have this true faith. The faith of the church is not made by our faith, but by our assent, which assent cometh of us, and is the work of our soul.

After these considerations, the preacher turned more directly to the teachings of Luther, and particularly to his doctrine of justification by faith alone. He found his text in the epistle of the day, 1 Cor. xiii. 1-13.

> Saint Paul in the Epistle this day plainly condemneth this opinion, for he saith that faith, hope and charity be three diverse things: *Fides, spes, et charitas, tria haec*: these be three diverse things, faith, hope and charity. He saith further: *Si habuero omnem fidem, ita ut montes transerram, charitatem autem non habuero, nihil sum*: If I had all and every faith, so that I might by my faith remove any great mountain, yet if I have not charity, I am nought. Wherefore if a man have all manner of faith, and wanteth charity, he is

never the more justified. Withouten charity therefore no man can be justified; but who that bath charity hath also good works; as the same Saint Paul also proveth at length in the same Epistle. Wherefore withouten good works, either done, or in a full will to be done, no man can be fully justified.

The first half of the sermon was concluded with a prayer "that these poor brethren of ours (which have been out of the way) may the better be confirmed and established" in the truth.

The second half could not unfairly be described as a separate discourse as there is no direct link with what has gone before. It opens with the parable of the Sower, and this provides an admirable scheme for a more direct attack on Luther's teaching. We need not follow this in detail as the exposition is on familiar lines, but one passage repeats the unusual argument he had used in his book on Peter at Rome.[8] The preacher has been discussing the pre-eminence of the Papal See.

> If he consider that the true Christian people which we have at this day, was derived by a continual succession from the See of Peter; for where is now the Christian people of the region of Scythia which came of the succession of Saint Andrew? Be they not now infidels? Where is now the people of Ephesus and of all Asia, which came of the succession of Saint John? Be they not infidels? Where is now the people of both Ethiopias which came of the succession of Saint Matthew and Saint Mathias? Be they not infidels? And briefly to say, where is all the other people which came of the succession of the other Apostles? Either

---
[8] See above, p. 120.

they now be infidels or else schismatics or otherwise divided from the church of Christ. Finally, if he put unto these that only the succession of Peter, in despite of all their enemies doth yet continue, and yet beareth the name of the very catholic church, and so shall do unto the world's end, he shall see evidently that this multitude and this succession is the very church of Christ, against the which the gates of hell shall never prevail.

The preacher did not scold the abjurors who stood before the pulpit; there are no fulminations against them. In the final words where he at length returns to the Gospel of the day, he appealed to them in the spirit of a true pastor of souls.

> And now henceforth (as that man did) follow ye Christ in the right way. For it is said there of him: *Confestim vidit et sequebatur eum*; he forthwith had his sight and followed Christ. Do ye in likewise and beware that ye return not to your old errors again nor that ye look not back unto those heresies nor stop in the way by any wavering of your faith, but go forth right in meritorious works wherein the church walketh which bath with them the continual presence of Christ and of his most Holy Spirit, that one to sow this gracious doctrine, that other to give his influence with the same unto the hearers. And doubt not but this way shall finally bring you unto the glorious country of heaven where ye shall have the presence of Almighty God with endless joy and bliss; to the which he bring us all, *Qui cum patre et spiritu sancto vivit et regnat deus.* Amen.

CHAPTER XIV
THE BISHOP IN HIS DIOCESE—II

IN spite of the increasing burden of grave problems of Church and State, the last decade of John Fisher's episcopate shows no lessening of his devotion to his diocese. He seems to have spent more time at Rochester than at his manors during his last years; this was probably due to declining health.

The aggravation of heresy, particularly after the publication of Tyndale's New Testament in 1526 and of the translator's subsequent polemical works, would alone have brought anxious preoccupation, but to this was added the prolonged struggle on behalf of Catherine of Aragon, followed by the heroic defence of the authority of the Church. In both conflicts, John Fisher had few to support him, while against him were the most powerful leaders in the country. To most his resistance must have seemed a foolish attempt to stop the inevitable "progress" of the times; yet he wrote an imperishable page in the history of the Church, and, with his fellow-martyr, Thomas More, added to the glory of the saints.

The Rochester Register records his assiduity as a bishop. We need not record the normal ordinations and appointments in detail;[1] two call for mention. On 6th

---

[1] The following figures of ordinations (deacons and priests only) have been compiled from the Register, 1506-33. Deacons, II; priests, 23: of the deacons, 10 were regulars (7 of Rochester Priory), and of the priests, 20 were regulars (7 of Rochester Priory). Of the total number of these ordinations, 22 come within the period 1516-23. For other dioceses the bishop ordained 12 deacons (including 9 regulars), and 19 priests (15 of

October 1525 the bishop at Rochester admitted William Ticehurst, the former abbot of the dissolved abbey of Lesnes, to the living of Horsmonden.[2] The early biographer made use of the recollections of Robert Truslove, one of the bishop's chaplains; his name first appears under the date 11th March 1530 when he was collated to the free chapel of Halling.[3]

A letter dated 30th September 1526 from Wolsey[4] ordered that all Lutheran books containing translations from the New Testament in the vulgar tongue were to be surrendered by a date to be fixed by the bishop. A similar letter from Archbishop Warham was dated 3rd November; this required such books to be given up within thirty days.

By a letter dated 30th June 1527 Wolsey[5] ordered processions, prayers and vigils in every church for the liberation of the pope—Rome had been sacked on 6th May by the starving imperialist troops.

On 8th October 1527 the bishop held a diocesan synod in the cathedral chapter house.

He began a visitation of the diocese on 5th April 1529 in the cathedral.[6] On 1st August he received the monastic profession of a monk at Rochester Priory and clothed him.

A summons (9th August 1529) to a Parliament to meet on 3rd November was received by the bishop; this was to

---

them regular). One or two of this latter group may have been for men remaining in the diocese, but the information is not always precise. In these figures, deacons are counted only if there is no record of later ordination to the priesthood.

[2] 131r.
[3] 159v.
[4] 135r.
[5] 137V.
[6] 145V.

prove to be the "Reformation Parliament"; the Canterbury Convocation was also summoned for 5th November in St. Paul's. The clergy met in Rochester Cathedral on the Thursday after the Feast of St. Francis (4th October) to elect their two representatives; a tax of one penny was imposed to cover expenses.[7]

A letter from the bishop (14th April 1530)[8] appointed collectors for a tax demand made in a letter from the king containing a list of the places and the amount each had to pay. On 10th May, the bishop wrote to the Barons of the Exchequer to point out that one of the places mentioned was not in his diocese, and that another, Stone, had not been a vicarage "from time immemorial."[9]

The bishop issued a licence on 21st April 1530 to Thomas Godfrey, Lector of Sacred Theology, Prior of Blackfriars, Canterbury, to preach in the diocese.[10] A case of heresy was dealt with on 2nd May when the Bishop held a chapter in his palace at Rochester. John Pilcher of Cuxton had declared that his soul would arise at the day of judgment but not "my body and bones"; having abjured this opinion, John Pilcher was ordered to do penance in the usual form at Hailing Church, and he had to promise to do no harm to his accusors. One of the commissaries was John Addison (Adeson) whose name first appears in the Register under the date 10th May 1522[11] when he was

---

[7] 152r.

[8] 153V.

[9] Probably the outstanding amounts due under the Amicable Grant of 1525. "Warham and his fellow commissioners did not show themselves at any time over-enthusiastic for the loan; they do not seem to have pressed for payment." F. C. Dietz, English Government Finance, 1485-1558 (5925), p. 96.

[10] 158r.

[11] 108r.

collated to St. Nicholas, Rochester; he was one of the bishop's chaplains and was later involved in the affair of the Holy Maid of Kent.

The Register records that on 7th January 1531 the bishop left Rochester to attend Parliament. He was back in his palace by 17th March and was at Rochester at dates in April, May and June of that year.[12]

A case of heresy on 10th February 1531 was dealt with by the bishop's official Robert Johnson.[13] It concerned John Beeching, rector of Ditton near Aylesford. He admitted that he had not believed in the sacrament of penance, that he had celebrated Mass for half a year in that state of mind when he "might have had priests for to hear my confession." Before several persons he had said that a priest in deadly sin might take upon himself to consecrate the Blessed Sacrament; he had also said to a layman that a layman might just as well hear his confession as a priest, meaning thereby that he had as little authority as the other; to several persons he had said that he was not bound to go to confession. At his abjuration the usual penance was imposed, and he was forbidden to leave England for two years under penalty of being treated as a relapsed heretic.

Under the date 3rd June 1531, it is recorded that the bishop conferred the subdiaconate on Sebastian Newdigate of the London Carthusians. No later ordination is given. He was one of those who o suffered at Tyburn on 14th June 1535; a week later, the bishop who had ordained him a subdeacon was led to Tower Hill.

The bishop himself dealt on 10th August 1532 with an accusation of heresy brought against John Dissenger,[14] a

---

[12] 160r-162V.

[13] 163r.

[14] 167r.

joiner, who had said that priests should deliver the Gospel to the people in the mother tongue and that Christ was "a wroth and a angry fellow and did naught in casting down the poor man's goods in the Temple." When the bishop questioned him about this, Dissenger admitted that he had said these things and added "I have heard say in the city of London that we should not worship saints but God only for they said that the images be but stocks and stones and therefore I suppose I should not worship them. Also I have heard say that a man should not shew his confessor all his sins that he had done." After his abjuration he was ordered to refrain from such blasphemous statements and behave himself: The penance was that he should go to the cathedral on the Sunday after the feast of St. Bartholomew (24th August) and as a true penitent stand before the preacher bare legged and bare footed with a lighted candle. The rest of the penance the bishop reserved to himself.

Another case of heresy came before the bishop on 16th September 1532.[15] The accused was Peter Durr of Gravesend who seems to have been known by several other names; he was literate as he signed his name on the document recording his abjuration. He had declared that St. Augustine was not in heaven, that the pope and archbishops had no authority to make laws, that Luther was not a heretic, and that "my prayer is as good as Our Lady's." A book in his possession contained invective against the pope with praise of Luther; it taught that in trouble we should ask help of God alone, and that by faith all sin is pardoned. He was absolved from excommunication and ordered to carry the faggot in the church at Milton, after which he was to leave the diocese with all speed.

---

[15] 167v.

The Register gives an account of the election on 21st October 1532 of a prior to Rochester.[16] After a sermon by the bishop, Laurence Dann, the sub-prior, certified to him that the community had acted on his letter of the 19th summoning all members to take part in the election. Twenty-three monks were present. The election was by scrutiny, that is the votes were cast separately and apart by each monk. The bishop examined the votes and declared that the Sub-prior, Laurence Dann, had been elected. He then promised obedience to the bishop; the community, after reciting the *Te Deum* proceeded to the cathedral choir, and, prostrate before the altar, received the episcopal blessing. The bishop then installed the new prior.[17]

There is nothing of particular note in the remaining part of the Register; the matters recorded are part of the normal life of a diocese—admissions, collations, ordinations, disputes about patronage, and so on.

The last entry is dated 28th February 1534 when the bishop collated William Hodgeson to Wouldham on the resignation of John Addison (Adeson) his chaplain. That resignation brings us close to the final tragedy.

The abjuration of Peter Durr mentioned above is the last recorded case of heresy in the Register. It will have been noticed that the abjurors during John Fisher's episcopate were treated with lenity. Appearing in church as a penitent was the least an abjuror could expect; those who, in addition to this, were restricted in their movements about the diocese could not complain of undue harshness.

---

[16] 173r.

[17] Laurence Dann (or Mereworth) took the oath of supremacy on 10th June 1534; he resigned in 1538. His successor surrendered the Priory on 20th March 1540.

There is no record of anyone in the diocese of Rochester being handed over to the secular authorities; certainly no case is mentioned by Foxe in his Book of Martyrs of a heretic being sent to the stake in the diocese, and even the rumour of such an event would have been used by him. Such extreme measures may have been avoided owing to the smallness of the area which made it possible for the bishop and his priests to keep a more watchful eye on heretics than was possible in the greater dioceses where the bishop was rarely in residence.

The County of Kent—most of it under Canterbury—tells A different story. In 1511 Archbishop Warham indicted forty-six heretics; most of these were from the region stretching from Benenden to Ashford, a cloth-making area. Forty-one abjured and five were burned. The archbishop may have been aided by his suffragan, the Bishop of Rochester, in dealing with some of these cases. The records, however, lack details. Foxe in his Book of Martyrs gives one case from this period in which John Fisher sat with the Archbishop.[18] John Browne, so Foxe reported, told his wife "how by the two bishops, Warham and Fisher, his feet were heated upon hot coals, and burned to the bones." He was tried at Canterbury and burned at Ashford. The difficulty with much of Foxe's work is that his statements cannot always be checked; much of the documentary evidence he used has perished, and he so colours his accounts with his lurid imagination that it is sometimes difficult to distinguish between Fact and Foxe.

One case involving John Fisher can be checked by a contemporary opinion. The case of Thomas Hitton (1530?) is the better known because it was dealt with by Sir

---

[18] *Foxe* (ed. Pratt), IV, p. 582.

Thomas More in his Confutation of Tyndale, and more briefly in his Apologye.[19]

Foxe's version was that Hitton was a "preacher of Maidstone whom the bishop of Canterbury, William Warham, and Fisher, bishop of Rochester, after they had long kept him in prison and tormented him with sundry torments, and that he notwithstanding continued constant, at last they burned him at Maidstone." Foxe added that "nothing remaineth in writing," so he was speaking from hearsay.[20] The accusation of "sundry torments" and of torture in Browne's case savours more of fancy than of fact, for torture was not used in Catholic England in cases of heresy; such an allegation is out of keeping with all we know of the characters of Warham and Fisher. In his *Apologye*, Sir Thomas More wrote of "Sir Thomas Hitton that was waxen a joiner and in many a day neither said matins nor mass, but raged and railed against the Blessed Sacrament."[21]

The account in the Confutation adds to this brief picture; it is probable that More got his information from the bishops. Thomas Hitton was a priest who had fallen into heresy and fled abroad. He returned as a colporteur for Tyndale and was arrested at Gravesend. He was brought before Warham and Fisher on five different days but remained obdurate; he was therefore handed over to the secular power and burned at Maidstone. An apostate priest who had returned from the land of Luther and persistently spread heretical teaching and literature could not expect to be treated like an illiterate labourer who repeated in a muddle-headed way notions that he had picked up at random. Yet five sessions were devoted to

---

[19] *E.W.* (1557), pp. 344-5.

[20] *Foxe* (ed. Pratt), IV, p. 659.

[21] *Apologye* (ed. Taft), p. 127.

Hitton's case before it was certain that he was irreconcilable.

The fact that John Fisher, as far as the records show, had not to make such fearful decisions in his own diocese, does not mean that he disapproved of handing over obdurate heretics to the civil authorities with all that such an action implied. His views were definite. They were stated without equivocation in his *Confutatio*;[22] it was lawful, he maintained, to deliver up to the secular arm those who had been convicted as relapsed heretics. That opinion, too, was as firmly held by Sir Thomas More; indeed it was shared by the Reformers themselves when they exercised authority.

An earlier case of heresy outside the diocese of Rochester was that of Thomas Bilney in 1527.[23] There are similarities with that of Robert Barnes. Little Bilney, as he was known for his short stature, was also a member of the group of Cambridge who met at the White Horse Tavern and walked on Heretic's Hill. With his friend Thomas Arthur he was brought before Wolsey in 1526 and they then abjured their offending teachings. A series of sermons they preached in and near London in 1527 brought them again before Wolsey who remitted the case to a smaller court consisting of the bishops of London (Tunstal), Norwich (Nix), and Rochester (Fisher). Five meetings of the court were held over a period of ten days as Tunstal wished to give Bilney time to consider his views and to consult his friends. Bilney and Arthur abjured and were absolved. It is not known what part Fisher took in the proceedings save that Bilney said that

---

[22] Article XXIII.

[23] See E. G. Rupp, *English Protestant Tradition* (1947), pp. 22-31 for a sympathetic account.

he agreed with the bishop of Rochester's condemnation of Luther.

The early biographer had little to say of the bishop's dealing with heresy in his diocese; more than two thirds of the book are occupied with the grave matters that led to his martyrdom. The most precious pages tell us of John Fisher's devout and holy life, and before we pass on to consider the events of those last years, it would be well for us to see the saint as he was known to those who served him and whom he served. In an earlier chapter[24] we saw something of his pastoral care of his flock; his own devotions are described in the following words:

> He never omitted so much as one collect of his daily service, and that he used to say commonly to himself alone without the help of any chaplain, not in such speed or hasty manner to be at an end as many will do but in most reverent and devout manner so distinctly and treatably [deliberately] pronouncing every word that he seemed a very devourer of heavenly food, never satiated nor filled therewith. In so much as talking on a time with a Carthusian monk who much commended his zeal and diligent pains in compiling his book against Luther, he answered again saying that he wished that time of writing had been spent in prayer, thinking that prayer would have done more good and was of more merit. And to help this his devotion he caused a great hole to be digged through the wall of his church of Rochester whereby he might the more commodiously have prospect into the church at mass and evensong-time.
>
> When he himself would say mass, as many times he used to do, if he were not letted [prevented] by

---

[24] See above, pp. 66-7.

some urgent or great cause, ye might then perceive in him such earnest devotion that many times the tears would fall from his cheeks. And lest that the memory of death might slip from his mind, he always accustomed to set upon one end of the altar a dead man's skull which was also set before him at his table as he dined or supped, and in all his prayers and other talk he used continually a special reverence and devotion to the name of Jesus. Now to those his prayers he adjoined two wings, which were alms and fasting by the help whereof they might mount speedier to heaven.[25]

His hospitable reception of guests has already been described. The early biographer also tells us of the customary regulation of meals.

And when he had no strangers, his order was now and then to sit with his chaplains, which were commonly grave and learned men, among whom he would put some great question of learning, not only to provoke them to better consideration and deep search of the hid mysteries of religion but also to spend the time of repast in such talk that might be (as it was indeed) pleasant, profitable and comfortable to the waiters and standers by. And yet was he so dainty and spare of time that he would never bestow fully one hour at any meal. His diet at table was for all such as thither resorted, plentiful and good, but for himself very mean. For upon such eating days as were not fasted, although he would for his health use a larger diet than at other times, yet was it with such temperance that commonly he was wont to eat and

---

[25] *Ortroy*, pp. 99-101.

drink by weight and measure. And the most of his sustenance was thin pottage, sodden with flesh, eating of the flesh itself very sparingly.[26]

This account calls to mind the order of meal times in the household of Sir Thomas More. We are given further details of John Fisher's ascetic life.

> The ordinary fasts appointed by the church he kept very soundly and to them he joined many other particular fasts of his own devotion, as appeared well by his thin and weak body, whereupon though much flesh was not left, yet would he punish the very skin and bones upon his back. He wore most commonly a shirt of hair and many times he would whip himself in most secret wise. When night was come, which commonly brings rest to all creatures, then would he many times despatch away his servants and fall to his prayers a long space. And after he had ended the same, he laid him down upon a poor hard couch of straw and mats (for other bed he used none) provided at Rochester in his closet near the Cathedral church, where he might look into the choir and hear divine service; and being laid, he never rested above four hours at one time but straightways rose and ended the rest of his devout prayers. Thus lived he till towards his latter days, when being more grown into age, which is (as Cicero saith) a sickness of itself, he was forced to relent of these hard and severe fasts, and the rather for that his body was much weakened with a consumption. Wherefore by counsel of his physician and license of his ghostly father [confessor] he used

---

[26] *Ortroy*, pp. 102-3.

upon some fasting days to comfort himself with a little thin gruel made for the purpose.[27]

The references to the cathedral raise a problem. The palace was not adjacent. Had he a room in the monastery from which he was able to see the monks in the choir? Or has the writer confused the cathedral with the chapel in the palace? His care of his own household is also recorded.

The care that he had of his family was not small, for although his chiefest burden consisted in discharge of his spiritual function, yet did he not neglect his temporal affairs. Wherefore he took such order in his revenues that one part was bestowed upon reparation and maintenance of the church, the second upon the relief of poverty and maintenance of scholars, and the third upon his household expenses and buying of books, whereof he had great plenty. And lest the trouble of worldly business might be some hindrance to his spiritual exercise, he used the help of his brother Robert, a layman, whom he made his steward so long as his said brother lived, giving him in charge so to order his expenses that by no means he brought him into debt. His servants used not to wear their apparel after any courtly or wanton manner, but went in garments of a sad and seemly colour, some in gowns and some in coats as the fashion then was, whom he always exhorted to frugality and thrift and in any wise to beware of prodigality. And where he marked any of them more given to good husbandry than others, he would many times lend them money and never ask it again, and commonly when it was offered him, he did forgive it. If any of his household had committed a

---

[27] *Ortroy*, pp. 103-4.

fault (as sometimes it happened) he would first examine the matter himself, and finding him faulty, would for the first time but punish him with words only; but it should be done with such severity of speech that whosoever came once before him, was very unwilling to come before him again for any such offence. So that by this means his household continued in great quietness and peace, every man knowing what belonged to his duty. Some among the rest (as they could get opportunity) would apply their minds to study and learning, and those above others he specially liked, and would many times support them with his labour and sometimes with his money. But where he saw any of them given to idleness and sloth, he could by no means indure them in his house, because out of that fountain many evils are commonly wont to spring. In conclusion, his family was governed with such temperance, devotion and learning that his palace for continency seemed a very monastery and for learning an university.[28]

William Rastell recorded an incident that shows both sides of the bishop's nature—his hospitality and his personal frugality.

> "Three or four years before his death, when in a Christmastime he had caused to be prepared worshipful fare and honest pastimes for his kinsfolk and friends that then came to visit him (as that manner was then much used in England in the Christmas), he commanded his officers to entertain gently and make hearty good cheer unto friends and kinsfolk so repairing to him, and came also among them and

---

[28] *Ortroy*, pp. 104-106.

cheered them very heartily. And leaving them at their pastimes, went himself away into his study to his prayers and meditations. Which one of his chief officers and trusty servants perceiving, came unto him and said, 'My lord, I pray you, leave of your study for this merry time of Christmas, while your friends be here, and come among them, and keep them company, or else will they think themselves not welcome to you.' 'Why,' quoth the bishop, 'have they not all such things as was prepared for them?' 'Yea,' quoth his servant, 'they have, but what then? Your lordship's presence shall more cheer your friends than all your meat and their pastimes.' 'Well,' quoth the bishop, 'I pray you be content, and let me alone here in my study. For my friends, I dare say, will be content that I follow herein mine own mind in mine own house. And therefore pray them, in my name, to be as merry without me as though I were with them. For as for me, I have other things to do than to cheer my guests, or to be present at their worldly pastimes, for I tell you in secret, I know I shall not die in my bed. Wherefore it behoveth me to think continually upon the dreadful hour of my account.'"[29]

When his great trials came upon him he had passed his sixtieth year—a considerable age for the times—and he was in weak health. It was against this old and sick man that the king was to vent his anger. The faithful service of long years to the Crown, to Cambridge, and above all to the Church was to count as nothing when the bishop dared to oppose the king.

---

[29] *Harpsfield*, p. 247.

CHAPTER XV
THE KING'S CONSCIENCE

ON three days in May 1527,[1] a bizarre transaction was staged at York Place,[2] Wolsey's mansion at Westminster. No less a person than the king himself was there to answer a complaint brought against him that, for the past eighteen years, he had been living in sin with his brother's widow. The assessors were Cardinal Wolsey and Archbishop Warham; the case was stated and argued. Catherine was not there, nor was she represented; she was not even aware of what was happening.

Such was the first scene in the tragedy which is popularly, though inaccurately, known as the Divorce.

This secretly convened court reached no conclusion; its purpose had been, presumably, to enable the legate to pronounce a decision that could later be confirmed by the pope. There is no reason to think that such a procedure would have succeeded; the one-sided investigation was cut short by the news that the pope was the prisoner in Rome of the undisciplined troops of the queen's nephew Charles V. In view of this unprecedented situation, it seems to have been decided that Wolsey should deal with the papal problem and also collect the opinions of the bishops. Henry had the delicate task of informing Catherine of his intentions; this he did three weeks later, and the abrupt announcement momentarily unnerved the queen.

---

[1] 17th, 20th, 31st May. *L.P.*, IV, 3140.
[2] *The future Whitehall.*

She had come to England in 1501 to be the bride of Arthur, Prince of Wales. Six months after their marriage, the fifteen-year old husband died. Catherine's parents, Ferdinand of Aragon and Isabella of Castile, negotiated with Henry VII for their daughter to marry the king's second son, Henry. Owing to the affinity between Henry and his brother's widow, it was necessary to obtain a papal dispensation for the marriage; this was, after some difficulty, granted. It is true that some doubts were expressed as to the power of the pope to grant such a dispensation, and Henry himself; at the age of fourteen, had made a protest, but this had obviously been part of the intricate manoeuvres—partly political and partly financial—between the two fathers. Within seven weeks of his accession, Henry VIII, of his own volition, married Catherine of Aragon.

It is not necessary here to review once more the many problems raised by this tragic story, nor to follow in detail its development step by step. We cannot now know when it was, or at whose instigation, Henry first became aware of the significance of the words in Leviticus, "He that marrieth his brother's wife doth an unlawful thing . . . they shall be without children."[3] Nor is it possible to determine to what degree he was moved by reasons of state—the lack of a legitimate male heir—or by his passion for Anne Boleyn. It soon became apparent that events were to be dominated by Henry's dogmatic assumption that what he wanted must be right and just, and that any hint of opposition was a form of treason. He made his conscience the servant of his appetites.[4]

---

[3] XX, 21.

[4] There is a considerable literature on the divorce. After studying much of it—I dare not say all—I consider the most balanced account to be Chapter VIII in Volume X of Pastor's *History of the Popes* (Eng. trans.

Our concern here is with the part taken by John Fisher. In reading the records it is indeed a relief to come across his name. It spells for us integrity of mind and spirit; for a space we can breathe the air of truthfulness; we shall not need to look for hidden motives or equivocation; then we plunge back into the fog of lies and chicanery, of arrogance and time-serving. In cynical mood we can relish the spectacle of the king and the cardinal double-crossing each other, but that mood vanishes when we recall the tragedy of a much-wronged woman and when we consider the lamentable consequences of those meetings in York House in May 1527.

Part of the cardinal's task was to gather the opinions of the bishops—not apparently on the specific case of the king, but as to the power of the pope to grant a dispensation for a man to marry his brother's widow. It is doubtful if any of the bishops could have regarded the question as an academic one in which the cardinal happened to be interested. Rumours of the king's wish to be rid of the queen had been circulating for some time; their origin can no more be traced than that of the whole business. Even the York House meeting, in spite of the great secrecy, was soon a subject of common talk and gossip.

The results were not as favourable as had been hoped. John Fisher's opinion was forwarded to the king by Wolsey on 2nd June 1527 with the comment that "his said opinion proceedeth rather of affection than of sincerity, of his learning or scripture." With these words the cardinal may have hoped to temper a judgment that must have been little to the king's desire.

1910). The most important collection of documents is Mgr. S. Ehses, Römische Dokumente (1893). Fr. Philip Hughes, *The Reformation in England*, vol. I (1950), chap. IV, is most valuable.

Having consulted all those silent masters[5] I have by me, and diligently discussed their opinions and weighed their reasons, I find there is a great disagreement among them, a great many asserting that[6] it is prohibited by the divine law, whilst others on the contrary affirm that it is by no means repugnant to it; and having truly weighed the reasons on both sides in an even scale I think I see it easy to unravel all the arguments which they produce who deny it to be lawful by the divine law, but not so easy to answer the others; so I am fully persuaded that it cannot be proved by any solid reason that it is prohibited by the divine law now in force that the brother of a brother deceased without children shall take his wife; which, if true, as I do not doubt of its being most certain, who is there now that considers the plenitude of power which Christ has conferred on the pope, who can deny that the pope may dispense for some great cause with a brother of a brother deceased without issue taking his wife? But that granting the reasons on both sides equal and that neither weighed down the other, yet would that oblige me to be more inclined and yielding to the pope's side; I know it is allowed by both parties as a part of the amplitude of the pope's power that it is lawful for him on hearing the opinions of divines and lawyers concerning the matter to interpret ambiguous places of scripture, for that otherwise in vain had Christ said to him, *Whatsoever thou shalt loose on earth shall be loosed in heaven, and whatsoever thou shalt bind on earth shall be bound in heaven*, that therefore since it manifestly appears that the pope has more

---

[5] That is, the books of learned authorities.

[6] That is, marriage of a brother to the widow of a deceased brother.

than once declared by his proceedings that he may in the aforesaid case dispense with the second brother, this alone would powerfully move me to give my assent, although I have not produced the best proofs and reasons but that both parties were equal in their assertions. But that now, since I plainly perceive, both that the reasons on their side who defend the pope's power in this matter are more convincing and that I observe besides in what words and how very fully the power is given by Christ to the pope, and that lastly I understand by the clearest evidences that a dispensation of that nature took effect, I have no scruple remaining, but that it is lawful for the pope to grant such a dispensation that a brother may take the wife of another brother that is deceased without issue.[7]

John Fisher never moved from that position: the pope had the power of dispensation in such a case.

On 3rd July 1527 Wolsey left London on his way to France to negotiate a "perpetual peace" with that country, and, at the same time, to form an alliance against Charles V—a strange proceeding in view of the influence of Catherine's nephew.

George Cavendish described the cardinal's procession as he rode over London Bridge.

> And before him he had his two great crosses of silver, two great pillars of silver, the great seal of England, his cardinal's hat, and a gentleman that carried his valaunce, otherwise called a cloakbag, which was made altogether of fine scarlet cloth, embroidered over and over with cloth of gold very

---

[7] *L.P.*, IV, no. 3148 gives a summary which is quoted in *Bridgett*, p. 150. The above is a full translation.

richly, having in it a cloak of fine scarlet . . . . The next day he rode to Rochester, and lodged in the bishop's palace there; and the rest of his train in the city, and in Strood on this side the bridge.[8]

Sir Thomas More was in Wolsey's train, but it is not known what dealings there were between him and John Fisher.

Cavendish says nothing of the real purpose of this stay at Rochester, but Wolsey had a great deal to say about it to the king. His letter, dated 8th July from Canterbury,[9] is so important that the greater part must be quoted. The cardinal discussed with the bishop the validity of the king's marriage, no longer as an academic question but as a matter of policy. He explained that the Bishop of Tarbes on his recent embassy to negotiate a marriage between the King of France and the Princess Mary, had expressed doubts of the validity of Henry's marriage; the king's conscience was troubled and he wished the difficulty to be resolved.

> [Wolsey] shewed unto him [Fisher] the bull of dispensation which after he had deliberately perused and read, noting and marking every material point thereof, although he said, for the first sight, he supposed the bull was not sufficient as well for that this impediment was of divine law, wherewith the pope could not dispense unless on the most urgent grounds. And thus declaring the whole matter unto him at length, as was devised with your highness in York Place, I added that, by what means it was not yet

---

[8] *Cavendish*, p. 59.

[9] *S.P.*, I, p. 196. The original is in English: I have translated a few Latin phrases.

apprehended, an inkling of this matter is come to the
queen's knowledge; who, being suspicious, and casting
further doubts than was meant or intended, hath broke
with your grace thereof, after a very displeasant
manner, saying that by my procurement and setting
forth, a divorce was purposed between her and your
highness.

Certain points may be noted. There is no evidence to support the statement that the Bishop of Tarbes had raised this issue; he may have done so, but it is doubtful; if he did, he was only echoing thoughts already in the king's mind. The words "as was devised with your highness in York Place" indicates that the king and the cardinal had discussed how best to win over the Bishop of Rochester, for they recognized the weight that people would give to his opinion. The professed ignorance of how the queen had heard of the matter is a lie; Henry himself had told her some weeks before the cardinal set off for France. The queen's charge against Wolsey that he had started the business has found many supporters, but, here again, conclusive evidence is lacking; the weight of opinion today is against that view.[10]

In his interview, Wolsey went on to blame the queen for having talked about such a secret matter.

And I assure your grace, my lord of Rochester,
hearing the process of the matter after this sort, did
greatly blame the queen, as well for giving so light
credence in so weighty a matter as also when she
heard it to handle the same in such fashion as rumour
and bruit should spread thereof.

---

[10] For a full discussion, see chapter IV of Philip Hughes, *The Reformation in England*, vol. I.

[The bishop] doubted not, but that if he might speak with her and disclose unto her all the circumstances of the matter as afore, he should cause her greatly to repent, humble and submit herself unto your highness; considering that the thing done by your grace was so necessary and expedient and the queen's act so perilous. Howbeit I have persuaded him that he will nothing speak or do therein, or anything counsel her, but as shall stand with your pleasure; for, he saith, although she be queen of this realm, yet he acknowledgeth you for his high sovereign lord and king, and will not therefore otherwise behave himself, in all matters, concerning or touching your person, than as he shall be by your grace expressly commanded.

The cardinal returned to the scruples said to have been mentioned by the French embassy, and explained "the difficult points that might be objected."

First that the impediment was of divine law, whereunto he said, as he then thought, answer might be made, that it is not, but not sticking with him much thereupon, I said that an impediment of marriage there was, which must be taken away by dispensation sufficient; and he assented thereunto. Then I showed him the fault of the bull, in the suggestion, which was false, forasmuch as it was showed unto the pope therein that your grace should desire the marriage in order to preserve the peace, not being at that time twelve years of age, and my lord of Winchester [Fox] deposeth, not made privy to the impetration thereof. As hereunto he said it was not his faculty anything to judge in that matter; nevertheless he misliked it much, and said he had ever heard that a dispensation is nought if the grounds on which it is granted do not agree with the facts, and greatly lamented the negligence of them that so handled that thing in the beginning being of so high importance and great weight, whereupon might insurge doubt or question upon the succession of your highness. And more and more as I showed him of your protestation made, and the death of the king your father before the execution[11] of the bull, and so if the reasons are false, the grant also fails. He noted the matter to be more and more doubtful and the bull diminute [lessened] marvelling that none other bull was purchased than that, being so slenderly couched and against which so many things might be objected. He would not reason the matter, but noted great difficulty in it.

This visit was a clever attempt to conciliate one whose opposition could prove embarrassing, not only in his own country but in Europe where his learned controversial works had brought considerable prestige.

Wolsey's letter repays careful study. We must keep in mind that as he was writing to the king he put the best construction possible on what was evidently a difficult interview. Even so, the result could not have been pleasing either to the cardinal or to the king. John Fisher put his finger on the weak point in the Bull; if it should prove that it was granted on inadequate or factitious grounds then there was a case for inquiry. That was to be one of the leading arguments on the king's side, until Catherine produced a copy of a brief of dispensation from the Spanish archives which was phrased in wider terms.

---

[11] Presumably before the marriage; the Bull was obtained early in 1505, four years before the death of Henry VII.

It will be noted that John Fisher did not express any definite opinion; all he would admit was that here was something that called for careful examination. He evidently accepted Wolsey's slur on the queen's discretion; his offer to speak to Catherine shows that he was on sufficiently close terms with her and believed she would listen to him. Wolsey, however, urged him not to do so without the king's approval; a consultation between the queen and the bishop at this stage would have revealed the falseness of the cardinal's accusation. Finally, "he would not reason the matter, but noted great difficulty in it."

John Fisher was not a simpleton; the fact that the cardinal at the head of an important embassy should break his journey to discuss this question at some length must have seemed strange if not suspicious. The bishop could not know that the cardinal himself was bewildered; the king had revealed his intentions only shortly before the meeting at York Place and had not shown his full mind on the matter; even while the cardinal was on his way to France, Henry was planning to appeal to the pope without consulting Wolsey. Moreover, at this time it seems certain that the cardinal was unaware of the part Anne Boleyn was playing. He was in France for two months, and during that time the Boleyns strengthened their position.

The early biographer recorded that the king later discussed the problem with John Fisher. This must have been after the cardinal's return in the middle of September 1527.

> Wherefore consulting again with the cardinal what way were best to use to bring him [Fisher] to favour his desire, it was advised by my lord cardinal that the king should call unto him my lord of Rochester and by

fair means work him to incline to his mind. Wherefore the king on a day sent for him, and when he came, the king, using him very courteously gave him many reverend and good words and at last took him with him into the long gallery at Westminster. And there, walking awhile with him, after divers words of great praise given him for his worthy learning and virtue, he at last break with him of this matter in the presence of the dukes of Norfolk and Suffolk and certain bishops alledging there how sore his conscience was tormented and how for that cause he had secretly consulted with his ghostly father [confessor][12] and divers other learned men by whom he was not yet satisfied. And therefore said that upon special confidence in his great learning he had now made choice of him to use his advice above all others, praying him to declare his opinion freely, so as with hearing thereof he might sufficiently be instructed in his conscience and remain no longer in this scruple wherewith he was so much unquieted.

My lord of Rochester hearing all this case proponed by the king never stuck long in answering the matter, which he both knew and thought to be good and true; but, falling straightways upon his knees, offered to speak to the king. But the king immediately lifted him up again with his own hands and blamed him for so doing. Then spake this learned prelate with a reverend gravity after this or the like sort: "I beseech your grace in God's name to be of good cheer and no further to dismay yourself with this

---

[12] John Longland, Bishop of Lincoln. The belief that it was Longland who first stirred up doubts in Henry's mind is preserved in Shakespeare's *Henry VIII*, II, iv. It will be noted that the king, according to this account, made no reference to the Bishop of Tarbes.

matter, neither to unquiet or trouble your conscience for the same. For," said he, "there is no heed to be taken to these men that account themselves so wise and do arrogate to themselves more cunning and knowledge in divinity than had all the learned fathers and divines both of Spain and of this your realm in your late father's time, neither yet so much credit to be given unto them as is to the see apostolic by whose authority this marriage was confirmed, dispensed and approved for good and lawful. Truly, truly," said he, "my sovereign lord and king, you may well and justly ought to make conscience of casting any scruple or doubt of this so clear and weighty a matter in bringing it by any means into question; and therefore, by my advice and counsel you shall with all speed put all such thoughts out of your mind. And as for any peril or danger that to your soul may ensue thereby, I am not afraid in giving you this counsel to take upon my own soul all the danger, and will not refuse to answer against all men in your behalf either privately or openly that can anything object against this matter nothing doubting but there are many right worthy and learned persons within this your realm that be of this mind with me and think it a very perilous and unseemly thing that any divorce should be spoken of. Unto which side I rather wish your grace to hearken than to the other. And what colour or show they may seem to have in this their motions to your highness, yet God forbid that your majesty upon so small a foundation should so easily incline yourself or hearken to any person living in so weighty a case passed and established by so great authority as the see apostolic."

These and divers like words he there uttered to the king, which might have satisfied his sick mind had he

THE KING'S CONSCIENCE 191

not been otherwise perversely bent, and therefore all was in vain . . . . And so for that time my lord of Rochester departed from the king who from that date forward never looked on him with merry countenance as the good bishop did well perceive for that his grudge daily increased towards him.[13]

The words put into John Fisher's mouth are no doubt an historical reconstruction; the writer safeguards himself by the phrase, "after this or the like sort." They are in agreement with the opinions he expressed in speech and writing.

At this time he seems to have had no doubt that the king's talk of a troubled conscience was the expression of honest scruples. A letter[14] to an unidentified correspondent which was probably written in the latter part of 1527 makes this clear. In it he declared that he believed that the king meant to do nothing against the law of God, but that he would be quite justified in submitting his difficulties to the pope, especially as kings, from the fullness of their powers, are apt to think that right which suits their pleasure.

John Fisher had yet to learn that Henry had no doubt whatever that what suited his pleasure must, *ipso facto*, be right.

---

[13] *Ortroy*, pp. 176-9. Bridgett presumably thought this interview had no basis in fact as he did not use it. Ortroy accepted it as probably authentic in substance, although there is no other record. The king must have had many discussions of this kind that have not been officially recorded. There is nothing improbable about the incident; indeed some of the minor details suggest an observer's recollections.

[14] *L.P.*, IV, no. 3232.

XIII - King Henry VIII

XIV - Katherine of Aragon
The contrast between Henry above and Catherine here should indicate well the physical motivations for Henry seeking a divorce. Being older, she was now past child-bearing years, and frequent miscarriages had altered her figure from Henry's youth.

CHAPTER XVI
KING AND POPE

HENRY opened his "great matter" with Sir Thomas More for the first time in September 1527.[1] The king pointed out the crucial text in Leviticus and asked his councillor's opinion, but More begged for time to study the problem. He turned to the relevant passages in the works of the early Fathers, and later suggested to the king that St. Jerome and St. Augustine and other "old holy doctors" would be his best councillors, but, for himself, he would prefer not to be drawn into the discussion. The king had, reluctantly, to accept this decision. From that time, Sir Thomas More refused to argue the question one way or the other; he could not in conscience support the king, but his strong sense of his duty to his prince, constrained him to keep silent. Silence is not, however, negative. When other councillors found that he would not express an opinion on a subject of common talk, they drew the obvious conclusion. So did the king, though for a time he was to make greater use of Sir Thomas More's services; Henry had a long memory.

John Fisher could not take up a similar position; both as bishop and theologian he was concerned with the interpretation of the Scriptures and of the authority of the Church, and this matter touched both. The king's scruple, if he was to believed, was entirely due to reading that verse in Leviticus; had this indeed been the case, then the authoritative opinion of a learned theologian like John

---

[1] See my *Saint Thomas More*, pp. 202, 233.

Fisher should have been sufficient to set conscience at rest; but the king was looking for a partisan, not a judge; he wanted theological reasons for doing what he knew was wrong.

While the prolonged and confused negotiations were going on with Rome, John Fisher gave his mind to a renewed study of these problems of Scripture and canon law. He later on wrote that "the matter was so serious, both on account of the importance of the people concerned, and on account of the injunction given me by the king, that I devoted more attention to examining the truth of it, lest I should deceive myself and others, than to anything else in my life."[2]

At the same time he stated that he did not see the queen until he was appointed one of her counsellors in 1529. This was evidently in conformity with his promise to Wolsey that he would not discuss the question with her unless the king gave permission. Later he was again warned by Wolsey not to interfere.[3]

While Wolsey was in France, the king decided to send one of his secretaries, Dr. William Knight (later Bishop of Bath and Wells) to Rome with private instructions to ask for a Bull allowing him, without the dissolution of his marriage with Catherine, to take a second wife. Knight saw Wolsey at Compiegne, and the cardinal managed to worm out of the secretary the nature of his secret mission, and when he returned to England he persuaded the king to withdraw the scandalous proposal that he should be licensed to commit bigamy. By the time he reached Rome, Knight had been overtaken by fresh instructions; Wolsey wanted to be made the imprisoned pope's vicar-general,

---

[2] *L.P.*, VIII, pp. 335-7.

[3] *Cal. Span.*, III, ii, no. 377. See also G. Mattingly, *Catherine of Aragon* p. 325 n. 20 for a correction of the entry in the calendar.

and Henry this time (unknown to Wolsey) asked for a dispensation which, after his divorce from Catherine, would remove the impediment of his earlier adulturous relations with Mary the sister of Anne Boleyn. What Knight eventually obtained (when the pope had escaped from Rome) was a Bull that stipulated that the marriage with Catherine must first be proved invalid before any fresh dispensation could be granted. Henry could no longer argue that the pope had no power to grant such dispensations, since he now asked for another.

The original ground for the annulment of the marriage had been that the pope had no power to dispense the case of a brother marrying his brother's widow. John Fisher's opinion, as given to Wolsey, was that the pope had the necessary authority, and other theologians then and since have supported that view; he had, as we have seen, pointed out that the validity of the dispensation, could only be shaken if it had been granted on inadequate grounds, or by misrepresentation. The king and the cardinal now argued that the original plea that the marriage was necessary to preserve peace between England and Spain was baseless, and that as Henry was only twelve years old at the time, he could not have had an effective voice in the matter, indeed, he had protested against it. This ignored the plain fact that the marriage did not take place until he was king, and he had then eagerly pressed for its celebration. The pope was again asked to allow Wolsey to investigate the case and to be given power to make an irrevocable decision. It was an unprecedented and even outrageous proposal to put before the pope. All that he would grant was a commission for Wolsey and a papal representative to carry out an inquiry.

Wolsey by this time was getting desperate; he could see that unless he could meet the king's wishes, his own power would be endangered. So two more envoys were sent to Rome; one was his secretary, Stephen Gardiner (later Bishop of Winchester) and the other was Edward Fox (later Bishop of Hereford). Once more the demand was made that the verdict should be given in England without being afterwards reviewed in Rome; this time, Wolsey suggested that Cardinal Campeggio, a noted canonist, should be joined with him in the commission. Gardiner's own account of his interviews with the pope makes sorry reading; few envoys have dared to speak with such arrogance or insolence. Perhaps Gardiner was exaggerating his own part in order to impress the king and the cardinal. It was agreed that Campeggio should go to England, but no public assurance was given that the pope would confirm their decision. Campeggio brought with him, however, a Bull which he was not to let out of his possession; this he read to the king and to Wolsey and later destroyed. Its contents are not known, but presumably it granted final powers of decision to the two cardinals; the pope had yielded in a weak moment, and later bitterly regretted his action. Campeggio was fortunately a man of balanced judgment and safeguarded the pope's reputation.

They both agreed to draw out the negotiations as long as possible in the hope that time might bring its own solution.

Campeggio arrived in London in October 1528. It was no longer possible for the king to refuse Catherine the advisers she desired. These included Archbishop Warham, Bishop John Fisher, Bishop Standish who was a Franciscan, and Bishop Tunstal. To them she gave a copy of the Brief found in the Spanish archives. This changed the situation, as the Brief was not so rigid in its terms as the Bull. Every effort was made by Wolsey to get the original of the Brief sent to England, but Catherine[4] managed to get a messenger through to the emperor warning him not to part with it. She feared that her enemies would destroy it. Then Wolsey tried to get the pope to declare that the Brief was a forgery; this he refused to do on hearsay only.

Meanwhile Campeggio had discussed the matter with the king, and, later, with the queen. He wanted if possible to reach some kind of agreement that would prevent an open rupture. Henry, it was soon clear, was not looking for an impartial inquiry, but assumed that the decision must be in his favour. Campeggio's impression of the king was given in a letter to Rome dated 26th October. "His majesty has so diligently studied the whole subject that I believe he knows more than a great theologian or jurist . . . . I believe that if an angel came down from heaven, he could not persuade the king to the contrary."[5]

When he saw Catherine, he suggested that if she were to withdraw to a convent and take vows, it would ease the situation; she however declared that she would live and die in her vocation as a married woman. The cardinal then saw John Fisher and suggested that he should use his influence with the queen to persuade her to enter religion. In reporting this conversation, Campeggio wrote, "I had a long talk with him on the 25th [Oct.] and begged him, for many reasons, to support this policy, and he appeared to me, at parting, to be favourable to it."[6] Evidently John

---

[4] The adventures of her messengers (one was the future martyr, Thomas Abell) are well told by G. Mattingly in his *Catherine of Aragon*, pp. 185-6, and, 202-3.

[5] *Ehses*, p. 54.

[6] *Ehses*, p. 57.

Fisher was not prepared to commit himself definitely; he had shown the same prudence when Wolsey had tried to persuade him to support the king.

The all but fatal illness of the pope at the end of the year meant a further delay. Wolsey was becoming more and more apprehensive as the king grew more and more restive. To his credit it must be said that Wolsey not only feared his own ruin if the king were thwarted, but, as he warned the pope, and now Campeggio, the king would probably break from Rome and go his own way.

In a letter dated 18th February 1529, Campeggio reported that Wolsey had implored him to bring the matter to a swift conclusion in favour of Henry and so prevent the threatening calamities. "So far as I can see," he wrote, "'this passion of the king' is a most extraordinary thing. He sees nothing, he thinks of nothing but Anne; he cannot do without her for an hour and it moves one to pity to see how the king's life, the stability and downfall of the whole country hang upon this one question."[7]

At last the emperor began to move; it is quite contrary to the facts to think of him as springing to the defence of his aunt and bringing strong pressure to bear on the pope. Charles, a typical monarch of the period, was quite ready to sacrifice anyone in the interests of what he thought were his political needs, and at that period he wanted to keep on good terms with Henry. In spite of Catherine's appeals, her nephew did not send her the expert advisers she begged for in the early days of her trouble; and, indeed, at the critical time, during the trial itself, there was no imperial ambassador in England.[8]

Catherine did not believe that her English counsellors would dare to oppose the king's known wishes. So little

---

[7] *Pastor*, IV, p. 267.

[8] *Cal. Span.*, IV, no. 739.

did they seem to do for her, she was led to speak slightly of their efforts. On one occasion she complained that Warham would not say more than, "The wrath of the king is death" (*Indignatio principis mors est*),[9] and that John Fisher could only tell her to be of good courage. Herein she misjudged her strongest supporter, but she was kept isolated from all outside influence. It was only with difficulty that she could have private conversation with the imperial ambassador, and even her appointed counsellors were not allowed free access to her, nor were they permitted to see her alone.

It must be recognized that the king and Wolsey had created an atmosphere of terror; those who were near the king were well aware that he was self-centred and ruthless. In the glory of his young manhood when he preferred outdoor sports to indoor politics, the vicious elements in his character had been masked by a surface conviviality. The executions of Edmund de la Pole, of Richard Empson and of Edmund Dudley at the beginning of the reign were old tales by 1529, but the more recent execution of Buckingham was a warning to many. Sir Thomas More had seen what was beneath the surface. "Son Roper, if my head could win him a castle in France it should not fail to go."[10] Wolsey, in disgrace, voiced the same opinion of his master. "Rather than he will either miss or want any part of his will or appetite, he will put the loss of one half of his realm in danger."[11]

It was little wonder that men shrank from incurring the king's wrath, and John Fisher knew the dangerous

---

[9] *Proverbs*, xvi. 14. Norfolk was to use the same text in warning Sir Thomas More of the king's anger; see *Roper*, p. 75.

[10] *Roper*, p. 20.

[11] *Cavendish*, p. 245.

road he would tread when he resolved to speak out in the queen's defence. The opportunity was soon to come.

At this trying period, John Fisher received a tribute from the University of Cambridge that must have brought some comfort to his distressed spirit. A statute was passed by the senate to give honour to the chancellor in perpetuity. It acknowledged his many benefactions, not only as adviser to the Lady Margaret in her foundations and in his labours to carry out her wishes, but also as a generous patron of the university and especially of St. John's College. All this, it was felt, numbered him amongst the founders. The senate had therefore decided to establish an annual requiem on the anniversary of the day of his death. The statute ends by calling him "most learned father, head and glory of this our republic of learning."

In his reply John Fisher declared that such an honour was more fitting for a king than for a poor bishop (*pauperculo pontifici*). He had only been the minister or agent of the Lady Margaret; as her confessor he had advised her, for her soul's health, to bequeath part of her wealth to the training of young men in learning and virtue so that they could the more effectively preach the Gospel of Christ. He assured the senate that he would be more than content if they would link his name in their prayers with the name of the Lady Margaret.[12]

The senate's decision did not go unchallenged. One of the Fellows of St. John's was Richard Croke, the most learned Greek scholar of his day. It was through the influence of John Fisher that Croke had been kept at Cambridge instead of moving to Oxford as he had been urged to do by Archbishop Warham and Sir Thomas More; indeed, at first, John Fisher had himself paid Croke's salary. This fact should have restrained the

---

[12] *Lewis*, II, pp. 301-7.

scholar from writing an ungracious letter objecting to the senate naming John Fisher one of the college founders.

The bishop's reply gives us a glimpse of the sterner side of his character. He exclaimed against anyone suggesting that he himself had put forward pretensions to the title of a founder. "I, who have striven, as I shall strive, by every means to ensure that the glory of the Foundress shall shine, and her name be everywhere renowned!" Then he wrote as a chancellor. "I hear you neither lecture, nor go to the common table, and also that you entertain guests from among the fellows in your room, against the statutes of the College, which I will not tolerate." Then, recalling perhaps recent happenings, he declared that he would willingly lay down the chancellorship. "Perhaps some other person will take it who likes the Lutheran doctrines . . . . I do not doubt that the fathers and seniors of the University are much opposed to heresy, although there many of you who are suspect, and some whose names are already noted."[13]

---

[13] Hymer's edition (1840) of the funeral sermon on the Lady Margaret, pp. 210-17.

XV: Pope Julius II
Raphael di Urbino

Julius was famously shut out of heaven in Erasmus' poem *Julius Exclusus* (Julius Excluded) for managing a worldly pontificate devoted to the arts and war. He issued the dispensation for Catherine to marry Henry, which would become "the King's great matter."

XVI - Pope Leo X
Raphael di Urbino

The first Medici Pope, Leo condemned the doctrines of Luther with the bull *Exsurge Domine*, and conferred upon Henry the title of *Fidei Defensor* for his short lived defense of the Church. English monarchs to this day use this title.

XVII: Pope Clement VII
Sebastiano del Piambo
Pope Clement belatedly declared the marriage between Henry and Catherine valid.

CHAPTER XVII
BLACKFRIARS

THE king issued his warrant to permit the legatine court to open on 31st May 1529 at Blackfriars. The hall of this Dominican house had been used for the meeting of Parliament in 1523; it was conveniently near the new palace of Bridewell just across the Fleet River.

The first meeting was formal; the commission was read, and the king and queen were cited to appear at the next session on 18th June, but their personal presence was not expected until the routine pleadings had been made. Queen Catherine, however, had made up her mind to act promptly. It is not known on whose advice she had reached this decision. Every effort had been made to prevent her supporters, and even her appointed counsellors, from seeing her in private. The king and Wolsey certainly suspected that she had had messages, if not letters, from John Fisher. Her conduct throughout the tragic and prolonged agony from May 1527 until May 1533 shows that she had the firmness of will and of character to make her own decisions.

So, at this second session,[1] the queen made a strong protest against the constitution of the court. Reading a prepared statement, she questioned the competency and impartiality of the court, and stated that, as the matter had been put to the pope it should remain with him for decision. A record was made of her protest. This unexpected intervention of the queen herself made it clear to all that she was not prepared to acquiesce in the proceedings.

---

[1] *Ehses*, p. 103.

At the next meeting, on 21st June, both the king and the queen were present. The king's counsellors were in place—all of them were favoured in later years. "Now on the other side," wrote Cavendish, "stood the counsel for the queen, Doctor Fisher Bishop of Rochester, and Doctor Standish, some time a Grey Friar, and then Bishop of St. Asaph in Wales, two notable clerks, in divinity, and especial the Bishop of Rochester, a very godly man and a devout person."[2]

Campeggio was shocked at the irregularities of the proceedings: "in the house of a foreigner one cannot do all one wishes," he wrote. This time the king started off with a long and wordy speech in his own defence, repeating the well-known plea of the sensitiveness of his conscience and of his desire for the truth, and adding a solemn protestation of his devotion to the Apostolic See. The legates were then able to proceed with the business. In reply to the queen's objections at the previous session, they stated that the court was regularly constituted under the authority of the pope and was thus competent to proceed.

Catherine once more surprised the court by her immediate intervention. Cavendish gives a picture that is clearly that of an onlooker. She "rose up incontinent out of her chair, where as she sat, and because she could not come directly to the king for the distance which severed them, she took pain to go about unto the king, kneeling down at his feet in the sight of all the court and assembly."[3]

The dignified and pathetic plea she made to the king cannot be read even now, four centuries later, without deep compassion.

---

[2] *Cavendish*, p. 107.

[3] *Cavendish*, p. 108.

When Shakespeare came to dramatize the scene in Blackfriars for Henry VIII, he followed Cavendish closely.

> Sir, I desire you do me right and justice,
> And to bestow your pity on me; for
> I am a most poor woman, and a stranger,
> Born out of your dominions; having here
> No judge indifferent, nor no more assurance
> Of equal friendship and proceeding. Alas, sir,
> In what have I offended you? what cause
> Hath my behaviour given to your displeasure,
> That thus you should proceed to put me off?
> And take your good grace from me? Heaven witness,
> I have been to you a true and humble wife,
> At all times to your will conformable,
> Ever in fear to kindle your dislike,
> Yes, subject to your countenance, glad or sorry
> As I saw it inclined: when was the hour
> I ever contradicted your desire,
> Or made it not mine too? Or which of your friends
> Have I not strove to love, although I knew
> He were mine enemy? what friend of mine
> That had to him derived your anger, did I
> Continue in my liking? nay, gave notice
> He was from thence discharged? Sir, call to mind
> That I have been your wife, in this obedience,
> Upward of twenty years, and have been blest
> With many children by you: if in the course
> And process of this time you can report,
> And prove it too, against mine honour aught,
> My bond of wedlock or my love and duty,
> Against your sacred person, in God's name,
> Turn me away, and let fount contempt
> Shut door upon me, and so give me up

To the sharp'st kind of justice. Please you, sir,
The king, your father, was reputed for
A prince most prudent, of an excellent
And unmatch'd wit and judgment: Ferdinand,
My father, king of Spain, was reckon'd one
The wisest prince that there had reign'd by many
A year before: it is not to be question'd
That they had gather'd a wise council to them
Of every realm, that did debate this business,
Who deem'd our marriage lawful: wherefore I humbly
Beseech you, sir, to spare me, till I may
Be by my friends in Spain advis'd, whose counsel
I will implore: if not, I' the name of God,
Your pleasure be fulfill'd![4]

"And even with that," wrote Cavendish, "she rose up, making low courtesy to the king, and so departed from thence.[5] She refused to return."

The king felt it necessary to declare to the court how true and obedient and virtuous a wife Catherine had been, a fact that no one had questioned. He went on to refer to the secret court of May 1527 and to the support he had from the bishops. "I moved you first my Lord of Canterbury, asking your licence, forasmuch as you were our metropolitan, to put this matter in question; and so I did of all you my lords [bishops] to the which ye have all

---

[4] *Henry VIII*, II, iv, 11-54. Most authorities agree that this scene is by Shakespeare. Dr. Johnson's note is worth quoting: "The meek sorrows and virtuous distress of Catherine have furnished some scenes which must be justly numbered among the greatest efforts of tragedy. But the genius of Shakespeare comes in and goes out with Catherine."

[5] The early biographer follows Cavendish closely, but here adds a passage attacking Wolsey: Shakespeare introduced this later in the scene. It was derived from Hall and really relates to an interview the two cardinals had with the queen.

granted by writing under all your seals, the which I have here to be showed."

Then followed a curious episode.

"That is truth if it please your highness," quoth the Bishop of Canterbury, "I doubt not but all my brethren here present will affirm the same."

"No, sir, not I," quoth the Bishop of Rochester, "ye have not my consent thereto."

"No! ha' the!" quoth the king, "look here upon this, is not this your hand and seal?" and showed him the instrument with seals.

"No, forsooth, sire," quoth the Bishop of Rochester, "it is not my hand nor seal!"

To that, quoth the king to my Lord of Canterbury: "Sir, how say ye, is it not his hand and seal?"

"Yes, sir," quoth he.

"That is not so," quoth the Bishop of Rochester, "for indeed you were in hand with me to have my hand and seal, as other of my lords had already done; but then I said to you, that I would never consent to no such act, for it were much against my conscience; nor my hand and seal should never be seen at any such instrument, God willing, with much more matter touching the same communication between us."

"You say truth," quoth the Bishop of Canterbury, "such words ye said unto me; but at the last ye were fully persuaded that I should for you subscribe your name, and put-to a seal myself, and ye would allow the same."

"All which words and matter," quoth the Bishop of Rochester, "under your correction, my lord, and supportation of this noble audience, there is no thing more untrue."

"Well, well," quoth the king, "it shall make no matter; we will not stand with you in argument herein, for you are but one man."[6]

The only existing document[7] that was signed and sealed by some of the bishops (including Rochester) is dated 1st July 1529; this is more than a week later than the episode assigned by Cavendish to 21st June. Tunstal who signed it left that very day for France in company with Sir Thomas More on an embassy. It goes no further than saying that the king had consulted them and that they considered the matter should be referred to the pope; it makes no judgment on the problem at issue. It would not seem that John Fisher could have objected to this. Five of the other seven signatories were also counsellors appointed to the queen. The date rules this document out as the one over which Warham and Fisher disagreed. It may be that Cavendish's memory betrayed him and the dispute arose, not in the legate's court, but at some later audience the bishops had with the king. This illustrates the difficulty of following the proceedings from day to day without an official report. We have to piece together the notes made by various persons.

On 22nd June there was a wrangle between John Fisher and Wolsey. The point in dispute was the exact relations between Catherine and her first husband, Prince Arthur. The king's supporters maintained that the marriage had been consummated; but this was denied by the queen and her counsellors.

"So that it was said that no man could know the truth." "Yes," quoth the Bishop of Rochester, "I know

---

[6] *Cavendish*, pp. 113-14.

[7] *L.P.*, IV, no. 5751.

the truth." "How know you the truth?" quoth my lord Cardinal. "Forsooth, my lord," quoth he, "I am a professor of the truth; I know that God is truth itself, nor he never spake but truth; which said, What God hath joined together let not man put asunder. And forasmuch as this marriage was made and joined by God to a good intent, I say that I know the truth the which cannot be broken or loosed by the power of man upon no feigned occasion."

"So much doth all faithful men know," quoth my lord cardinal, "as well as you. Yet this reason is not sufficient in this case; for the king's counsel doth allege divers presumptions to prove the marriage not good at the beginning, ergo, say they, it was not joined by God at the beginning, and therefore it is not lawful."[8]

The sting of John Fisher's intervention lay in his final words, "upon no feigned occasion." He and the other counsellors of the queen were in a difficult position. As the queen refused to recognize the court and kept aloof, they had no standing, but this was not to prevent John Fisher from speaking his mind. He was present at each meeting of which there is record, and a few days after his brush with Wolsey, he spoke out clearly before the legates. Campeggio's secretary gave an account of the speech.

Yesterday [28th July] the fifth audience was given. While the proceedings were going on as usual, owing to the queen's contumacy, the Bishop of Rochester made his appearance, and said, in an appropriate speech, that in a former audience he had heard the

---

[8] *Cavendish*, p. 15.

king's majesty discuss the cause, and testify before all that his only intention was to get justice done, and to relieve himself of the scruple that he had on his conscience, inviting both the judges and everyone else to throw some light on the investigation of the cause, because on this account he found his mind much distressed and perplexed. If on this offer and command of the king he [the bishop] did not come forward in public and manifest what he had discovered in this matter after two years' most diligent study [he would be failing in his duty].[9] Therefore, both in order not to procure the damnation of his soul, and in order not to be unfaithful to the king, or to fail in doing the duty which he owed to the truth, in a matter of such great importance, he presented himself before their reverend lordships to declare, to affirm, and with forcible reasons to demonstrate to them that this marriage of the king and the queen can be dissolved by no power, human or divine, and for this opinion he declared he would even lay down his life. He added that the Baptist in olden times regarded it as impossible for him to die more gloriously than in the cause of marriage, and that as it was not so holy at that time as it has now become by the shedding of Christ's blood, he could encourage himself more ardently, more effectually, and with greater confidence to dare any great or extreme peril whatever. He used many other suitable words, and at the end presented a small book (*libellus*) which had been written by him on the subject.

---

[9] The writer did not complete the construction of his sentence. The words in brackets suggest the line of thought he may have been following.

> After him the Bishop of St. Asaph's (Standish) of the Minorite order, spoke, and expressed nearly the same opinion, but with less polished eloquence and in briefer terms, and he offered several comments. Then followed a doctor (Ligham) who alleged various arguments from the sacred canons in favour of the marriage, which were not very cogent....
>
> This affair of Rochester was unexpected and unforeseen, and consequently has kept everyone in wonder. What he will do we shall see when the day comes. You already know what sort of man he is, and may imagine what is likely to happen.[10]

It is a pity that the secretary did not enlarge on the last sentence. In his letter was enclosed a note from a friend which refers to John Fisher as a man of high reputation both for his learning, and his good life, and goes on to suggest that since such a man spoke in favour of the queen it would be difficult for the king to hold his ground. This was an optimistic view, but evidently this Italian onlooker had been deeply impressed by John Fisher's bold pronouncement.

The French Ambassador, Du Bellay, wrote to his own king on the same occasion.

> The cause was called again yesterday, when the king's proctor appeared, and the queen was a second time put in default for non-appearance. The Bishop of Rochester, however, who is accounted one of the best and most holy divines in England, especially in his opposition to these last heresies of Luther, was there with other counsellors, but not as her proctor, only to

---

[10] *Ehses*, pp. 116-17. L.P., IV, no. 5732, mistakenly assigns the letter to Campeggio himself and the enclosed note to his secretary.

remonstrate with the judges, offering to prove that she had a good cause by a little book which he had made thereon jointly with his companions, which he then presented, enlarging upon the queen's cause with many wise words. A rather modest answer was made by the judges, that it was not his business to pronounce so decidedly in the matter as the cause was not committed to him.[11]

The small book or statement handed in by John Fisher enraged the king and a written reply was prepared.

---

[11] *L.P.*, IV, no. 5741.

CHAPTER XVIII
THE KING'S ANGER

COUNSEL on both sides submitted to the legatine court statements of opinion, sometimes on points of canon law raised in argument, and sometimes on the general issues. Thus on 9th July 1529, eight "libels" (*libelli*) were presented on behalf of the king, and six in support of the queen. Of these six, two were from the Bishop of Ely (West), one from the Bishop of London (Tunstal), one from R. Gwent (a learned canonist and later Archdeacon of London), and two from John Fisher.[1]

Part of the document that John Fisher handed in on 28th June is now preserved at Cambridge.[2] Fortunately he followed the plan he used, as we have seen, in his controversial works; he began by stating six axioms or truths that he proposed to establish. These give us the main line of his argument; the manuscript as we now have it, does not go beyond the detailed consideration of the first two axioms. Here are the six.

1. There is no obstacle to marriage between the two parties that cannot be removed by the authority of the pope.
2. Since the pope has this power, there can be no doubt that he exercised it by the dispensation.
3. Once these obstacles had been removed, there was nothing to prevent them marrying according to established law.

---

[1] L.P., IV, 5768.
[2] Cambridge University Library, MS. 1315.

4. The contract of marriage and the marriage itself were celebrated according to the rites and ceremonies of the Church, as many can testify.
5. God, by the sacrament of marriage, gave his assent to this union, and consecrated it by his invisible power; that, no one can question.
6. This sacramental union and connexion, by which God formed a bond between these persons, made legitimate by the dispensation, is unbreakable by any power.

It will be seen how, in these fundamental propositions, John Fisher went to the heart of the matter; arguments about defects in the Bull were to him no longer relevant; all that was needed was the pope's assent, and that Julius II had undoubtedly given. In his talk with Wolsey at Rochester, John Fisher it will be recalled, had suggested[3] that the circumstances should be examined in which the Bull was obtained; evidently his later intensive study of the question had cleared his mind of such qualifications, and now he based his deliberate opinion on first principles.

Such a reduction of the problem to a few plain truths must have surprised the legatine court where subtle distinctions and conflicting witness obscured the real issue: had the pope power to grant this dispensation? John Fisher's answer was, "Yes."

Henry's anger at this forthright opinion is understandable. He still believed that the court would not dare to oppose his wishes, but this return to simple issues could be fatal to his cause unless answered effectively and

---

[3] This assumes that Wolsey's report was correct.

immediately. He instructed Stephen Gardiner to prepare the reply.[4]

Stephen Gardiner was fifteen years younger than the man he was to attack. He had a brilliant career at Cambridge where he distinguished himself in civil and canon law; he became Master of Trinity Hall in 1525. We have no knowledge of his relations with the chancellor of his university, but there is an animosity in Gardiner's attitude that suggests a discordance between them. Gardiner's association with Robert Barnes has already been mentioned, so also has his mission to Rome when his arrogant behaviour to the pope was scandalous. On his return he had been in Wolsey's service, and was now on the point of becoming the king's secretary. No doubt Henry indicated the lines along which he wanted the attack to be made and must have approved of Gardiner's unworthy attack on John Fisher. This reply is significant not so much for its arguments, which are not impressive, as for its bitterness. The manuscript was handed to John Fisher; he wrote a few comments in the margin.

The opening passages are here given in full with the bishop's comments italicized within parenthesis.

> Since in this matrimonial cause now to be investigated, or in the controversy now to be determined, we have attempted or designed nothing, on our own authority, which were unsuited to the office of a true Christian prince; but on the contrary have always had regard before everything to equity, justice and truth, and have everywhere held that the

---

[4] Pierre Janelle in his edition of Stephen Gardiner's *Obedience in Church and State* (1930) has established that Stephen Gardiner was the author of this reply. See also his *L'Angleterre Catholique a la Veille du Schisme* (1935). This chapter owes much to these two books.

judgment of the church was to be deferred to with great respect; relying upon our consciousness of this our innocence, we hoped, O Judges, that we should have all the best men as supporters of our honour, our efforts and our purposes, and hardly thought that there might come forth anyone to disparage such a dutiful mind of ours, show enmity to our virtue, and jealousy of our fame. If this was to be (*and we are not ignorant how many things have deceived the wisest, even in regard to their own concerns, and to public affairs*), yet we never supposed, O Judges, that the bishop of Rochester would take up before your tribunal that accusation against ourselves, which would rather befit the hatred, or better still the fury, of bad citizens, and a multitude seditiously roused, than his own virtue and dignity. Of a certainty, O Judges, we did unfold to this Rochester, and this already some months ago (*nearly a year ago*), and more than once, how far we had been from purposely seeking out or rashly devising those reasons, which long before had engendered in us scruples of conscience, in regard to this illegitimate and incestuous marriage. Which reasons this very Rochester thus far then approved, and deemed so weighty and powerful, that unless we applied to the oracle of our most serene Lord [the pope] (*which he then thought it necessary to consult upon those matters*) he did not believe that our former peace of mind could be restored to us (*I did not say so, but the cardinal would have been glad if I had said so*). Now when this same our most holy Lord (*yet not without the advice and opinion of some of the most reverend cardinals of the apostolic see, and of other members of the Roman court, most eminent for their worthiness and erudition*) has judged that these same reasons made the cause of our marriage so intricate and ambiguous, that only through the ruling of the best chosen and most discreet judges could it be treated and set forth according to its dignity and magnitude; and when he has, most in accordance with your deserts, entrusted it to you, O Judges, and to your scrupulousness, to be wholly determined; and has sent thee here, O most reverend Campegius, for no other reason, to the great charges indeed of his Holiness, and to thy huge peril and travail through the dangers of so many things and ways; what shall we believe, O Judges, to have come into the mind of this Rochester, or by what spirit shall we think he has been led, to come forward here so impudently and so much out of season (*I was obliged to this by the protestation of the king and the cardinal*), in order to declare his own personal view of the matter, now at length after so many months, and even here before such a great and illustrious assembly as that of your court.

It had been of constancy on his part, not to ascribe now at last in public those scruples of conscience, which he had once thought we were right in harbouring, to mere commonplaces (*as he calls them*), to subtleties only probable in appearance, and other gilded persuasions of rhetoricians. It had been of Christian piety (*if indeed by the study of many opinions he had succeeded in ascertaining thoroughly what in this cause was just, what true, what lawful*), to have reminded us of it again and again in private, and not to proclaim with such huge self-confidence, to the great blemishing of our conscience; it had been of his duty, of his faith and of his loyalty (*which every good citizen owes to his king*) to protect and vindicate our innocence from the calumnies of evil men; and since

THE KING'S ANGER 221

he saw, by tokens in no wise obscure, our conscience labour and fluctuate, to hasten to its help by all possible means; it had been of pious reverence and observance which he owes to the supreme Pontiff, when the later had decreed that this cause was exceedingly intricate, and especially necessary to the preservation of this our realm, so that he could weigh everything by yourselves judging supremely,—to acquiesce in his decision, rather than publicly to charge his Holiness with levity, as if the truth of the cause he had committed to you for investigation, and was so obvious (*it is not obvious to all, but only to those who are compelled to study it*) easy, plain, and open, that it would be foolish to call it into question.

Lastly it had been of wisdom and modesty, when you had commenced in this cause assigned to you according to the most ample authority of your jurisdiction, to allow to you a free order of trial, and not to prescribe to you so to say a new formula for judging, and to bring forward of his own authority a pre-judgment before your sentence.

But it is in vain that we require those things of this bishop, O Judges, whose breast and heart are so filled and stirred up by two most evil advisers, namely a certain immoderate arrogance, and a too self-confident temerity. (*Arrogance—temerity.*) For else whence did these words proceed, O Judges, that he would by sound and unanswerable arguments, at once place before your eyes, and those of all men, the naked truth of this cause, without deceit and colouring of words; and that indeed he would defend it constantly, and defend it indeed as far as the stake (*I said nothing of that*); and that he had now a juster cause, in withstanding the dissolution of this marriage than

Saint John the Baptist had once had against Herod. O voice devoid of all modesty and gravity! (*What more did I attest than the cardinal who [affirmed] he would be burnt or torn limb from limb rather than act contrary to justice?*) As if indeed, alone of all men, Rochester was gifted with discernment, and alone had investigated and illuminated the truth of this cause.

And what need was there for him to declare himself ready to endure fire and flame for that reason, when such manifest tokens gave him evident proof of our clemency and our zeal to protect, and not oppress, truth? And lastly how unjust is that comparison, by which he labours to couple together his cause and that of the holy Baptist! Unless perhaps he has conceived that opinion of ourselves, that apparently we were somehow playing the Herod, or daring some crime akin to the crime of Herod (*I don't understand this*). To be sure, O Judges, never did Herod's impiety bear a pleasing aspect for us; and certainly we did learn from the rule of the gospel and the voice of the Baptist that this in him was to be condemned, that he had taken to his wife the sister of his brother.[5] But whichever of the two things Rochester may think in regard to us, we were always far removed from Herod's cruelty. If ever we proceeded with any severity against those who appeared to look upon this divorce with little favour, and did not rather lovingly draw them to ourselves with the highest favours, in proportion to their virtues, let Rochester come, and justly cast Herod's tyranny in our teeth. But let this man's evil-speaking against us his prince, be his own punishment. Yet, O Judges, lest

---

[5] The king (or Gardiner) was at fault here. Herod Antipas divorced his first wife to marry Herodias, the wife of his half-brother Philip who was still alive.

you might be steeped in darkness, and lest your judgment might be hindered, by his assertion, uttered with great haughtiness, that he has now at last found the very truth, and plucked it out of darkness, it behoves us to examine this bragging, and more than thrasonical pomposity of words.[6]

Did Henry—or Stephen Gardiner—remember, six years later, that Herod had beheaded John the Baptist?

After this amazing introduction, Gardiner, still speaking for the king, went on to consider the case put forward by John Fisher. There was nothing new in the arguments advanced; both sides had time and again stated their opinions. Once more the validity of the dispensation was questioned on the grounds that the pope had been misled; there had been no danger of war between England and Spain so the marriage was pointless; when his brother died, Henry was too young to make a responsible decision; the text in Leviticus and its alleged abrogation by a text in Deuteronomy[7] were again examined. It had all been said before.

This document reveals very clearly the mentality of the king; it will be noted that, in spite of his talk of his "dutiful mind," he prejudged the question by speaking of this "illegitimate and incestuous marriage." The quick anger at any sign of opposition is manifest. John Fisher's calm and impersonal consideration of the principles involved was interpreted as a personal insult to be answered by insults. It is also to be noted that the reply contains an acknowledgment, all but fulsome, of the authority of the pope and of the legatine court. Henry was

---

[6] *Obedience in Church and State*, ed. Pierre Janelle, pp. 2-9. The above is Janelle's translation.

[7] Deut. xxv. 5.

still expecting that he would gain the verdict, but when he was robbed of that, his dutiful sentiments towards the pope suffered an immediate reversal.

John Fisher could no longer doubt the king's animosity towards him, but the attack was also meant as a warning to others.

While the legatine court was sitting, the queen's appeal was being considered by the pope, and on 16th July he advoked the cause to Rome. The news of this decision may have reached Wolsey, and this would explain his increased urgency for a decision. Campeggio was not so well informed. He had been shocked at the way in which the consideration of such a grave matter was being hustled along regardless of the due observances and procedure of a judicial inquiry. He could do nothing to lessen what he thought was an indecent forcing of the pace. It was not only the king who was in a hurry; Anne Boleyn and her relations stood, at his elbow; and now Wolsey saw that unless the desired result could be reached speedily, his own position was in danger. But Campeggio had one unsuspected resource in reserve. On 30th July[8] he adjourned the court for the two months of the Roman vacation. Before that period expired, the pope's decision to recall the case was known; the legatine court did not meet again.

John Fisher was not content to allow the queen's cause to be lost for lack of support from his pen. When he was in the Tower he was asked how many tractates or books he had written in her defence.[9] He replied, "I am not certain of the number, but I think seven or eight. The matter was so serious both on account of the importance

---

[8] I accept Janelle's argument in favour of 30th July as against the usually given 23rd July. See *Veille*, p. 130n. I.

[9] *L.P.*, VIII, no. 859. Also *Lewis*, II, pp. 403-7, for Latin text of answers.

of the persons concerned, and on account of the injunction given me by the king, that I devoted more attention, to examining the truth of it, lest I should deceive myself and others, than to anything else in my life." He was further asked how many copies had been made and who possessed them. He answered, "I do not know, nor was I very careful about them, except for the last two, which went to the heart of the matter. One; of these is now in the hands of the Archbishop (Cranmer)." He avoided giving any names save that of one who was in the king's favour. He added, "I never sent them or any copies of them out of the country, nor consented to this being done." He repeated this statement with emphasis.

One of these short books was printed in Spain in the summer of 1530 and the manuscript may have been sent there by Eustace Chapuys, the Emperor's ambassador, who was most active in support of the queen and knew the value of anything written by John Fisher on her behalf. It is from the dispatches of Chapuys or of Dr. Ortis, the Emperor's representative in Rome, that it is possible to get information about these writings.[10]

A careful study of these references suggests that John Fisher was correct in his recollection of the number as it is possible to distinguish seven, and perhaps eight. There were three that he handed in for the consideration of the legates in July 1529. In February 1530 Chapuys wrote that the bishop had finished revising his book; this may have been an expanded version of the earlier court opinions. Then in August the ambassador reported the publication of the Spanish book, which, he noted, was printed without the permission of the bishop; many thought, wrote Chapuys, that the bishop would go in fear of the king's displeasure, but in fact he seemed indifferent to what

---

[10] *L.P.*, IV, nos. 5729, 5768, 6199, 6596, 6738; V, nos, 207, 460, 553.

Henry might think. In April 1531, Dr. Ortis in Rome wrote that he had received two books (manuscripts) different from that published in Spain. As will be explained presently, a book summarizing the opinions of the universities was prepared at the king's order in the latter part of 1530. John Fisher wrote a reply to this; the first part was sent to Rome by Chapuys in October 1531, and the second part a month later. Nicholas Harpsfield used this reply to the universities in *his Treatise on the Pretended Divorce of King Henry VIII from Queen Catherine of Aragon* which was written in the reign of Queen Mary.[11]

Amongst those who wrote for the king was Robert Wakefield; he recalled that "about eighteen years ago" he had instructed John Fisher in the rudiments of Hebrew, and it was on the Hebrew text of the verses from Leviticus and Deuteronomy that he based his arguments; it does not seem that the bishop replied to him.

The early biographer wrote, "it was once told me by a reverend father that was Dean of Rochester many years together, named Mr. Phillips,[12] that on a time in the days of King Edward VI when certain commissioners were coming towards him to search his house for books, he for fear burned a large volume which this holy bishop had compiled containing in it the whole story and matter of the divorce; which volume he gave him with his own hand a little before his trouble."[13]

The work published in Spain, *De Causa Matrimonii*, brought together a host of witnesses ranging from the Early Fathers to the later Schoolmen in support of the dispensation granted by the pope. This display of learning

---

[11] First published by the Camden Society in 1878.

[12] Walter Philips, last prior, and first dean, 1540-70.

[13] *Ortroy*, p. 365.

and reason was a beating of the air. It was hopeless to struggle against the relentless determination of the king.

Some of the bishops were alarmed at John Fisher's advocacy of the queen's cause. In December 1530, Warham, supported by other bishops, urged John Fisher to retract his writings, but he refused to deny what he believed to be the truth.

Wolsey's fears were realized. On 16th October 1529, the Great Seal was taken from him, and a year later he died on his way to the Tower. Sir Thomas More succeeded him as Lord Chancellor.

The king's next move after the recall of the case to Rome, was to adopt a suggestion made by Dr. Thomas Cranmer, a forty-year old Cambridge scholar, that the opinions of the universities on the validity of the dispensation should be obtained. These, if favourable, could be used at Rome to influence opinion.

Stephen Gardiner was sent to Cambridge to persuade the regents and scholars there to express their support for the king. It does not seem that the chancellor, John Fisher, was consulted; his views must have been well known, for, in addition to the reports of his defence of the queen and his written opinions, the Master of St. John's College at that time was his archdeacon, Nicholas Metcalfe, who openly opposed the king's suit and was later to suffer for his opinions.

Gardiner did not have an easy passage.[14] The first general meeting ended in an uproar. By judicious selection of so-called delegates, and by wearing down and frightening the opposition, he at length got an opinion that went some way, but not all the way, to satisfy the king. The University affirmed that by divine and natural law a man might not marry his brother's widow; nothing

---

[14] L.P., IV, nos. 6218 and 6259.

was said of the pope's powers of dispensation. This document was signed by the vice-chancellor, ten doctors, seventeen Masters of Arts, and the two proctors.

When one considers the pressure that was brought to bear on the heads of the colleges by the man who was now the king's secretary, and the ever-growing terror that cowed all men, it is possible to appreciate the courage of the University in not giving the king all he wanted. That must have been a little consolation to John Fisher in the unhappiness that the result brought him.

By the summer of 1530, the king felt he had sufficient support from some of the universities to influence Rome. He persuaded some of the lords and bishops to sign a petition setting out the support so far received and asking for the pope's favourable consideration. Both John Fisher and Sir Thomas More refused to sign the petition. The king was so annoyed that Chapuys believed the Great Seal would be taken away from the new chancellor.

CHAPTER XIX
PRÆMUNIRE

IN August 1529 John Fisher was summoned to Parliament and Convocation which were to meet in November. The Parliament was to prove the longest so far held in the country's history; there were eight sessions between 3rd November 1529 and 14th April 1536; it stood prorogued during 1530 and 1535. It is no exaggeration to say that the relations between Church and State were revolutionized during what has come to be known as the Reformation Parliament.

The often repeated statement that this was a packed House of Commons needs qualification. When it assembled in November 1529 there were 310 members; there is little evidence that any exceptional pressure was used in the election. Some of the boroughs were under court influence; others, as well as the counties, were more or less controlled by the great peers, and others were independent; this was the normal situation. The length of the Parliament, however, meant that in the course of years, the membership changed considerably. In January 1531, for instance, there were forty vacancies; gradually, under the skilled management of Thomas Cromwell, the number of king's men, as they may be called, increased, so that by 1534 when the main statutes were passed, the Commons were more submissive than in 1529; even so, there was opposition from the bolder spirits to a new Act of Treason.[1] The Lords numbered about ninety; here again events helped the king; during the period of the

---
[1] See below, p. 361.

Parliament, thirteen sees became vacant and were filled with safe men.

It must be admitted that there was no widespread opposition to the legislation of this Parliament. There was no interference with the teaching and practice of religion; most of the matters dealt with did not directly affect the bulk of the population and as some of the statutes dealt with popular grievances, the legislation did not rouse strong opposition. Even the crucial question of the authority of the pope did not stir up opposition; for most people, this was a matter for the king and his council, and was an old story; time and again there had been quarrels between king and pope; and, after all, if the bishops said it was all right, how could ordinary folk dispute the matter? That question indicates the tragedy of the whole situation; if the leaders of the church failed to recognize their responsibilities, it was little wonder that the lay population accepted the position. It was not until the last days of this Parliament with the dissolution of the smaller monasteries that men began to wonder what was happening; here was something they could see at work in their own neighbourhoods. It was then that popular feeling was aroused.

John Fisher was concerned directly with the first half of the life of this Parliament during which changes were made by degrees, but he was quick to see, as did Sir Thomas More, the direction in which things were moving; had they been given even a moderate measure of support the catastrophic legislation of 1534 and 1535 might have been modified.

The responsibility for policy lay with the king. It is a mistake to place too much emphasis on the influence of Thomas Cromwell during the two years after Wolsey's fall. He did not become a councillor until 1531 and

PRÆMUNIRE 231

Chapuys made no reference to him in his dispatches before the beginning of 1533 when he became the king's secretary. From that date until his execution in 1540 he had considerable influence, but Henry had the last word.

During the few weeks of the 1529 session, the Commons passed bills dealing with probate, mortuaries, and pluralities.[2] The significance of this legislation was not in the details of the regulations which were moderate and aimed at what were undoubted grievances; the importance lay in the fact that the Commons were encroaching upon what had hitherto been ecclesiastical territory. This innovation alarmed John Fisher; he saw that if this first step were permitted, a greater advance would follow. So when these measures came before the Lords, he urged that the Commons should be checked at once. The speech put into his mouth by the early biographer is a reconstruction; there is no verbatim record of the proceedings.

My lord of Rochester stepped up among the other lords and said in effect as followeth:

> "My lords, I pray you for God's sake, consider what bills are here daily preferred from the Commons. What the same may sound in some of your ears I cannot tell, but in my ears they sound all to this effect, that our holy mother the Church, being left unto us by the great liberality and diligence of our forefathers in most perfect and peaceable freedom, shall now by us

---

[2] For a clear guide to the somewhat involved proceedings of this year, the reader is referred to *Report of the Ecclesiastical Courts Commission* (1883), especially to the historical appendices by Bishop Stubbs. The fourth is particularly useful as it gives in parallel columns summaries of the proceedings in the Convocations and in Parliament with extracts from State Papers and other contemporary documents.

be brought into servile thraldom like a bondmaid, or rather by little and little to be clean banished and driven out of our confines and dwelling places. For else to what end should all this importunate and injurious petitions from the Commons tend? What strange words be here uttered, not to be heard of any Christian ears and unworthy to be spoken in the hearing of Christian princes? For they say that bishops and their officials, abbots, priests and others of the clergy are covetous, ravenous, insatiable, idle, cruel, and so forth. What? Are all of this sort, or is there any of these abuses that the clergy seek not to extirpate and destroy? Be there not laws already provided by them against such and many more disasters? Are not books full of them to be read of such as list to read them if they were executed? But, my lords, beware of yourselves and your country, nay, beware of the liberty of our mother the Church. Luther, one of the most cruel enemies to the faith that ever was, is at hand, and the common people study for novelties and with good will hear what can be said in favour of heresy.

What success is there to be hoped for in these attempts other than such as our neighbours have already tasted, whose harms may be a good warning to us? Remember with yourselves what these sects and divisions have wrought among the Bohemians and Germans, who, besides an innumerable number of mischiefs fallen among them, have almost lost their ancient and catholic faith. And what by the snares of John Huss and after him of Martin Luther (whom they reverence like a prophet) they have almost excluded themselves from the unity of Christ's Holy Church? These men now among us seem to reprove the life and doings of the clergy, but after such a sort as they endeavour to bring them into contempt and hatred of the laity. And so finding fault with other men's manners, whom they have no authority to correct, omit and forget their own, which is far worse and much more out of order than the other. But if the truth were known, ye shall find that they rather hunger and thirst after the riches and possessions of the clergy than after amendment of their faults and abuses. And therefore it was not for nothing that this motion was lately made for the small monasteries to be taken into the king's hands. Wherefore I will tell you, my lords, plainly what I think. Except ye resist manfully by your authorities this violent heap of mischief offered by the Commons, ye shall shortly see all obedience withdrawn first from the clergy and after from yourselves. Whereupon will ensue the utter ruin and danger of the Christian faith, and in place of it (that which is likely to follow) the most wicked and tyrannical government of the Turks. For ye shall find that all these mischiefs among them riseth only through lack of faith."

This speech being ended, although there were divers of the clergy that liked well thereof, and some of the laity also, yet were there some again that seemed to mislike the same, only for flattery and fear of the king; insomuch as the Duke of Norfolk reproved him half merrily and half angrily saying that many of these words might have been missed; adding further these words, "I wis, my lord, it is many times seen that the greatest clerks be not always the wisest men." But to that he answered merrily again and said that he could not remember any fools in his time that had proved great clerks.³

Hall's brief account⁴ of this speech may have been used by the early biographer as the basis for his more elaborate version. The reference to the smaller monasteries indicates that the writer incorporated material that could not have been applicable in 1529. The sequel is best told in Hall's words.

When these words were reported to the Commons of the nether house, that the bishop should say that their doings were for lack of faith, they took the matter grievously, for they imagined that the bishop esteemed them as heretics, and so by his slanderous words would have persuaded the temporal lords to have restrained their consent from the said two bills which they before had passed as you have heard before.

Wherefore the Commons after long debate determined to send the speaker of the Parliament to the king's highness with grievous complaint against the Bishop of Rochester, and so on a day when the king was at leisure, Thomas Audley the speaker for the Commons and thirty of the chief of the Common House came to the king's presence in his palace at Westminster, which before was called York Place, and there very eloquently declared what a dishonour to the king and the realm it was to say that they which were elected for the wisest men of all the shires, cities and boroughs within the realm of England should be declared in so noble and open presence to lack faith,

---

³ *Ortroy*, p. 217.

⁴ *Hall* (a. Whibley), II, p. 167.

which was equivalent to say that they were infidels and no Christians, as ill as Turks or Saracens, so that what pain or study soever they took for the commonwealth, or what acts or laws soever they made or stablished, should be taken as laws made by paynims and heathen people, and not worthy to be kept by Christian men: wherefore he most humbly sought the king's highness to call the said bishop before him and to cause him to speak more discreetly of such a number as was in the Common House.

The king was not well contented with the saying of the bishop, yet he gently answered the speaker, that he would send for the bishop and send them word what answer he made, and so they departed again. After this the king sent for the Archbishop of Canterbury and six other bishops, and for the Bishop of Rochester also, and there declared to him the grudge of the Commons, to the which the bishop answered that he meant the doings of the Bohemians was for lack of faith, and not the doings of them that were in the Common House, which saying was confirmed by the bishops being present, which had him in great reputation, and so by that only saying the king accepted his excuse and therefore sent word to the Commons to Sir William Fitzwilliam, knight treasurer of his household, which blind excuse pleased the Commons nothing at all.[5]

To overcome the opposition of the spiritual lords, the king called a conference of the two Houses, thus putting the prelates in a minority; so the Bills became law.

The early biographer followed his account of John Fisher's opposition in the Lords with a speech in

---

[5] *Hall* (ed. Whibley), II, p.167.

Convocation against a proposal to suppress the smaller monasteries and grant revenues to the king. It has already been noted that this is a matter that, as far as records show, did not arise in that year; the first overt step was not taken until 1536 but it was probably mooted before that year. This speech in Convocation must therefore be read with the caution that it is misplaced, though it is difficult to suggest when it could have been given. As however it preserves some words and opinions of John Fisher, it is quoted here.

My lords, I pray you take good heed what you do in haste granting to the king's demand in this great matter. It is here required that we should grant unto him the small abbeys for ease of his charges, whereunto if we condescend, it is like the great will be demanded or it be long after. And therefore considering the manner of this dealing, it putteth me in remembrance of a fable, how the axe that lacked a handle came on a time to the wood and making his moan to the great trees how that for lack of a handle to work withal he was fain to sit idle, he therefore desired of them to grant him some young sapling wood to make him one. They, mistrusting no guile, forthwith granted him a young small tree whereof he shaped himself a handle, and being made at last a perfect axe in all parts, he fell to work and so laboured in the wood that in process of time he left neither great tree nor small standing. And so, my lords, if we grant to the king the small monasteries, ye do but make him a handle and so give him occasion to demand the rest ere it be long after. Whereof cannot but ensue the displeasure of Almighty God in that ye

PRÆMUNIRE

take upon you to give the thing that is none of your own.[6]

A month before this Parliament an event took place that presaged a policy that was to affect the whole body of the clergy and to put them at the mercy of the king.

On 9th October 1529 a writ known as Præmunire was issued against Cardinal Wolsey.

> *Surrey.* Lord cardinal, the king's further pleasure is—
> Because all those things you have done of late,
> By your power legatine, within this kingdom,
> Fall into the compass of a præmunire
> That therefore such a writ be sued against you;
> To forfeit all your goods, lands, tenements,
> Chattels, and whatsoever, and to be
> Out of the king's protection.[7]

We are not here concerned with the process against Wolsey except so far as it suggested the method used for coercing the clergy. The term "præmunire" was a convenient label for statutes passed in the fourteenth century to check the direct exercise of papal authority in England by prohibiting appeals that might "touch our lord the king, against him, his crown and his royalty, or his realm."[8] The penalty in case of conviction was forfeiture

---

[6] *Ortroy*, p. 223; the fable is from Phaedrus.

[7] *Henry* VIII, III, ii, 337-344.

[8] It is worth noting that such a process in itself did not then derogate from the Pope's proper authority even in Ecclesiastical cases. Rather, it is based on the expediency of appeals to Rome. This was a problem that was also debated in the early Church. What was novel was the way in which Henry used it to prepare for a formal break with Rome. -Editorial note.

of all possessions and life imprisonment. The application of this statute to Wolsey had its justification as he had, as cardinal legate, undoubtedly ignored its provisions while at the same time using the threat of Præmunire against others, including Warham. On his behalf it can be said that what he did was under the authority permitted to him by the king. There was, however, no justification whatever for the next application of these statutes.

The first intention was to indict certain bishops (including John Fisher) and abbots and other ecclesiastics for breaches of the Præmunire statutes.[9] This course was not followed; if selected clergy were guilty, why not all? So in December 1530 (Parliament was not sitting) a writ was issued in the King's Bench indicting the whole body of clergy for having accepted Wolsey's legatine authority, and thereby being as it were, accessories after the fact. It is interesting to speculate what would have happened to any rash person who might have dared to challenge Wolsey's authority when he was in power.

It was with this threat hanging over its head that the Convocation of Canterbury met in the Chapter House of Westminster Abbey[10] on 21st January 1531.

A way out had been proposed; let the clergy purchase their pardon. This they offered to do for the sum of £40,000. They made this grant, as it was speciously called, in recognition of the benefits conferred on the Church by the king, especially for his defence of the faith against heretics. A warning was conveyed to them that this sum was insufficient, so on 24th January they more than

---

[9] *L.P.*, IV, no. 6488.

[10] An interesting preliminary may be noted. The abbot formally protested against any infringements of his privileges, and the Archbishop declared that by using the Chapter House, it was not intended to derogate from the immunities or exemptions of the monastery.

PRÆMUNIRE 239

doubled their original offer and agreed to raise £100,044 8s. 8d.[11] But this still did not satisfy the king. It was as if, finding the clergy easier prey than he had expected, he was now determined to keep them on the run. It may be that had they shown resolute opposition at the outset, the course of events might have been far different, for it is difficult to see what Henry could have done at that stage against a steadfast prelacy and clergy.

On 9th February Convocation was informed that the royal pardon would be granted provided they accepted as an addition to the king's titles the words, "Protector and Supreme Head of the English Church and Clergy."

The early biographer gives us the most detailed account that survives of the discussion in Convocation.

> When this matter was come to scanning in the Convocation House, great hold [contention] and stir was made about it. For among them there wanted not some that stood ready to set forth the king's purpose; and for fear of them, many others durst not speak their minds freely. But when this holy father [Fisher] saw what was towards and how ready some of their own company were to help forward the king's purpose, he opened before the bishops such and so many inconveniences by granting of this demand, that in conclusion all was rejected and the king's intent clean overthrown for that time.
>
> Then the king hearing what was done, and perceiving that the whole Convocation rested upon

---

[11] It is perhaps risky to suggest a modern equivalent, but 42,000,000 would not be an excessive estimate. However wealthy some sections of the church may have been, the exaction of this sum must have meant grievous hardship to a great majority of the clergy; see above,. 63, 99. The Convocation of York later taxed itself to the additional sum of £18,840 os. 10d.

this worthy bishop, he wrought by sundry means to bring this matter about. And yet doubting that, with overmuch haste and rigour at the beginning' he might easily at the first overthrow all his intent, he sent his orators[12] at another time to the Convocation House who in their own names moved the clergy to have good consideration of this gentle and reasonable demand, putting them in mind what danger and peril they stood in at this present against his Majesty for their late contempt in accepting the legatine power of the cardinal, whereby they had also deeply incurred the danger of the law that their bodies and goods were wholely at his highness' will and pleasure, which notwithstanding he hath hitherto forborne to execute, upon hope of their good wills and conformities to be showed to him again in this matter.

Then the king sent for divers of the bishops and certain others of the chief Convocation to come to him at his palace of Westminster, to whom he proponed[13] with gentle words his request and demand, promising them in the word of a king that if they would among them acknowledge and confess him for supreme head of the Church of England, he would never by virtue of that grant assume unto himself any more power, jurisdiction or authority over them than all other kings of this realm, his predecessors, had done before, neither would take upon him to make or promulgate any spiritual law or exercise, any spiritual jurisdiction, nor yet by any kind of means inter-meddle himself among them in altering, changing, ordering or judging of any spiritual business. "Therefore having now made

---

[12] The chief "orator" was Lord Rochford (George Boleyn), the brother of Anne Boleyn.

[13] That is he "put forth". -Editorial note.

you," said he, "this frank promise, I do expect that you shall deal with me as frankly again whereby agreement may the better continue between us." And so the bishops departed with heavy hearts to talk further of this matter in the Convocation among themselves. But still it stuck sore among them upon certain inconveniences before showed by my lord of Rochester, who never spared to open and declare his mind freely in defence of the Church, which many others durst not so frankly do for fear of the king's displeasure, although they were for the most part men of deep wisdom and profound learning.

Then came the king's counsellors again from the king to know how the matter sped, seeming as though they had not known what was said or done in the Convocation house before their coming. So hotly they followed this matter once begun for many causes, the king having indeed a further secret meaning than was commonly known to many, which in few years broke out to the confusion of the whole clergy and temporality both. These counsellors there repeated unto the Convocation the king's words which he himself had spoken to some of them, saying further that if any man would stick now against his Majesty in this point, it must needs declare a great mistrustfulness they had in his highness's words seeing he had made so solemn and high an oath. With this subtle and false persuasion the clergy began somewhat to shrink and for the most part to yield to the king's request, saving this holy bishop who utterly refused to condescend thereunto, and therefore earnestly required the lords and others of the Convocation to consider and take good heed what mischiefs and inconveniences would ensue to the whole Church of Christ by this unreasonable and unseemly grant made to a temporal prince, which never yet to this day was once so much as demanded before, neither can it by any means or reason be in the power or rule of any temporal potentate. "And therefore," said he, "if ye grant to the king's request in this matter, it seemeth to me to pretend an imminent and present danger to hand. For what, if he should shortly after change his mind and exercise indeed the supremacy over the Church of this realm, or what, if he should die and then his successor challenge the continuance of the same; or what, if the crown of this realm should in time fall to an infant or a woman, that shall still continue and take the same name upon them, what shall we do then? Whom shall we sue, or where shall we have remedy?"

The king's counsellors to that replied and said that the king had no such meaning as he doubted and there alleged again his royal protestation and oath made in the word of a king. "And further," said they, "though the supremacy were granted to his Majesty simply and absolutely according to his demand, yet it must needs be understood and taken that he can have no further power or authority by it than *quantum per legem dei licet*. And then if a temporal prince can have no such authority and power by God's law (as his lordship had there declared) what needeth the forecasting of all these doubts?"

Then at last the counsellors fell into disputation among the bishops of a temporal prince's authority over the clergy, but thereunto my lord of Rochester answered them so fully that they had not list to deal that way any further. For they were indeed but simple smatterers in divinity to speak before such a divine as he was. And so they departed in great anger, showing themselves openly in their own likeness and saying that, whosoever would refuse to condescend to the king's demand therein, was not worthy to be accounted a true and loving subject.

The lords and others of the Convocation seeing this kind of threatening persuasion besides many other false practices and fearing the report of the counsellors to be made to the king (whom they knew and perceived to be all cruelly bent against the clergy) grew at last to a conclusion and so, after sundry days' argument in great striving and contention, agreed in manner fully and wholely among them to condescend to the king's demand that he should be supreme head of the Church of England and to credit his princely word so faithfully and solemnly promised unto them.

My Lord of Rochester, perceiving this sudden and hasty grant only made for fear and not upon any other just ground, stood up again all angry and rebuked them for their pusillanimity in being so lightly changed and easily persuaded. And being very loath that any such grant should pass from the clergy thus absolutely and yet by no means able to stay it for the fear that was among them, he then advised the Convocation that seeing the king both by his own mouth and also by the sundry speeches of his orators had faithfully promised and solemnly sworn in the high word of a king that his meaning was to require no further than *quantum per legem dei licet*, and that by virtue thereof his purpose was not to intermeddle with any spiritual laws, spiritual jurisdiction or government more than all his predecessors had always done before, "If so be that you are fully determined to grant him this demand (which I rather wish you to deny than grant), yet for a more true and plain exposition of your meaning towards the king and all his posterity, let these conditional words be expressed in your grant *quantum per legem dei licet*, which is no other wise (as the king and his learned counsel say) than yourselves mean."

But then the counsellors (who by that time were returned to the Convocation House for speed of their business) hearing of my lord of Rochester's words, cried upon them with open and continual clamour to have the grant passed absolutely and to credit the king's honour in giving them so solemn a protestation and oath. Howbeit the clergy having gotten new courage by this good man's words, nothing could after that prevail among them, for then they answered with full resolution that they neither could nor would grant this title and dignity of supremacy without these conditional words *quantum per legem dei licet*. And so the orators departed making to the king relation of all that was done. Who, seeing no other remedy, was of necessity driven to accept it in this conditional sort, and then granted to the clergy pardon for their bodies and goods, so that they should pay him a hundred thousand pounds; which was paid to the last penny.[14]

Archbishop Warham put this qualified title to the clergy; no one spoke. "He that is silent seems to consent," he said. One voice was heard, "Then we are all silent," and the matter was concluded. More than twenty days were spent in discussing this royal demand; the granting of the actual subsidy was done after three days, but the discussions over the title and the negotiations with the

---

[14] *Ortroy*, p. 238.

king were long drawn-out.[15] Even so the king had not got exactly what he wanted; the new title ran, "only and supreme lord of the Church and the English Clergy, and as far as is allowed by the law of Christ, also their supreme head."

Convocation was not solely concerned with this matter; other subjects under discussion were the appointments to benefices, the apparel of the clergy, trials for heresy, the reform of abuses, the reform of grammar schools, universities studies, and simony. Convocation was adjourned on 4th May.

Chapuys, reported to the Emperor on 21st February,[16] said that John Fisher was very ill with disappointment at the decision of Convocation; "he opposed it as much as he can, but, being threatened that he and his adherents should be thrown in the river, he was forced to consent to the king's will."

The Convocation of York did not agree to the new title so quickly. Tunstal as Bishop of Durham[17] was the most influential prelate there during the vacancy of the Archbishopric. He did not like the vagueness of the proposed title and he put his doubts in writing to the king suggesting that the words "in temporal affairs" should be added. Henry's reply[18] was a clever argument that avoided the main issue; he claimed that the saving clause added by the southern Convocation excluded such spiritual matters

---

[15] It may be noted that this account by the early biographer is the only one of any length; he may have assigned too dominant a role to John Fisher but this account explains the delay (twelve or thirteen sittings) between the grant of the money and the grant of the title.

[16] *L.P.*, V, no. 112.

[17] He had been appointed in 1530; Stokesley succeeded him in London.

[18] *Wilkins*, III, pp. 762-5. There is a good discussion of this letter in Philip Hughes, *The Reformation in England*, pp. 230-2.

as the sacraments and the priestly office. He put the point that what Fisher had accepted should surely satisfy Tunstal. The speciousness of this plea was to appear when the saving phrase "as far as is allowed by the law of Christ" was dropped in subsequent legislation.

The direct question of papal supremacy was not raised in these proceedings, nor was any reference made to the pope's power of dispensation. Henry was still negotiating with Rome. Warham and Fisher, and the new chancellor, Sir Thomas More must have accepted the qualifying phrase in the king's title in the sense put to Tunstal by Henry; they would certainly not have approved a denial of the papal supremacy. When the true nature of the claims became clear, Warham was on his deathbed; Fisher and More resolutely opposed the king's revealed intention. Tunstal continued to believe that Henry's letter to him was an acceptable interpretation, and remained valid.

When Parliament reassembled early in 1531, the Commons were asked to ratify the pardon to the clergy of the southern province; some were quick to see that the king might be disposed to treat the laity in the same way as he had treated the clergy, so they first asked that the laity should be granted a pardon lest they too should be found to "fall within the compass of a præmunire." They got their pardon for nothing.

On 28th February the king himself went to the Lords and asked them to consider a recent attempt that had been made to poison the Bishop of Rochester. This incident which happened on 18th February is related by the early biographer, but the account given by Chapuys was written at the time.[19]

---

[19] *L.P.*, V, no. 120.

There was in the bishop's house about ten days ago some pottage, of which all who tasted it, that is, nearly all the servants, were brought to the point of death, though only two of them died, and some poor people to whom they had given it. The good bishop, happily, did not taste it. The cook was immediately seized at the instance of the bishop's brother, and it is said, confessed that he had thrown in a powder which, he had been given to understand would only stupify the servants without doing them any harm. I do not yet know whom he has accused of giving him this powder nor the issue of the affair. The king has done well to show dissatisfaction at this; nevertheless, he cannot wholly avoid some suspicion, if not against himself; whom I think too good to do such a thing, a least against the lady [Anne Boleyn] and her father.

The said Bishop of Rochester is very ill, and has been so ever since the acknowledgement made by the clergy of which I wrote. But, notwithstanding his disposition, he has arranged to leave to-morrow by the king's leave. I know not why, being ill, he is anxious to go on a journey, especially as he will get better attendance of physicians here than elsewhere, unless it be that he will no longer be a witness of things done against thee; Church, or that he fears there is some more powder in reserve for him. If the king desired to treat of the affair of the queen, the absence of the said Bishop and of the Bishop of Durham [Tunstal] would be unfortunate.

The king was seriously alarmed; the plague frightened him and poisoning terrified him; it was probably not out of regard for the Bishop of Rochester that he persuaded Parliament to pass a law declaring poisoning to be treason, with boiling as the form of death. The Grey Friars' *Chronicle* records:

> This year was a cook boiled in a cauldron at Smithfield, for he would have poisoned the Bishop of Rochester with divers of his servants, and he was locked in a chain and pulled up and down with a gibbet at divers times till he was dead.

The early biographer recorded what he regarded as another attempt on John Fisher's life. This was also at Lambeth.

> Suddenly a gun was shot through the top of his house not far from his study where he accustomably used to sit. Which made such a terrible noise over his head and bruised the tiles and rafters of the house so sore, that both he and divers others of his servants were suddenly amazed thereat. Wherefore speedy search was made whence this shot should come and what it meant. Which at last was found to come from the other side of the Thames out of the Earl of Wiltshire's house who was father to the Lady Anne. Then he perceived that great malice was meant towards him and calling speedily unto him certain of his servants, said, "Let us truss up our gear and be gone from hence, for here is no place for us to tarry any longer."[20]

Whether Anne Boleyn and her relatives, as Chapuys and the early biographers believed, were responsible for these mishaps is a matter of conjecture. Chapuys was of a

---

[20] *Ortroy*, p. 226. One can accept the fact without accepting the explanation; the direct distance would be at least 1200 yds.

PRÆMUNIRE   249

sanguine temperament and was apt to see things as he
would like them to be. He was probably on more secure
ground when he reported on 9th October 1531.

The lady fears no one here more than the Bishop
of Rochester, for it is he who has always defended the
queen's cause, and she has therefore sent to persuade
the bishop to forbear coming to this Parliament that he
may not catch any sickness as he did last year, but it is
no use, for he is resolved to come and to speak more
boldly than he has ever done should he die a hundred
thousand times.[21]

Another mischance reported by the early biographer,
but seen by him in the same lurid light, was probably
plain robbery.

On a night as he lay at his manor of Hailing near
Rochester, a company of thieves brake privately into
his house and robbed him of all his plate, which being
in the morning perceived and known to his officers
and servants they were much vexed and sorry through
the mischance. Wherefore pursuit was speedily made
after the thieves and such diligence was used that
before my lord knew anything thereof, some part of
the plate was found again in a wood joining to the
house where the thieves had passed; which through
haste in flying they scattered behind them and durst
no more return for it. When dinner time was come, my
lord perceived unquietness and heaviness among his
servants more than was wont to be, for no man durst
open to him the case thinking he would have taken it
so ill. At last my lord mistrusting more and more by

---

[21] L.P.,V, no. 472.

their countenances of some great harm, he asked one of them what this matter meant. But his servants for fear durst not open unto him the mischance. "No," said my lord, "I mean not to dine this day before I know what it is." Then said he [the servant], "This night a certain number of thieves have robbed you of your plate, which is all lost and gone saving a little quantity that was recovered in a wood by following them and that was brought back again." "Is that all?" said my lord. "Then let us go to dinner and be merry and thank God for that we have still remaining and look better to it than we did to the rest before." And so eat his dinner very merrily and quietly.[22]

This episode may perhaps be dated in September 1532 as the bishop's Register shows that he was at Hailing during that month, apparently his first visit for six years.

---

[22] *Ortroy*, p. 229.

XVIII - Thomas Cromwell, Earl of Essex
Hans Holbein the Younger

Little is known about Cromwell's early life. He was a secretary to Wolsey and survived Wolsey's fall, rising to become Henry's secretary. He would himself be beheaded over the Cleves Marriage later in Henry's reign.

XIX: Thomas Cranmer, Archbishop of Canterbury
Gerlach Flicke

Cranmer was an obscure Cambridge doctor at the time of his elevation to Archbishop of Canterbury. He was chaplain to Anne Boleyn, which placed him inside Henry's circle. It was Cranmer who first suggested to Henry that the Papacy was merely a ceremonial institution of men, and that it lacked the authority to dispense from the verse in Leviticus.

XX - Stephen Gardiner, Bishop of Exeter

Gardiner, as we've seen, served Henry's policy both in England and abroad. He was among the bishops urging Fisher to swear the Act of Supremacy, and later, perhaps as a fruit of Fisher's martyrdom, returned to the Catholic faith in the reign of Queen Mary. He was never fully trusted by the latter on account of his advocacy of the divorce.

CHAPTER XX
THE KING HAS HIS WAY

IF the bishops and clergy of the two Convocations imagined that the payment of £120,000 would bring them peace and security they were soon disillusioned. Parliament and the Convocation of Canterbury met in January 1532.

Shortly before the meeting of Parliament, Chapuys reported to the emperor that,

> respecting the Bishop of Rochester, I will inform him as soon as possible of the paragraphs in your majesty's letter that concern him. This will be done in writing and through a third person, as there is no other means at present of communicating with that prelate, for he has lately sent me word that, should we meet anywhere in public, I must not appear to know him, or make any attempt whatever to speak. He himself would do the same, and begged to be excused if he took no notice of me until the present storm had blown away. As I have sure means, without the least danger of maintaining the bishop in his good intentions, I will omit no trouble to keep him to his purpose.[1]

Sir Thomas More had made a similar request some months earlier.

On 22nd January the ambassador wrote,

---
[1] *L.P.*, V, no. 472.

THE KING HAS HIS WAY 255

The assembly (Parliament) is numerous, being attended by almost all the lords, temporal as well as spiritual. Only the Bishop of Durham [Tunstal], one of the queen's good champions, has not been called in; no more has Rochester,[2] as I have been informed, though this last has not failed to come, and is actually in town, intending to tell the king the plain truth about the divorce and speak without disguise. No sooner did the king hear of this bishop's arrival than he sent him word he was very glad at his coming, and had many important things to say to him. The bishop, fearing lest the communication which the king said he had to make should be for the purpose of begging him not to speak on the subject, seized the moment when the king was going to mass, attended by the gentlemen of his household, to make his reverence and present his respects, thus avoiding, if possible, the said communication. The king received him more graciously, and put on a better mien than ever he had done before, deferring the conversation till after the mass; but the good bishop, owing to the above fears, prudently retired before mass was over.[3]

Convocation continued its discussion of the various reforms that had occupied part of the time of the previous session, and a number of regulations were framed dealing with such matters as appointments to benefices, the qualifications of ordinands, clerical garb, simony, and misconduct of several kinds. Meanwhile the Commons had passed a Bill to restrain the payment to Rome of annates, that is, the first year's revenue of a benefice. This

---

[2] The Bishop's Register does not record his summons to Parliament; it shows that he was at Lambeth during January.

[3] *Span. Cal.*, IV, no. 883.

was not a measure of relief for the clergy as in future they would have to pay the amounts in to the Exchequer. Archbishop Warham himself drew up a protest against the several Acts passed by Parliament, or known to be in contemplation, which he felt were designed to weaken the authority of the pope and the hierarchy. The bishops opposed the Annates Bill, but it became law on 18th March; its operation was suspended until the king, by letters patent, chose to apply it. This was used as a threat to the pope whose decision on the validity of Henry's marriage was still awaited.

On the same day that this Act was passed, the Commons presented to the king a Supplication against the Ordinaries, that is, the bishops. At the same time the members begged to be allowed to go home so that they could attend to their own affairs. Henry pointed out that they could not at one moment ask for reforms and at the next ask to leave Westminster. So they had to stay. This lack of logic suggests that the Commons did not regard their Supplication as of pressing importance; the drafts that survive show that the document had not originated with the Commons but with the Court; most of the alterations are in the handwriting of Thomas Cromwell, and these may have been made at the king's desire. It was customary for the king and council to propose measures for legislation so it is not necessary to see anything sinister in the production of this Supplication. The complaints were mostly directed against the working of the ecclesiastical courts which were certainly unpopular on account of delays and the fees exacted. We do not know what part John Fisher played in the consideration of the Supplication when it was laid before Convocation.

He was certainly present in March as he was one of the bishops who judged the case of Hugh Latimer, another of the Cambridge group that included Robert Barnes and Thomas Bilney. On this occasion Latimer subscribed to a recantation.

The Supplication was discussed in both houses of Convocation during April. Stephen Gardiner, now Bishop of Winchester, was closely concerned with the drawing up of the answer, and thereby forfeited the patronage of the king. The bishops made a spirited defence of their authority and of the conduct of their courts; they pointed out that Convocation was already dealing with some of the complaints and had proposed remedies where these were justified. This reply was presented to the king at the end of April; in handing it to the Speaker he said, "We think this answer will smally please you, for it seemeth to us very slender; you be a great sort of wise men; I doubt not but you will look circumspectly on the matter, and we will be indifferent between you." The claim to be impartial was not consonant with the first part of his comments. He took the opportunity of once more explaining how his scruples of conscience had led him to question the validity of his marriage. This repetition of an old story was prompted by the boldness of a member named Temse who had suggested that the Commons should beseech the king to take back his queen and so avoid all the complications of bastardizing the Princess Mary and of possible trouble with the emperor.[4]

On 10th May the king sent further demands to Convocation; no canons were in future to be promulgated without his consent, and canon law was to be revised by a royal commission. The significance of these was seen by Chapuys who wrote, "Churchmen will be of less account

---

[4] *Hall* (ed. Whibley), II, pp. 209-10.

than shoemakers who have the power of assembling and making their own statutes."⁵

The apprehensions of the clergy were increased, no doubt deliberately, when the king on 11th May once more called some of the Commons together and announced to them a discovery he had made after having been on the throne for over twenty years. Hall's report of the king's words reads:

> Well-beloved subjects, we thought that the clergy of our realm had been our subjects wholly, but now we have well perceived that they be but half our subjects, yea, and scarce our subjects: for all the prelates at their consecration make an oath to the pope clean contrary to the oath that they make to us, so that they seem to be his subjects, and not ours.⁶

In their alarm at these fresh attacks on their authority the clergy decided to send a deputation to John Fisher who was lying ill at his Lambeth house. There is no record of the advice he gave them, but his subsequent actions are evidence of his attitude.

There was some further going to and fro between the Court and Convocation, but at length the clergy gave way; an additional clause provided that Convocation could be summoned in future only with the king's consent. So the clergy made their submission and from that date, 15th May 1532, lost the initiative in legislating for the spiritual welfare of the people.

John Fisher was not the only one to oppose this surrender; Sir Thomas More resigned the Great Seal. He had had an uneasy task as Lord Chancellor; he was in a

---

⁵ *L.P.*, V, no. 1013.

⁶ *Hall*, II, p. 120.

position to know what further steps were being planned, and, rather than acquiesce, he withdrew into private life.

There were some of the clergy too who did not willingly accept the decision of Convocation. On 22nd May, Chapuys wrote to the emperor, "Four days ago the ecclesiastics of the archdiocese of York and the diocese of Durham have sent to the king a great protest against the sovereignty which he would claim and usurp over them. Those of the archdiocese [province] of Canterbury have also published a protest, of which I send a copy. The king is greatly displeased."

Amongst the names who signed the protest from the province of Canterbury may be noted two that have already been mentioned—Rowland Phillips of Croydon, and Nicholas Metcalfe, Archdeacon of Rochester and Master of St. John's College, Cambridge. Robert Johnson signed on behalf of the Chapter of Rochester, and John Willo (?) for the clergy of the diocese.[7]

No break with Rome had yet been made nor was such a possibility discussed in Convocation or Parliament. The king was impatient at the delay in reaching a settlement of the marriage question, but he was not yet prepared to give up hope of a favourable decision from Rome. He had undermined the authority of the clergy of England; if the pope annulled the marriage, there would be many delicate adjustments to be made in defining the relations between the papacy and the monarchy; could the pope, for instance, accept the submission of the clergy? Or the new title of Supreme Head? Could the king retrace his steps? If the pope's verdict went against Henry, then all was ready for the separation.

Henry had not seen Catherine since July 1531, and there were many signs that she had many sympathizers

---

[7] Friedmann, *Anne Boleyn*, I, p. 142.

amongst the people. Temse's voice in the Commons was not the only one raised on her behalf. Early in 1532 a priest had dared to preach at St. Paul's against the king's proceedings; he was arrested before his sermon was ended. The king ordered that sermons should be preached everywhere in favour of the annulment; some who did so were roughly handled. Then at Easter, Henry himself had to listen to a sermon preached by William Peto, the provincial of the Observant Friars; he dared to suggest a topical application of the story of Achab. One of the royal chaplains preached on the following Sunday and attacked Peto, whereat Elstow, the warden of the Observants at Greenwich, openly objected. Both Peto and Elstow were reprimanded by the Council and told that they deserved to be thrown into the river.

When John Fisher had sufficiently recovered from his illness, he felt that he too must speak out. In his report to the emperor on 21st June 1532, Chapuys wrote, "About twelve days ago the Bishop of Rochester preached in favour of the queen, and has been in danger of prison and other trouble. He has shut the mouths of those who spoke in the king's favour, but the treatment of the queen is not improved."[8] No action seems to have been taken against John Fisher, and he was back in Rochester in July. The early biographer tells us nothing of this period.

The king then turned his attention to Warham. The archbishop, now over eighty, had not played an heroic part in these affairs, but the strain of the months of argument in Convocation and of the unremitting pressure of the king's will, had told upon him. He was threatened with a writ of præmunire for having in 1518 consecrated Henry Standish as Bishop of St. Asaph's before the royal confirmation had been given. Warham was too ill to speak

---

[8] *L.P.*, VI, 1109. See below, p. 381.

in his own defence, but he dictated a statement for the Council that reveals a bolder spirit than he had hitherto shown. He pointed out that the Archbishops of Canterbury had always exercised the right to consecrate without their authority being questioned. He reminded the lords of the council that it was for this undoubted right that St. Thomas of Canterbury had suffered martyrdom. "I think it more better for me to suffer the same than against my conscience to confess this article to be a præmunire for which St. Thomas died."[9] It was too late; had that note been sounded earlier the clergy might have rallied round their archbishop. William Warham died on 23rd August 1532.

His death removed one obstacle from the king's path. The old archbishop had been unyielding on one point; without the consent of the pope, Warham would not consider the marriage question in his court. Threats and arguments were used to no effect; he stood firm.

A more complaisant archbishop might be found.

In October the king set out for France. Anne Boleyn, now curiously styled Marquis of Pembroke and wearing the jewels of Queen Catherine, accompanied Henry across the Channel, but she was left behind at Calais when he went to Boulogne to meet Francis. The two kings swore the customary oaths of perpetual peace and friendship; Francis was not as warm in support of Henry's cause as was hoped, but he promised to use what influence he could with the pope to hasten a favourable verdict. A letter to John Fisher from Peter Ligham, dean of arches of Canterbury, refers to Henry's outward journey.

> I thank you for your venison. The king left Canterbury on Thursday last at 12 noon, and reached

---

[9] *L.P.*, V, no. 1247.

Calais on Friday about 10 in the morning. I was named by the prior of Christchurch to be his vicar-general and master of the prerogative, but the king will none of me, saying that he heard I was a good priest, but he would have more experience of me whether I were *plene conversus* ere I should have any such room. I am well content. I am very desirous to hear how our good, gracious queen doth, and where she is, for I have not heard of her grace this many days, nor how her cause doth at Rome.[10]

Peter Ligham had spoken on behalf of Catherine and signed the protest against the submission of the clergy.[11]

Having made sure of the sympathy of the king of France, Henry next used all his skill in propitiating the pope; it was noticed, for instance, that the papal nuncio and the French ambassador twice accompanied Henry to Parliament; he sat between them and showed a cordiality that deceived onlookers, as it was meant to do, into thinking that all would yet be arranged between the king and the pope. In this way a favourable atmosphere was created in which Henry could make his next moves.

The first, however, was made in secret. On 25th January 1533 he married Anne Boleyn; this was necessary if her child was to be of legitimate birth. Next he chose Thomas Cranmer to be Archbishop of Canterbury, an appointment that still needed papal approval. The speed with which the necessary Bulls were obtained from Rome was due to the improved relations with the Papal See. Cranmer was consecrated on 30th March. That key appointment having been secured, Henry could move swiftly. At his request, or rather command (was he not

---

[10] *L.P.*, V, 110. 1411.

[11] See above, p. 212.

THE KING HAS HIS WAY

Supreme Head?) both Convocations passed, with some dissentients, two propositions: that the pope had no power to grant a dispensation for a man to marry his childless brother's widow, and, that the marriage between Catherine and Arthur had been consummated. The first proposition was certainly a proper one for theologians and canonists, but they were not competent to decide the second. "No one," wrote Chapuys, "dared open his mouth to contradict except the Bishop of Rochester. His single voice cannot avail against the majority."[12]

After some opposition, of which John Fisher was again the leader in the Lords, Parliament passed an Act in Restraint of Appeals; this prohibited the taking of cases to Rome. The immediate application of this Act was to make Catherine's appeal to Rome invalid in English law.

Chapuys thought that three bishops, whose names he did not record, had not been summoned to Parliament. He may have been misinformed; John Fisher was certainly summoned to Convocation as his Register records, and it is difficult to see how he could have been excluded from the Lords except by a deliberate act of the king of which there is no evidence other than the ambassador's report. Be that as it may, Henry was determined to prevent any interference from this obstinate prelate for the critical period that was opening. So on 6th April John Fisher was placed under house-arrest in the care of the Bishop of Winchester (Gardiner).

---

[12] *L.P.*, VI, 296. The only bishops who voted against the propositions were Rochester and Llandaff. The latter was Jorge de Athequa, the Spanish confessor to Queen Catherine. Nicholas Metcalfe also voted against the proposition with five other canonists. The nineteen divines who voted against included the Abbots of Winchcombe, Sherborne, Pershore and Reading, and the Prior of Walsingham. For full lists, see Pocock, *Records*, vol. II, pp. 449-59.

The excuse was that he had said that Lord Rochford (George Boleyn) had been guilty of bribery in securing adherents for Henry's cause in France.[13]

While John Fisher was thus kept out of the way, the new Archbishop of Canterbury as *legatus natus* sought the king's permission to try the "great cause of matrimony" in his court. To this request the king graciously gave his consent. The Act for Restraint of Appeals had ensured that the case could now be dealt with in England.

The court met on 8th May at Dunstable conveniently near Ampthill where Catherine was living in enforced retirement. She ignored the summons to attend. On 10th May Cranmer declared her contumacious, and on 23rd May he annulled the marriage between Henry and Catherine.

Five days later at Lambeth he pronounced the marriage between Henry and Anne to be valid.

On 1st June, Anne Boleyn was crowned queen in Westminster Abbey, a ceremony that Sir Thomas More refused to attend. A fortnight later John Fisher was allowed to go to Rochester. On 11th July the pope, abruptly disillusioned after the St. Martin's summer of Henry's assumed friendliness, declared the marriage with Anne Boleyn to be null and void.

---

[13] *L.P.*, VI, no. 296. Was this the second time he had been under restraint? Bridgett, p. 189, refers to two entries in the State Papers (Venetian) dated 29th Oct. and 22nd Nov. 1530 where it is said that three bishops (Fisher, Clerk and West) had been imprisoned because they had appealed to the Apostolic See against a prohibition of pluralities. Parliament was prorogued during 1530 and no such prohibition was declared. Chapuys made no mention of this arrest (as one would expect him to do), nor is there any other reference to it. The Rochester Register shows that John Fisher was in his diocese during October. I therefore think that the report was made under a misapprehension.

CHAPTER XXI
THE NUN OF KENT

THE coronation of Anne Boleyn dismayed the many sympathizers of Queen Catherine, who, by the king's command, was in future to be known as the Princess Dowager. It was true that the pope had threatened Henry with excommunication unless he put away Anne, but the major question had not yet been answered. The situation must have seemed intolerable to those who had waited so long for a decision from Rome. What could be done? The clergy had surrendered their authority; a subservient archbishop, still *legatus natus*, sat in St. Augustine's chair at Canterbury. The king so dominated affairs that it needed heroic courage to oppose his wishes.

Eustache Chapuys had no doubt what should be done; the emperor must declare war on England. For some months the ambassador had been urging this policy on Charles. Thus on 10th April 1533 he wrote,

> Considering the great injury done to Madame your aunt, you can hardly avoid making war now upon this king and kingdom ... an undertaking which would be, in the opinion of many people here, the easiest thing in the world at present, for this king has neither horsemen nor captains and the affections of the people are entirely on the side of the queen and your majesty.[1]

As an immediate step Chapuys advised the suspense of "all carrying out of commerce between your dominions

---

[1] *Span. Cal.*, IV, no. 592.

and this kingdom, whereat the people would rise against this accursed marriage." Such a policy might very well have had more effect than a declaration of war, but the emperor showed no sign of adopting either policy.

In September, Chapuys could report that John Fisher was in favour of armed intervention.

> As that excellent and holy man, the Bishop of Rochester, told me some time ago, the pope's weapons become very pliable when directed against the obdurate and pertinacious, and therefore, it is incumbent on your majesty to interfere in this affair, and undertake a work which must be as pleasing in the eyes of God as war upon the Turk.[2]

On 10th October he wrote again.

> That good and holy Bishop of Rochester advises prompt action on the part of your majesty such as I recommended in one of my last despatches. Indeed, not many days ago he sent me word to say that strong measures must now be taken. In this opinion of the good and pious bishop, the majority of the English nation, as I am told, concur; no one doubts that your majesty will take the affair in hand; otherwise they fear the mere suspension of the intercourse of trade will be the cause of revolt and much trouble and confusion in this country. To obviate this the smallest sea force will suffice; innumerable people from all ranks of society who wish for the prosperity and welfare of their country keep telling me so, and deafening my ears with their appeals.[3]

---

[2] *Span. Cal.*, IV, no. 1130.

[3] *Span. Cal.*, IV, no. 1133.

John Fisher would not have taken this extreme view unless he felt in conscience compelled to do so. In his day such an attitude would not seem as disaffected as it would today. Violent changes in dynasties had occurred in his childhood, and the Wars of the Roses were a living memory; the medieval idea that the Emperor of the Holy Roman Empire was the ordained temporal power had been weakened but it was not yet completely lifeless. This was not a matter of warring monarchies intent on territorial gains, but one that concerned the souls of the people. John Fisher could not doubt that separation from Rome must be the outcome of Henry's policy. Schism within the Catholic Church was an evil that must be prevented at all costs, even of armed intervention. It is indeed hard for us, in an age of indifferentism and after four centuries of Protestantism to understand the horror with which men recoiled from the idea of schism; it was unhappily true that not many saw, as did John Fisher and Sir Thomas More, that what at first seemed another phase of the old contention between papacy and monarchy was in fact something far more disruptive; while most men had their minds on the purely temporal aspects of the problem, these two saw that a separation of the Church in England from the authority of the pope must lead to schism and a divided Christendom.

The policy put forward by Chapuys was impracticable. His talk of "innumerable people" anxious to welcome the emperor's intervention was based on an ignorance of the facts; his knowledge of the English people was limited, and, although, no doubt, some discontented noblemen and courtiers voiced their complaints to him and made rash promises, there was no one to take an effective lead; the Wars of the Roses and Tudor policy had seen to it that no overmighty subject could threaten the throne. Moreover Charles had too many pressing difficulties of his own in his scattered dominions to take effective action against England and thus leave the way clear for France.

The decisive opposition to Chapuys came from Catherine. She made it clear to him and to her nephew that she would not countenance an armed rising which she said "would be a sin against the law and against my lawful husband of which I shall never be guilty."

There could, however, be no question that popular opinion was strongly in sympathy with her, and it was in dealing with this potentially dangerous feeling that Thomas Cromwell showed his increasing power. An example was needed that would overawe anyone who openly spoke in favour of Catherine. The reports of the sayings of Elizabeth Barton, the Nun or Maid of Kent, provided the needed opportunity.

At this distance of time it is impossible to construct an objective account of the life of this unhappy victim of Henry's vindictiveness. Still less is it possible to assess her character or the degree of her integrity. The records, it should be remembered, are from official sources and were designed to justify the action of the authorities. We have the case for the prosecution but not that for the defence. There was no open trial.

Elizabeth Barton was born about 1506 and was under thirty years of age at her execution. Her parish was Aldington, Kent, on Romney Marsh. This was the living to which Archbishop Warham had presented Erasmus; the priest, Richard Master, paid the scholar a pension of £20. He was described by Erasmus as a skilled theologian and man of upright character. Elizabeth was a domestic servant and a severe illness affected her personality. For long periods at a time she lay in a trance and would then

THE NUN OF KENT

give utterance to warnings against sin and vice. Her master and the neighbours considered that she was either possessed of the devil or was divinely inspired. The parish priest, Richard Master, listened to her words and watched her; he was convinced that she was the instrument of God. He at once reported the case to Archbishop Warham who, after some inquiry, accepted the genuineness of the young woman's messages. Here it may be noted that all who were concerned with the case acted correctly, either by referring it to superiors, or by instituting inquiries; there was no attempt at concealment.

Naturally the fame of Elizabeth's utterances spread widely, and in 1526 the archbishop thought it best to make a more thorough investigation, and he sent two monks of Canterbury, Edward Bocking and William Hadley, to see the young woman. It is important to know something of Bocking. He was probably in his early forties. He had taken his doctorate at Oxford in 1518, and for a time had been warden of Canterbury College until he found his vocation in the Benedictine Order. He was therefore a scholar and a man who had held a responsible position. The early biographer described him as "a learned and virtuous man."

Cranmer expressed a strongly adverse opinion of Dr. Bocking's character in 1533, but this was a superficial view as Cranmer had been archbishop for only a few months and had had little time to spare for Canterbury. In what followed, Dr. Bocking may have exercised undue influence over the young woman without realizing the dangers of the power a strong personality can have over an unformed mind. This, however, does not imply that he was the cunning rogue of official propaganda.

He was convinced that Elizabeth was divinely inspired, and he gave her more careful instruction in her faith than she had previously had. Her prophesying began to attract attention and many consulted her on their personal problems. It was wise to remove her from Aldington and to place her with the Benedictine nuns of St. Sepulchre's, Canterbury, where Dr. Bocking became her confessor and spiritual director. He wrote down her sayings and gave a copy to Archbishop Warham who showed them to the king. Henry was only mildly interested and asked Sir Thomas More for his opinion; he reported that there was nothing noteworthy: "a right simple woman might, in my mind, speak it of her own wit well enough."[4] There the matter might have rested had it not been for the widespread aversion to the king's desire to put away Queen Catherine. The Nun of Kent—as Elizabeth was commonly known—voiced this feeling in her prediction that if the king persisted in his intention, he "should no longer be king of this realm" and "should die a villain's death." Even in this matter it is not necessary to see any sinister plotting under the direction of Dr. Bocking; she was voicing sentiments that were commonplace amongst the people.

When she was allowed to move about, her influence increased. Earlier she had had an interview with Wolsey who was not greatly impressed. In October 1532 she was at Calais when Anne Boleyn was there during Henry's meeting with Francis at Boulogne. Did something happen at Calais to rouse the resentment of the would be queen? On Henry's return, Elizabeth spoke to him at Canterbury and upbraided him for deserting Catherine. She was also the guest at times of the Brigittines at Syon and it was there that Sir Thomas More was persuaded to see her; he warned her to keep silent on the king's affairs and

---

[4] See chapter XX of *Saint Thomas More* by the present author.

afterwards wrote to advise her to confine her thoughts to spiritual matters.

The Nun of Kent became the centre in Southern England of the popular support that undoubtedly was given to Queen Catherine. If discredit could be brought upon Elizabeth Barton and her associates, then the opposition to the king would be blunted and all sympathizers with Catherine warned of what might be their fate. Cranmer carried out the first inquiry in July 1533, and, in the course of several interrogations, he got from the nun a confession of simulation. During this prolonged questioning, the names of a number of important and well-known people were mentioned, including the Bishop of Rochester and Sir Thomas More. Attempts to implicate Queen Catherine failed. Chapuys reported:

> Many have been taken up on suspicion of having encouraged her [the Nun] to such prophecies to stir up the people to rebellion. It seems as if God inspires the queen [Catherine] on all occasions to conduct herself well, and avoid all inconveniences and suspicions; for the Nun had been very urgent at divers times to speak with her and console her in her great affliction, but the queen would never see her. Yet the council do not desist from making continual inquiry whether the queen has had any communication with her. She has no fear for herself, as she never had any, but she fears for the Marquis and Marchioness of Exeter and the good Bishop of Rochester, who have been very familiar with the Nun.[5]

---

[5] *Span. Cal.*, VI, no. 1419 (nth November 1533).

The Marquis and Marchioness were pardoned on this occasion, but, as the grandson of Edward IV, he was too dangerous to be allowed to live and he was executed in 1538; his wife lingered in the Tower in distressing conditions.

The nun, Dr. Bocking, Richard Master and six others were committed to the Tower; they were condemned in the court of the Star Chamber to stand in full view of the people at Paul's Cross and at Canterbury during the preaching of sermons describing their offences. The sermon on both occasions was given by a Benedictine, Dr. John Capon, later Bishop of Salisbury.[6] This, however, did not end the matter.

In January 1534 a Bill of Attainder was drafted including the names of John Fisher, Sir Thomas More, John Adeson, chaplain to John Fisher and Thomas Abell, who, as we have seen, had acted and written courageously on behalf of Queen Catherine whose chaplain he had been. The addition of Thomas Abell's name to the indictment (a document of over five thousand words) brings out more clearly than anything else the true purpose of the attainder. His name comes in the last paragraph almost like an afterthought; he is there charged that he was aware of the nun's proceedings (most people were equally aware), and also "caused to be printed and set forth in this realm divers books against the said divorce and separation, to the slander of our said sovereign lord, and also animated the said Lady Catherine obstinately to persist in her wilful opinion against the said divorce and separation, and after the said divorce lawfully had, to usurp and take upon her still to be queen."[7] It is

---

[6] The sermon at Canterbury is printed in *E.H.R.*, Oct. 1943, ed. the Rev. L. E. Whatmore.

[7] *Lewis*, II, pp. 339-352.

difficult to see the connexion between this charge against Thomas Abell and the Nun of Kent.

Sir Thomas More at once wrote to Cromwell showing how limited had been his association with the nun; he enclosed a copy of the letter to her in which he had told her to avoid the king's affairs. Sir Thomas asked to be heard by the Lords but the king preferred him to be examined by a commission of four—Cranmer, Audley, Norfolk and Cromwell. Here again the true purpose of the indictment was revealed; according to William Roper's account the main topic of the interview was not the Nun of Kent but Sir Thomas More's attitude towards the marriage question.[8] There was clearly no case against him as far as the nun was concerned, and the king reluctantly accepted the advice to delete Sir Thomas's name from the indictment.

Thomas Cromwell also had a letter from John Fisher. This has not survived, but a letter in reply gives an indication of the bishop's line of defence. He first complained of the "heavy words" and "terrible threats" Cromwell had used in a message delivered by Robert Fisher, the bishop's brother. To this Cromwell replied, "I sent you no heavy words, but words of great comfort, willing your brother to show you how benign and merciful the prince was, and that I thought it expedient for you to write unto his highness, and to recognize your offences, and desire his pardon, which his Grace would not deny you now in your age and sickness." It will be noted that Cromwell assumed that John Fisher was guilty though no investigation of his case had as yet been made. This was in keeping with the Tudor practice of taking guilt for granted unless the accused could establish his innocence—if given the opportunity. John Fisher had

---

[8] *Roper*, pp. 65-71.

written that he "had conceived a great opinion of the holiness of this woman" on the grounds of the reports he had received from many whose integrity he did not question, including that of Archbishop Warham; his chaplains too had visited her and were satisfied that her utterances were genuine. Cromwell argued that the bishop had approved of her sentiments because they were in agreement with his own. "My lord, all these things moved you not to give credence unto her, but only the very matter whereupon she made her false prophecies; to which matters ye were so affected, as ye be in all matters which ye enter once into, that nothing could come amiss for that purpose. And here I appeal your conscience, and instantly desire you to answer, whether if she had showed you as many revelations for the confirmation of the king's grace's marriage, which he now enjoyeth, as she did to the contrary, ye would have given as much credence to her."

John Fisher had pointed out that, as the nun had herself spoken to the king and others, including Warham, had also made reports, he could not himself be justly accused of deliberately concealing her messages. To this Cromwell replied that the bishop should have made quite certain that the king was indeed fully aware of all that the nun had said. If John Fisher would even now admit his "negligence, oversight and offence," the king "would benignly accept you into his gracious favour." He added, significantly, "men report that at the last convocation, ye spake things which ye could not well defend."

Parliament met on 15th January 1534. There was some discussion in the Lords as to the indictments, and, as we have seen, they persuaded the king that it would be difficult to go through with the charges against Sir Thomas More. John Fisher was summoned to appear.

The words of the indictment applying to him read as follows:

> And the said John Fisher, Bishop of Rochester and . . . having knowledge of the said false and feigned and dissembled Revelations, traitorously conspired against our said sovereign lord, did nevertheless make concealment thereof, and uttered not the same to our said sovereign, nor any his honourable council, against their duties and allegiance in that behalf.

He wrote to Thomas Cromwell to excuse himself.

> Master Cromwell,
> After my right humble commendations, I beseech you to have some pity of me, considering the case and condition that I am in; and I doubt not if ye might see in what plight that I am, ye would have some pity upon me. For in goodsooth, now almost this six weeks I have had a grievous cough, with a fever in the beginning thereof, as divers other here in this country hath had, and divers have died thereof. And now the matter is fallen down into my legs and feet with such swelling and ache that I may neither ride nor go, for the which I beseech you eftsoons to have some pity upon me and to spare me for a season, to the end the swelling and aches of my legs and feet may assuage and abate; and then, by the grace of Our Lord, I shall with all speed obey your commandment. Thus fare ye well.
> At Rochester the 28 day of January,
> By your faithful beadman,
>
> Jo. Roffs.[9]

---
[9] *L.P.*, VII, no. 116.

A few days later he wrote again, this time asking Thomas Cromwell not to trouble him with any more letters.

> After my right humble commendations, I most entirely beseech you that I no farther be moved to make answer unto your letters, for I see that mine answer must rather grow into a great book, or else be insufficient, so that ye shall still thereby take occasion to be offended, and I nothing profit. For I perceive that everything I writ is ascribed either to craft, or to wilfulness, or to affection, or to unkindness against my sovereign; so that my writing rather provoketh you to displeasure than it furthereth me in any point concerning your favour, which I most effectually covet. Nothing I read in all your long letters that I take any comfort of, but the only subscription wherein it pleased you to call you my friend; which undoubtedly was a word of much consolation unto me, and therefore I beseech you so to continue, and so to show yourself unto me at this time.
>
> In two points of my writing me thought ye were most offended, and both concerned the king's grace. That one was where I excused myself by the displeasure that his highness took with me when I spake once or twice until him of like matters. That other was where I touched his great matter. And as to the first, me think it very hard that I might not signify unto you such things secretly as might be most effectual for my excuse. And as to the second, my study and purpose was specially to decline that I should not be straited to offend his grace in that behalf, for then I must needs declare my conscience,

the which, as then I wrote, I would be 10th to do any more largely than I have done. Not that I condemn any other men's conscience. Their conscience may save them, and mine must save me. Wherefore, good master Cromwell, I beseech you for the love of God be contented with this my answer, and to give credence unto my brother in such things as he hath to say unto you. Thus fare you well.

At Rochester, the 31 day of January
By your faithful beadman,

Jo. Roffs.[10]

He did not follow Cromwell's earlier advice and write immediately a letter of submission to the king's mercy. The Bill of Attainder was introduced on 21st February and read again on 26th February. No doubt John Fisher was kept informed of how things were going; probably his brother Robert continued to act as his intermediary. On 27th February he at last wrote to the king, but it was not couched in the terms recommended by Cromwell.

> Please it, your most gracious highness, benignly to hear this my most humble suit, which I have to make unto your grace at this time, and to pardon me that I come not myself unto your grace for the same. For in good faith I have had so many perilous diseases one after another which began with me before Advent and so by long continuance hath now brought my body into that weakness that without peril of destruction of the same, which I dare say your grace for your sovereign goodness would not, I may not as yet take any travelling upon me. And so I wrote to Master Cromwell, your most trusty counsellor, beseeching

---

[10] *L.P.*, VII, no. 136.

him to obtain your gracious licence for me to be absent from this Parliament, for that same cause, and he put me in comfort so to do.

Now thus it is most gracious sovereign lord that in your most high court of Parliament is put in a bill against me concerning the Nun of Canterbury, and intending my condemnation for not revealing of such words as she had unto me touching your highness. Wherein I most humbly beseech your grace that without your displeasure I may show unto you the consideration that moved me so to do, which, when your most excellent wisdom hath deeply considered, I trust assuredly that your charitable goodness will not impute any blame to me therefore.

A truth it is this Nun was with me thrice in coming from London by Rochester, as I wrote to Master Cromwell, and showed unto him the occasions of her coming and of my sendings until her again.

The first time she came to my house, unsent for of my part, and then she told me that she had been with your grace and that she had shown unto you a revelation which she had from Almighty God; your grace I trust will not be displeased with this my rehearsal thereof; she said that if your grace went forth with the purpose that ye intended, ye should not be King of England seven months after.

I conceived not by these words, I take it upon my soul, that any malice or evil was intended or meant unto your highness by any mortal man but only that they were the threats of God, as she then did affirm.

And though they were feigned, that (as I would be saved) was to me unknown. I never counselled her unto that feigning nor was privy thereunto nor to any such purposes as it now is said they went about.

Nevertheless if she had told me this revelation and had not also told me that she had reported the same unto your grace I had been verily far to blame and worthy extreme punishment for not disclosing the same unto your highness or else to some of your council. But since she did assure me therewith that she had plainly told unto your grace the same thing I thought doubtless that your grace would have suspected me that I had come to renew her tale again unto you rather for the confirming of mine opinion than for any other cause.

I beseech your highness to take no displeasure with me for this that I will say. It sticketh yet most gracious sovereign in my heart, to my no little heaviness, your grievous letters, and after that your most fearful words that your grace said unto me for showing you my mind and opinion in the same matter [the marriage], notwithstanding that your highness had so often and so straitly commanded me to search for the same before. And for this cause I was right loth to have come unto your grace again with such a tale pertaining to that matter.

Many other considerations I had but this was the very cause why that I came not unto your grace. For in good faith I dreaded lest I should thereby have provoked your grace to fuither displeasure against me.

My lord of Canterbury also, which was your great counsellor, told me that she had been with your grace, and had shown you this same matter, and of him (as I will answer before God) I learned greater things of her pretended visions than she told me herself. And, at that same time, I showed unto him that she had been with me, and told me as I have written before.

I trust now that your excellent wisdom and learning seeth there is in me no default for not revealing of her words unto your grace when she herself did affirm unto me that she had so done, and my lord of Canterbury that then was confirmed also the same.

Wherefore most gracious sovereign lord in my most humble wise I beseech your highness to dismiss me of this trouble whereby I shall the more quietly serve God and the more effectively pray for your grace. This, if there were a right great offence in me, should be to your merit to pardon but much rather taking the case as it is, I trust verily ye will so do.

Now my body is much weakened with many diseases and infirmities and my soul is much inquieted by this trouble so that my heart is more withdrawn from God and from the devotion of prayer than I would. And verily I think that my life may not long continue. Wherefore eftsoons I beseech your most gracious highness that by your charitable goodness I may be delivered of this business, and only to prepare my soul to God, and to make it ready against the coming of death, and no more to come abroad in the world. This, most sovereign lord, I beseech your highness, by all the singular and excellent endowments of your most noble body and soul, and for the love of Christ Jesus, that so dearly with his most precious blood redeemed your soul and mine, and during my life I shall not cease (as I am bounden) and yet now the more entirely to make my prayer to God for the preservation of your most royal majesty.

At Rochester the 27th day of February
Your most humble beadman and subject

Jo. Roffs.[11]

It may be noted that John Fisher here accepted, as did Sir Thomas More, the opinion that the nun had gone beyond her proper vocation and had invented some of her political utterances. There is another important point about this letter. The reference to the king's "grievous letters" and "most fearful words" to John Fisher regarding the marriage question, put on record the manner in which Henry had tried to compel approval of his intention to put away his wife.

John Fisher also wrote to the Lords. The letter is undated and may have been written before his letter to the king.

> My Lords,
> After my most humble commendations unto all your good lordships that sit in this most high court of Parliament, I beseech in like manner to hear and to tender this my suit, which by necessity I am now driven to make unto all your lordships in writing because I may not by the reason of my disease and weakness at this time be present myself before you, without peril of destruction of my body, as heretofore I have written to Master Cromwell which gave me comfort to obtain of the king his grace respite for mine absence to then [till] I be recovered. If I might have been present myself I doubt not but the great weakness of my body with other manifold infirmities, would have moved you much rather to have pity of my cause

---

[11] *L.P.*, VII, no. 239.

and matter whereby I am put unto this grievous trouble.

So it is my good lords that I am informed of a certain bill that is put into this high court against me and others concerning the matter of the Nun of Canterbury, which thing is to me no little heaviness and most especially in this piteous condition that I am in.

Nevertheless I trust in your honours' wisdoms and consciences that you will not in this high court suffer any act or condemnation to pass against me to then [till] my cause may be well and truly heard. And thereof in my most humble wise, I beseech all you, my lords, in the way of charity, and for the love of Christ. And for the main reason it may please you to consider that I sought not for this woman's coming unto me, nor thought in her any manner of deceit. She was the person that by many probable and likely conjectures, I then reputed to be right honest, religious, and very good and virtuous. I verily supposed that such feigning and crafty compassing of any guile or fraud, had been far from her. And what default was this in me so to think when I had so many probable testimonies of her virtue?

First the bruit of the country which generally called her the holy Maid.

Secondly her entrance into Religion upon certain visions which was commonly said that she had.

Thirdly, for the good religion and learning that was thought to be in her ghostly father [Bocking], and in other virtuous and well-earned priests, that then testified of her holiness as it was commonly reported. Finally my lord of Canterbury that then was, both her ordinary [bishop] and a man reputed of high wisdom and learning, told me that she had many great visions. And of him I learned greater things than ever I heard of the Nun herself.

Your wisdoms I doubt not here see plainly that in me there was no default to believe this woman to be honest, religious and of good credence.

For sithen I am bound by the law of God to believe the best of every person unto then [until] the contrary be proved, much rather I ought so to believe of this woman that had then so many probable testimonies for her goodness and virtue. But here it will be said, that she told me such words as was to the peril of the Prince, and of the realm. Surely I am right sorry to make any rehearsal of her words, but only that necessity so compelleth me now to do. The words that she told me concerning the peril of the king his highness were these: she said that she had her Revelation from God, that if the king went forth with the purpose that he intended he should not be King of England seven months after; and she told me, also, that she then had been with the king and shown unto his grace the same revelation. Though this were forged by her or any other, what default is in me that knew nothing of that forgery? If I had given her any counsel to the forging this Revelation, or had any knowledge that it was feigned, I had been worthy great blame and punishment. But whereas I never gave her any counsel to this matter, nor knew of any forging or feigning thereof, I trust in your great wisdoms that you will not think any default in me touching this point.

And as I will answer before the throne of Christ, I knew not of any malice or evil that was intended her, or by any other earthly creature unto the king's highness: neither her words did so sound that by any temporal or worldly power such thing was intended, but only by the power of God of whom as she then said she had this Revelation to show unto the king.

But here it will be said, that I should have shown the same words unto the king his highness. Verily if I had not undoubtedly thought she had shown the same words unto his grace, my duty had been so to have done. But when she herself which pretended to have had from God this Revelation, had shown the same, I saw no necessity why I should renew it again to his grace. For her esteemed honesty, qualified, as I said before, with so many probable testimonies, affirming unto me that she had told the same unto the king, made me right assuredly to think that she had so shown the same words to his grace.

And not only her own saying thus persuaded me, but her Prioress's words confirmed the same, and the servants also reported unto my servants that she had been with the king. And yet besides all this I knew it not long after by some other that so it was indeed. I thought therefore that it was not for me to rehearse the Nun's words unto the king again, when his grace knew them already, and she herself had told them him before. And surely divers other causes dissuaded me so to do which are not here openly to be rehearsed. Nevertheless when they shall be heard I doubt not but they all together will clearly excuse me as concerning this matter.

My suit therefore unto all you my honourable lords at this time is that no act of condemnation concerning this matter be suffered to pass against me in this high court before that I be heard, or else some other for me, how that I can declare myself to be guiltless herein.

And this I most humbly beseech you all, of your charitable goodnesses, and also that if peradventure in the meantime there shall be thought any negligence in me for not revealing this matter unto the king his highness, ye for the punishment thereof which is now past, ordain no new law but let me stand unto the laws which have been heretofore made, unto which I must and will obey, beseeching always the king his most noble grace that the same his laws may be ministered unto me with favour and equity, and not with the straitest rigour. Me needeth not here to advertise your most high wisdoms to look up to God, and upon your own souls in ordaining such laws for the punishment of negligences or of other deeds which are already past, nor yet to look upon your own perils which may happen to you in like cases. For there sitteth not one lord here but the same or other like may chance until himself that now is imputed to me.

And therefore eftsoons I beseech all your benign charities to tender this my most humble suit as you would be tendered if you were in the same danger yourselves. And this to do for the Reverence of Christ, for the discharge of your own souls, and for the honour of this most high Court. And finally for your own sureties and others that hereafter shall succeed you, for I verily trust in Almighty God that, by the succour of his grace and your charitable supportations I shall so declare myself that every nobleman that sitteth here shall of good reason be therewith satisfied.

Thus our Lord have you all, and this most honourable court in his protection. Amen.

Your most humble petitioner.[12]

The Lords seem to have accepted this letter as a satisfactory alternative for the bishop's own appearance, or for that of his representative.

Two points should be noted in this letter. John Fisher asked that he should be tried according to the established law of the land and not by a Bill of Attainder. An attainder is a legislative act which goes through the same process as any other piece of legislation; it can be introduced in the Lords or the Commons provided the Crown approves. The procedure therefore is not that of a trial, and was, in fact, originally designed as a method for dealing with persons who had fled from justice and could not be produced in court. During the Wars of the Roses it was found to be a convenient and speedy way of removing opponents. It commended itself to Henry VIII for the same reason. John Fisher rightly claimed that the offence with which he was charged could be dealt with in the ordinary courts.

The second noteworthy point in this letter is the warning the writer gave "to look upon your own perils which may happen to you in like cases." Both Cromwell and Norfolk were to have reason to recall that warning when they too were attainted.

The Bill was agreed to in the Lords on 12th March, and on the 17th sent to the Commons where it was passed at once, *per communes expedita*; that probably means that they did not hear John Fisher's defence. The royal assent was given on 30th March, the last day of the session, and

---

[12] *L.P.*, VII, no. 240. Signature lacking; the letter is not in his hand, but is endorsed "from the Bishop of Rochester, the original."

one week after the pope had at last declared the marriage between Henry and Catherine to be valid.

The offence for which John Fisher and four others was condemned was misprison of treason; for this they were liable to imprisonment during the king's pleasure and to the forfeiture of their goods. Chapuys made the following comment: "The good Bishop of Rochester, who is a paragon of Christian prelates both for learning and holiness, has been condemned to confiscation of body and goods. All this injustice is in consequence of his support of the queen.'"[13]

The king remitted the penalty on John Fisher for a fine of £300, one year's revenue of his bishopric.

The fate of his chaplain, John Addison (Adeson), is not known beyond the fact that he lost his benefices. He was able to visit his bishop in the Tower, so he must have been at liberty.[14] Thomas Abell lingered in the Tower until his martyrdom in 1540.

Elizabeth Barton and four priests suffered at Tyburn on 10th April 1534.

The early biographer's comment on this tragic affair still holds good. "For mine own part, I will not for certain affirm anything either with her or against her, because I have heard her diversely reported of and that of persons of right good fame and estimation."[15]

---

[13] *L.P.*, vol. VII, no. 373.

[14] See above, p. 164.

[15] *Ortroy*, p. 247.

CHAPTER XXII
TEN WEEKS' WORK

THE first session of Parliament in 1534 had such decisive consequences that a review of its legislation is necessary if we are to understand the full significance of the position taken up by John Fisher and Sir Thomas More. Their protest was against the repudiation of the authority of the See of Peter, but they were, in effect, censuring the series of statutes passed between 15th January and 31st March.

These Acts of Parliament will be considered in the order in which they appear on the statute book.

Heresy

By this Act the bishops were restrained from initiating cases of heresy; there must now be a formal accusation by two witnesses before any such case could be heard. It was further enacted that speaking "against the said Bishop of Rome or his pretended power" was no longer to be deemed heresy.

Submission of clergy and restraint of appeals

This gave statutory form to the submission made by the clergy in 1532. Convocation was now by law forbidden to assemble except by the king's writ, and all its decisions were in future to be subject to the royal assent. A commission of thirty-two (sixteen clergy and sixteen laymen) was to be established to review canon law and recommend what should be retained and what abrogated[1]

---

[1] G. & H., p. 195. The commission first met in 1551 but the revision of canon law was never caned out.

Appeals to Rome were unconditionally forbidden, and any future appeals from the archbishops' courts were to be made to the king in chancery.

Ecclesiastical appointments and the absolute restraint of annates

This Act alone might be entitled "The repudiation of the authority of the pope." Annates and first-fruits were not to be paid to Rome (a later Act of 1534 provided that they should in future be paid to the king). Archbishops and bishops were to be "elected" by priors and convents or deans and chapters on the king's nomination alone, or, in default of such election, by letters patent. It would then be the duty of the archbishops and bishops to consecrate the bishop-elect, after which the new bishop would take an oath of fealty to the king. Failure to carry out this procedure would make the offender liable to the penalties of præmunire. Thus, in future, the pope was not to have any voice in the appointment of bishops and permission to consecrate was derived from the king.[2]

Dispensation

By this Act yet another link with Rome was broken. Its special importance as that it legalized retrospectively Henry's matrimonial position. In future all dispensations were to be within the power of the Archbishop of Canterbury, subject, in important matters, to the king's assent. It was also provided for the visitation of exempt monasteries by commissioners appointed by the king. The archbishops and bishops were specifically forbidden to

---

[2] G. &H., p. 201.

make such visitations; thus the king again took the place of the pope.³

First Act of Succession

This Act was "a constitutional innovation of the utmost importance."⁴ The Anglo-Saxon tradition of election had never been explicitly replaced by that of hereditary right; Parliament had given *ex post facto* recognition of successful contestants such as Henry VII. His son wanted to make the future as secure as possible. The Act is an extraordinary document; it might almost be described as an apologia and a manifesto. The preamble takes occasion to object to the "Bishops of Rome having presumed . . . to invest who should please them to inherit in other men's kingdoms and dominions;" then it goes on to declare that "the marriage heretofore solemnized between your highness and the Lady Catherine, being before lawful wife to Prince Arthur, your elder brother, which by him was carnally known, as does duly appear by sufficient proof in a lawful process had and made before Thomas, by the sufferance of God, now archbishop of Canterbury and metropolitan⁵ and primate of all this realm, shall be, by authority of this present Parliament, definitively, clearly, and absolutely declared, deemed and adjudged to be against the laws of Almighty God." Then follows the assent to the marriage of Anne Boleyn, which, it is declared, has been approved "by the whole clergy of this realm in both the Convocations," by the English universities and by many foreign universities, "and also by the private writings of many right excellent well-learned

---

³ *G.&H.*, p. 217. Exempt monasteries, etc., were not subject to the ordinary (bishop) but to the pope.

⁴ Pollard, *Henry VIII*, p. 257.

⁵ This term replaced "*legatus natus.*"

men." A denunciation of marriage within the prohibited degrees, including "the brother to marry his brother's wife," seems to have little bearing on the succession. Then comes the naming of the line of succession, first to the sons of Queen Anne, "and for default of such sons of your body begotten . . . to the eldest issue female, which is the Lady Elizabeth, now princess."

It was further enacted that those who "maliciously give occasion by writing, print, deed or act, whereby your highness might be disturbed or interrupted of the crown," or who did anything "to the prejudice, slander, disturbance, or derogation of the said lawful matrimony solemnized between your majesty and the said Queen Anne . . . shall be adjudged high traitors, and every such offence shall be adjudged high treason." Those who "by any words, without writing, or any exterior deed or act, maliciously or obstinately shall publish, divulge, or utter any thing or things to the peril of your highness, or to the slander or prejudice of the said matrimony . . . shall be taken and adjudged for misprison of treason."

"For the more sure establishment of the succession" it was enacted that all subjects of full age must make a "corporal oath . . , that they shall truly, firmly, and constantly, without fraud or guile, observe, fulfil, maintain, defend, and keep, to their cunning, wit, and uttermost of their powers, the whole effects and contents of this present Act." To refuse the oath was adjudged misprison of treason.[6]

The Act was proclaimed throughout the kingdom on 1st May 1534.

The form of the oath was not included in the Act itself, but the nature of the oath is indicated by the terms of the

---

[6] *G.& H*, p. 232.

Act, and it is essential that these should be clearly in mind when we come to consider the reasons for the refusal of John Fisher and Sir Thomas More to take the oath.

Each subject of the king had to accept "*the whole effects and contents of this present Act.*" That is the crucial phrase; it was not an oath simply accepting the line of succession; the statute goes far beyond the limits required to establish the succession, a matter that occupies less than a quarter of the whole.

An oath based on the contents of the Act implied acceptance of:

1. the invalidity of the marriage between Henry and Catherine, thereby bastardizing the Princess Mary;
2. the validity of the marriage between Henry and Anne, thereby legitimatizing the Princess Elizabeth;
3. the absolute interdiction of marriage within the prohibited degrees with the implication that neither the pope nor anyone else could grant a dispensation;
4. the absolute power of the bishops to annul unlawful marriages without appeal to Rome.

Further it should be noted that not only were overt acts declared to be treason, but any words that could be interpreted as tending to the peril of the king were condemned as misprision of treason. The original bill had proposed that words as well as acts should be condemned as treason. The Commons had insisted on the modification to "misprision of treason" for spoken words, and had intended the terms "maliciously and obstinately" as a further safeguard from too rigid an application of the law. In practice these merciful intentions were easily ignored.

These five Acts were passed within a matter of ten weeks, though not without some difficulties and after consultations and explanations between the king and groups of lords and members. The opposition, however, was not based on religious convictions or scruples but on more mundane objections.

A consideration of the scope and implications of these Acts will help us to appreciate the consternation with which the proceedings of Parliament must have been followed by John Fisher as he lay on his sick bed at Rochester. Not the least of his sorrows must have been the thought that he had not been able to take his place amongst the Lords and make his protest against the progressive encroachment on the authority of the Church and the papacy. No act had specifically denied the supremacy of the papacy, but on each Sunday during this session of Parliament "preached at Paul's Cross a bishop which declared the pope not to be head of the church."[7]

On the day after Parliament was prorogued, the Lower House of the Convocation of Canterbury was summoned to consider "whether the Roman pontiff has any greater jurisdiction bestowed on him by God in the Holy Scriptures in this realm of England than any other foreign bishop." Thirty-four replied "No," and only four "Yes." On 5th May the Convocation of York "unanimously and concordantly, with no dissentient" likewise abjured the papal supremacy.[8]

By this time the news had reached England that on 23rd March the pope had pronounced the marriage between Henry and Catherine to be valid. The king at

---

[7] *Hall* (ed. Whibley), II, p. 260.

[8] *G. & H.*, p. 252.

294   THE LIFE OF ST. JOHN FISHER

once ordered that the statutes passed in the recent session of Parliament should be promulgated, and on 9th June he made proclamation "abolishing the usurped power of the pope."

CHAPTER XXIII
THE OATH

JOHN Fisher was summoned to appear at Lambeth on 13th April 1534 to take the oath required by the Act of Succession. The other bishops and the lords had taken the oath at the end of the Parliamentary session. It might have been thought that, in consideration of his weak state of health, a commission could have been sent down to Rochester to administer the oath. The summons to London indicates how important his decision was regarded for otherwise there was no pressing need to trouble him.

The early biographer gives an affecting account of the last days at Rochester and of the journey to London; this is evidently based on recollections of the Bishop's servants.

> This letter [the summons] being once known and heard of within his house cast such a terror and fear among his servants and after among other his friends abroad in the country, that nothing was there to be heard of but lamentation and mourning on all sides. Howbeit the holy man nothing at all dismayed therewith (as a thing he daily and hourly looked for before), called all his family before him and willed them to be of good cheer and to take no care for him, saint that he nothing doubted but all this should be to the glory of God and his own quietness. "And for that," said he, "I being once gone, you may doubt of the time of my return hither to you again. I have willed my steward to consider every of you with a portion of my goods as far as they will extend, desiring God to send both you and me his grace." And so

turning his back left them all weeping and went about other business. And calling his officers to him to consult for the disposition of his goods, he first allotted to Michaelhouse in Cambridge (where he was brought up at learning) a hundred pounds which was after paid to the college in gold.[1] Another portion he caused to be divided among his servants, allowing to every one of them a rate according to his place and worthiness. Likewise to poor people in Rochester he assigned another sum to be distributed. The rest he reserved for himself to defend his necessity in prison whereof he counted himself sure as soon as he was come before the commissioners.[2] Always reserving to the College of St. John in Cambridge his books and such parcels of goods as he before had given them, and borrowed again of them by his writing, though indeed his good meaning in that point was never fulfilled, as after shall be declared.

The next day he set forward his journey towards Lambeth, and passing through Rochester, there were by that time assembled a great number of people of that city and country about to see him depart, to whom he gave his blessing on all sides as he rid through the city bareheaded. There might you have heard great wailing and lamenting, some crying that they should never see him again, some others said, "Woe worth they that are the cause of his trouble." Others cried out upon the wickedness of the time to see such a sight, every one uttering his grief to others as their minds served them.

---

[1] See Baker, *College of St. John*, p. 103

[2] He did not reserve sufficient to provide for the fourteen months he was to spend in the Tower. See below, p. 331.

Thus passed he till he came to a place in the way called Shooter's Hill, nigh twenty miles from Rochester, on the top whereof he rested himself and descended from his horse. And because the hour of his refection was then come (which he observed at due times) he caused to be set before him such victuals as were thither brought for him of purpose. And there dined openly in the air, his servants standing round about him, and so came to London that night. And this precise order of diet he used long before, because the physicians thought and he feared himself to be entered into a consumption.[3]

In his book *Pro ecclesiasticae unitatis defensione*, Reginald (Cardinal) Pole wrote of the physical weakness from which John Fisher suffered as a result of his long illness.

> Most certainly when I left England three years ago [1532] I thought that even then if he should use the greatest possible care about his health in his own house, considering what he suffered, he could not live another year. And I heard afterwards that when he was summoned to London to be imprisoned, on the journey he swooned away for some time from weakness.[4]

A letter written in the Tower by Sir Thomas More to his daughter Margaret Roper gives us an account of the procedure before the commissioners. Sir Thomas had been summoned to appear on the same day as John Fisher, but they did not see each other. The commissioners were

---

[3] *Ortroy*, pp. 276-9.

[4] Lib. III, f. cxviv.

Archbishop Cranmer, Sir Thomas Audley (Lord Chancellor), Thomas Cromwell (the king's secretary), and William Benson (Abbot of Westminster and, later, the first Dean). Sir Thomas More saw Rowland Phillips,[5] the vicar of Croydon, and Dr. Nicholas Wilson, Master of Michaelhouse; both refused to take the oath and were sent to the Tower. Sir Thomas More's account of what happened when he came before the commissioners is important.

> After the cause of my sending for declared unto me, I desired the sight of the oath, which they showed me under the Great Seal. Then desired I the sight of the Act of Succession which was delivered me in a printed roll.[6]

He studied the two carefully, and then declared that he could not take the oath. The terms of that oath are not known, but from the care with which Sir Thomas More examined the act after reading the oath, it may be assumed that he was required to accept "the whole effects and contents of this present Act." He would also note that the words of the oath were not incorporated in the Act and therefore had no statutory validity.

He was given a short time to think the matter over. When he was again called in, he declared that "to swear to the succession I see no peril," but he would not subscribe to an oath that included acceptance of the preamble of the Act.[7] He was then committed to the charge of the Abbot of

---

[5] We have seen how he clashed with Wolsey in Convocation; see above, p. 139.

[6] Rogers, p. 502.

[7] See above, pp. 288-289.

Westminster for a few days in the hope that he would change his mind.

In his letter Sir Thomas More wrote, "What time my lord of Rochester was called in before them, that can not I tell. But at night I heard that he had been before them, but where he remained that night and so forth till he was sent hither [the Tower] I never heard."

The early biographer gives the following account of John Fisher's interview with the commissioners:

> There my lord of Canterbury put him in remembrance of the late Act of Parliament, wherein is provided an oath to be ministered to all the king's majesty's subjects for the surety of his succession in the crown of his realm. "Which oath," said he "all the lords both spiritual and temporal have willingly taken, only your lordship except. And therefore his majesty holdeth himself greatly discontent with you and hath (by his commission) appointed us to call you before us and to offer you the oath once again, which we have here present." And therewith, laying the oath before him, demanded of him what he said to it. "Then" said my lord of Rochester, "pray you let me see the oath and consider a little upon it." Then the commissioners, consulting a little among themselves, granted him space for four or five days, and so he departed again to his own house in Lambeth Marsh where he lodged.[8]

John Fisher was put in the charge of the archbishop; his own house in Lambeth Marsh was next to the Archbishop's palace, so the early biographer may be correct in saying that he was allowed to go to his own place.

---

[8] *Ortroy*, p. 280.

It was on 17th April that the oath was again proferred to Sir Thomas More and John Fisher. Both again refused and were sent to the Tower.[9]

William Rastell gave this account of John Fisher's meeting that day with the commissioners.

> The Bishop of Rochester said he would not swear to that oath. "But," quoth he, "I will apply myself to the king's pleasure so far forth as I may with conscience and learning," offering that he would be content to swear unto some part of that oath, so that it were qualified, either with some conditions or exceptions or in some other manner than it was there set forth. But the commissioners, utterly misliking with his conditions and exceptions, as repugnant to the king's proceedings, and he, constantly refusing to swear that oath, being so contrary to God's word, was sent to the Tower where he was closely imprisoned and locked up in a strong chamber from all company saving one of his servants, who, like a false knave,[10] accused his master to Cromwell afterwards.

On the same day Cranmer wrote a letter to Cromwell suggesting a way out of the impasse.

---

[9] The early biographer gives 21st April as the date of John Fisher's imprisonment but this is not in agreement with the "space for four or five days" mentioned earlier as following the 13th April. Chapuys on the 16th April (*L.P.*, VII, no. 490) had heard that John Fisher and Sir Thomas More had been sent to the Tower that morning. It is evident from Sir Thomas More's letter to his daughter that he and John Fisher did not meet at Lambeth. Harpsfield says that the commissioners saw John Fisher before they saw Sir Thomas More on the 17th.

[10] When we come to examine the records (which Rastell did not see) it will be clear that this is not a fair comment.

THE OATH

Right Worshipful Master Cromwell.

After most hearty commendations, etc. I doubt not but you do right well remember that my lord of Rochester and Master More were contented to be sworn to the Act of the king's succession, but not to the preamble of the same. What was the cause of their refusal, I am uncertain, and they would by no means express the same. Nevertheless, it must needs be either the diminution of the authority of the Bishop of Rome, or else the reprobation of the king's first pretensed matrimony. But if they do obstinately persist in their opinions of the preamble, yet meseemeth it should not be refused, if they will be sworn to the very Act of Succession, so that they will be sworn to maintain the same against all powers and potentates.

For hereby shall be a great occasion to satisfy the princess-dowager and the Lady Mary, which do think that they should damn their souls if they should abandon and relinquish their estates. And not only it should stop the mouths of them, but also of the emperor and other their friends if they give as much credence to my lord of Rochester and Master More speaking or doing against them as they hitherto have done, and thought that all should have done, when they spake and did with them.

And, peradventure, it should be a good quietation to many other within this realm, if such men should say that the succession comprised within the said Act is good and according to God's laws. For then, I think, there is not one within this realm that would once reclaim against it. And whereas divers persons, either of a wilfulness will not, or of an indurate and invertible conscience cannot, alter from their opinions of the king's first pretensed marriage (wherein they have once said their minds, and percase have a persuasion in their heads that if they should now vary therefrom their fame and estimation were distained for ever), or else of the authority of the Bishop of Rome; yet, if all the realm with one accord would apprehend the said succession, in my judgment it is a thing to be amplected and embraced. Which thing, though I trust surely in God that it shall be brought to pass, yet hereunto might not a little avail the consent and oaths of these two persons, the Bishop of Rochester and Master More, with their adherents, or rather, confederates.

And if the king's pleasure so were, their said oaths might be suppressed but when and where his highness might take some commodity by the publishing of the same.

Thus Our Lord have you ever in his conservation.
From my manor at Croydon, the 17th day of April,
Your own assured ever,
Thomas Cantuar.[11]

This letter is evidence of the influence it was feared that John Fisher and Sir Thomas More might exercise over the minds of others. If only they could be persuaded to take the oath (apart from the preamble to the Act), then "not one within this realm would once reclaim against it." Moreover this would not only "stop the mouths of the princess-dowager and the Lady Mary . . but also of the emperor and other their friends." To achieve this, the archbishop proposed a subterfuge; let them take the oath to the succession alone; that this modified oath had been taken need not be announced until the king thought it a fitting time. Meanwhile others who were troubled by

---
[11] *L.P.*, VII, no. 499.

scruples would follow the lead of the bishop and of the former chancellor.

It is not necessary to see any deep cunning in the archbishop's sophistry; the very naivity of imagining that John Fisher and Sir Thomas More, or indeed the king himself, would be accomplices in such a scheme shows a lack of subtlety. Whatever hopes Cranmer may have had were dispelled by Cromwell's reply.

> My lord, after mine humble commendation, it may please your grace to be advertised that I have received your letter and showed the same to the king's highness, who, perceiving that your mind and opinion is that it were good that the Bishop of Rochester and Master More should be sworn to the king's succession and not to the preamble of the same, thinketh that if their oaths should be taken it were an occasion to all men to refuse the whole, or at least the like. For, in case they be sworn to the succession, and not to the preamble, it is to be thought that it might be taken not only as a confirmation of the Bishop of Rome's authority, but also as a reprobation of the king's second marriage. Wherefore, to the intent that no such things should be brought into the heads of the people by the example of the said Bishop of Rochester and Master More, the king's highness in no wise willeth but that they shall be sworn as well to the preamble as to the Act. Wherefore, his grace specially trusteth that ye will in no wise attempt or move him to the contrary, for, as his grace supposeth, that manner of swearing, if it shall be suffered, may be an utter destruction of his whole cause, and also to the effect of the law made for the same.[12]

---

[12] *L.P.*, VII, no. 500.

Cranmer had not understood (did he ever understand?) the king's fixity of purpose. Henry was determined that these two notable and influential subjects should accept all the implications of the Act of Succession, and that they should declare so openly. He would not permit picking and choosing; it was all or nothing.

Roper wrote that "Queen Anne by her importunate clamour"[13] hardened the king's mind towards John Fisher and Sir Thomas More. It has also been argued that Thomas Cromwell was the evil genius behind the throne. No doubt Anne and Cromwell spoke against any relaxation of the Act's requirements, but the more one studies the records of the reign, the more one is strengthened in the belief that the directing and ruthlessly controlling power was the king himself. Thomas Cromwell skilfully worked out the practical applications of the king's policy and found in the spoliation of the monasteries the essential resources, but he did not forget, until power had made him over-confident, that the king was his master. Cromwell's "remembrances"[14] or notes of things to be done, bear this out with such phrases as "what the king will have done . . ." and, "what the king mindeth." Even Cromwell had to learn in the end the truth of the advice given to him by Sir Thomas More. "You shall ever tell him what he ought to do, but never what he is able to do . . . . For if a lion knew his own strength, hard were it for any man to rule him."[15] This is not to deny that Cromwell suggested ideas to the king and carried them out when they were approved with complete thoroughness, but when he had served the king's purpose,

---

[13] Roper, p. 74.

[14] e.g. L.P., VIII, nos. 344 and 475.

[15] Roper, p. 56.

he was discarded, as Anne Boleyn had been four years earlier.

In 1534 Cromwell's influence was moving into the ascendant; it had not yet reached its apogee. Responsibility for the treatment meeted out to John Fisher and Sir Thomas More must be laid wholly on the shoulders of the king. He saw clearly that to relax the law to meet their scruples would be "an utter destruction of his whole cause." Nothing reveals more clearly Henry's malignity than his relentless persecution of this aged bishop whose life was drawing to an end.

On 22nd April Chapuys reported that it was feared the king would put John Fisher and Sir Thomas More to death.[16] It may also be noted that both of them when they set out for Lambeth assumed that the Tower and all that was implied lay before them. Men knew what the anger of the king meant; the possibility of being freed after a fair trial did not seem to enter their thoughts. *Indignatio principis mors est.*

Chapuys also reported that the archbishop had, on his own authority, consecrated three bishops, and that the king had appointed visitors to the exempt monasteries and other religious foundations.

The oath was tendered to Queen Catherine at Buckden in May.[17] She told the commissioners that she stood by the pope's decision. A second attempt was accompanied by threats of the penalties imposed by the Act. She replied, "If one of you has a commission to execute this penalty upon me, I am ready. I ask only that I be allowed to die in the sight of the people." She was later removed for greater security and seclusion to Kimbolton; faithful servants who

---

[16] *L.P.*, VII, no. 530.

[17] *Cal. Span.*, vol. IV, no. 524.

refused the oath were dismissed, and there she lingered until her death on 7th January 1536.

Soon after John Fisher and Sir Thomas More were confined in the Tower the opening scene of another tragedy was enacted. Commissioners arrived at the London Charterhouse to put the oath to the monks. The prior, John Houghton, explained that they were not concerned with such temporal matters as the king's marriage. On the demand being renewed, the prior said, "For my part I have not satisfied myself by what process a marriage duly celebrated according to canon law and long recognized without any objection on the score of right or law can be made void or of no effect." A similar answer was given by Humphrey Middlemore, the procurator. Both were at once sent to the Tower.

Archbishop Edward Lee of York and Bishop John Stokesley of London visited the two Carthusians and explained, or explained away, the nature of the oath. The news of the pope's verdict had probably not yet been made known to them, and they may not have seen the Act with its tendentious preamble. They were kept in the Tower for a month and then released without being committed to anything. On their return they discussed the problem with the community. The prior recommended that they should "yield this time to their will"; he added, "The end is not yet." Two more visits of the commissioners were necessary before the community accepted the prior's advice. The oath they took may have been qualified, *salva conscientia*.[18] On 29th May the senior

---

[18] This account is based on Dom Maurice Chauncy's Short Narration (1570). Some such qualification was allowed to Margaret Roper, and probably to others; but such relaxation could not be permitted to influential persons.

members took the oath, and on 9th June the others also subscribed. But, as the prior said, "The end is not yet."

It may be that the two Carthusians were released from the Tower because it was realized that they were imprisoned illegally. They were not of sufficient importance to attract public attention, and they would always be available at need. The holding of John Fisher and Sir Thomas More was also equally illegal, but their release might well have led to popular rejoicings at a time when neither the king nor Cromwell could yet be sure of the state of public opinion.

As a lawyer Sir Thomas More at once saw the illegality of their imprisonment. To his daughter he said, "I may tell thee, Meg, they that have committed me hither for refusing this oath not agreeable with the statute are not by their own law able to justify my imprisonment."[19]

A serious blunder had been made by not including in the Act of Succession the words of the required oath. This made it necessary to pass a second Act of Succession when Parliament reassembled in November 1534.

John Fisher was imprisoned in the Bell Tower and Sir Thomas More in the Beauchamp Tower. They were to be kept apart as they had been on the two days when they appeared before the commissioners at Lambeth. At first both were strictly confined and were not allowed books or writing materials or visitors. Each had one servant; Richard Wilson attended the bishop, and John a Wood on Sir Thomas More.

No time was lost after the committal of John Fisher in making sure that his goods were secured. According to the Act refusal to take the oath meant loss of property and imprisonment for life. So on 27th April commissioners went down to Rochester and to Hailing to make an

---

[19] *Roper*, p. 78.

inventory of the bishop's possessions. They must have been disappointed, but it may be hoped that they were also impressed by the fact that one who had been a bishop for thirty years had so little that was of any material value.

The main items in the inventory help us to picture the austere surroundings in which John Fisher was content to live. The lists are dated 27th April 1534.

In his own bedchamber. A bedstead and mattress, a counterpane of red cloth lined with canvas. A tester of old red velvet nothing worth. A leather chair with a cushion. An altar with a hanging of white and green satin of Bruges with Our Lord embroidered on it. Two blue silk curtains. A cupboard with a cloth. A little chair covered with leather and a cushion. A close stool with an old cushion upon it. An andiron, a fire-pan, and a fire shovel.

In the great study within the same chamber. A long spruce table and other tables. Three leather chairs. Fire irons. Eight round desks and shelves for books.

In the north study. Divers glasses with waters and syrups and boxes of marmalade. A table, four round desks and bookshelves.

In the south gallery. Fifty glasses of sorts with a curtain of green and red say.

In the chapel in the end of the south gallery. A cushion in the seat of the chapel, the altar cloths, two pieces of old velvet and an altar stone. Four gilt images with a crucifix.

In the broad gallery. Old hangings of green say. Old carpets of tapestry. An altar cloth painted with green velvet and yellow damask. A St. John's head standing at the end of the altar. A pontifical book. A painted cloth of the image of Jesus taken down from the Cross.

In the old gallery. Certain old books pertaining to divers monasteries.

In the wardrobe. A tunic of stamnel [coarse woollen cloth], a Spanish blanket, an alembic to distil *aqua vitæ*, with divers old trash. A trestle bedstead, a pair of sheets, six boards, two pair of trestles.

In the great chapel. The altar hung with white silk with red silk crosses, and under it two hangings of yellow silk of Bruges and blue damask; eight gilt images upon the altar; two latten candlesticks. A diaper cloth upon the altar and hanging over it. A pix with a cloth hanging over it garnished with gold with tassels of red silk and gold. At the ends of the altar two curtains of red silk upon the desk where he sits. Two pieces of tapestry and two cushions covered with dornick linen cloth. A mass book. An old carpet on the ground before the altar. Hangings of painted red say. An altar beneath in the same chapel hung with old dornick, and a painted cloth of the three kings of Cologne. Five images of timber. A table of Doomsday. A crucifix with the images of the Father and Holy Ghost.

In the little chamber next the great chapel. Hangings of old painted cloths, a great looking glass broken. An old folding bed.

In the old dining chamber. Two leather chairs. A black velvet chair. A table and trestles. Two cupboards. Two carpets in the windows. Two joined forms.[20]

---

[20] *L.P.*, VIII, no. 557.

The frequent use of the term "old" will be noticed. The nearest approach to elaborate furnishing was in the great chapel.

Another inventory of plate again shows a lack of ostentation. "Cruets, altar basins, &c, with the portcullis upon them" were probably the gifts of the Lady Margaret Beaufort. The total, weight of plate was just over two thousand ounces Troy weight; half of this was gilt plate and much of the remainder white silver. The plate was sent to "my master Cromwell to the king's use."[21]

The commissioners took away from Rochester the bishop's papers. This led to a lengthy series of questions about some of the letters.[22] John Fisher answered these in writing; a brief reference has already been made to some of his replies, but they are sufficiently important to be given again as part of the complete record to illustrate the attitude that was taken towards him.

Amongst the letters found in his study were several addressed to Queen Catherine by an unknown writer. The interrogatory opens with a quotation from one of them. It begins abruptly with the following extract:

> which things I showed to your Nobleness [Queen Catherine] in my Prince's name of late by the reverend father E.R., and what things your Nobleness gave unto me afterward by the same father, it needs not to rehearse here. That thing only I would your Nobleness

---

[21] *L.P.*, VIII, no. 888.

[22] These questions and answers (undated MSS) are printed in L.P., VIII, no. 859 as belonging to the first half of 1535, but Gairdner, the editor, suggested in a footnote, that they "perhaps belong to a time not long after Bishop Fisher's arrest." It seems to me that they would come soon after the visit to Rochester on 27th April 1534 when the inventory was made. The Latin text of the answers is given in *Lewis*, II, pp. 403-7. I have made use of this in the English version.

should believe, that I will be both so faithful and close in concealing these things that no mortal man shall ever know them besides them whom it behoveth. Of which thing, to the intent your Nobleness may the less doubt, know ye that I have sent over sea, now six clays since, one of my servants with that which I received of the bishop of Rochester.

It is not surprising that this obscure message roused the suspicion of the king. The questions put to John Fisher are here given with his replies italicized.

1. Who wrote them?
   Such a long time has passed since I received these letters that I have almost forgotten everything about them, nor do I recall the writer's name; I have not since heard a single word of him.

2. Who was the lord or prince of the writer?
   I cannot recall his name, but no doubt, as the writer said, he was a German Prince.

3. and 4. If E.R. means the Bishop of Rochester? What the writer showed in his Prince's name to the Lady Catherine by the bishop, and what she gave to the writer by the said bishop.
   Obviously E.R. and the Bishop of Rochester are not the same person, as the Bishop of Rochester is openly mentioned again later on. Besides, I have never addressed the Lady Catherine secretly since the king commanded me to be one of her counsellors in her affair.[23]

---

[23] October 1528.

5. He says they are trifles, why should the writer promise to keep such silence?
The writer promises that he can do just as he wishes, as many men do who promise the hills and the seas; all I know is that he made such promises without my knowledge or approval.

6. Who are they who should know those things which must be concealed from all other mortal men?
I have no idea.

7. What was it the writer received from the bishop and sent over seas?
Presumably some kind of token to be sent to one of the German Princes, but, God help me, I do not know what it was or to whom unless to Prince Ferdinand, now King of Hungary.[24]

8. How many books has he written concerning the king's matrimony and divorce?
I am not certain how many, but I can recall seven or eight that I have written. The matter was so serious, both on account of the importance of the persons it concerned, and the expressed command of the king, that I gave more labour and diligence to seeking out the truth lest I should fail him and others, than I ever gave to any other matter.

9. How many copies have been made of them and in whose hands are they?
I do not know, nor did I trouble about them except for the last two which contained the substance of the

---

[24] Brother of Charles V.

others. One of these is now in the hands of the Archbishop of Canterbury [Cranmer].

10. How many books or copies have been sent over sea?
   I never sent or consented to the sending of any of these books over sea, nor did the transcriber or his servant have them with my knowledge.

11. To whom were they sent?
   As is clear from the previous answer, to no one with my knowledge.

12. Whether he has given any of the books or copies to any foreigner that the contents might be published under a strange style by some one who was not the king's subject and feared not his indignation, though he wrote what was lewd and slanderous?
   Such an idea had never occurred to me.

13. Whether the book which was printed and born without certain author or father, and yet is said to be written either by Agrippa, or Lewis Vives, or Antony Pullion,[25] was published by Rochester's consent or approval.

---

[25] Henricus Cornelius Agrippa (von Netherheim) of Cologne, spent a year (1510) as guest of John Colet; there is no evidence that he wrote anything on the subject.
Juan Luis Vives, Spanish scholar, was tutor to the Princess Mary; he was allowed to be one of Queen Catherine's counsellors, but fell into disfavour with the king, and after a short imprisonment, left for Bruges. He had written in the Queen's defence, but, if the book was printed, it has not been traced. John Antony Pulles, papal nuncio in England, 1530-34, a smooth man who would not have defended anyone.

The book was not produced by my counsel or knowledge.

14. Let him be straitly examined who was the author.
I have no idea who was the author, but I suspect from the style and shrewdness that it was Cornelius Agrippa.

15. Whether he gave counsel or consent to Abell's[26] book against the king's cause.
I never counselled Abell or consented to his publishing his book; neither had he any book of mine as far as I know.

Then follows another quotation from the mysterious letter.

But as concerning these letters which I have unto the king's highness, I have decreed not to deliver them or cause them to be delivered before I shall have taken ship; for even then I intend to send one of mine servants to deliver them; and in the mean season so to order the matter that the king shall not perceive that those letters were brought by me.

This leads to the next question.

16. Let Rochester be asked if this messenger lurked in his house until he himself told the Lady Catherine what the messenger had from his Prince and if he brought an answer.
The messenger was never in my house for more than a quarter of an hour.

---

[26] See above, p. 265. Abell's book was entitled *Invicta Veritas* (1532).

A third quotation is then given from the letter.

"If there be anything therefore that your Nobleness will farther commit unto me as to go unto other princes of Germany, and so solicit them or to have anything done by me, etc."

17. Whether he knows what else the Lady Catherine committed to this messenger.
    I know nothing of this unless she wished it might be known to those princes that she had sworn she was never carnally known by the illustrious Prince Arthur.

18. Also he writes, "When I come into Germany I will show declare and defend amongst good men, and that by books written, the cause of your Nobleness most diligently and honestly, etc."
    I certainly gave no advice or consent to the writer to do anything with the German princes against the king, nor did these letters reach me before the messenger had left.

19 and 20. Whether, saving his faith and allegiance to the king, he could or ought to aid, counsel, or consent to him who went about such things with the German princes against the king? By what hope he was moved or for what reason he concealed so long so great a matter which he knew to be intended against the king?
    The letters were sent me by the Lady Catherine, to whose counsels I was sworn by the king's commands, nor was there anything in them, as I thought, except the declaration of the Lady Catherine's virginity.

21. For what cause the letters of the Lady Catherine came to his hand, who sent them, and who brought them to him?
I know no other cause unless it was to let me see she was not despised by the princes of other countries; but by whom they came to my hands I cannot remember, for she sent to me sometimes one person and sometimes another, although both then and long before I had abstained from giving her counsel except in some things touching her conscience.

22. Let the Bishop of Rochester be asked who wrote to him the three letters without name concerning Luther's business, the king's cause, and the translation of the New Testament into English, with other notable things.
I know not who wrote them unless it be in the hand of Dr. Adeson.[27]

23. Let him be asked if he wrote or sent a message to George Daye[28] of Cambridge that he was not a little grieved that Daye should seem to favour the king's cause.
I blamed neither George Daye nor any other man for favouring the king's cause. But I remember having said when I heard that he followed neither opinion that I was not pleased with him because he studied to obtain goodwill on both sides. Perhaps it was this that made him so anxious to purge himself by his letters.

---

[27] See above, p. 164.

[28] See above, p. 130.

THE OATH

24. Let him be asked whether it did not seem enough to him that he himself was against the king's cause with as great assaults as he might.
I never blamed anyone for defending the king's cause or advised anyone to advocate that of the king.

25. It is also written in Daye's letter, "I beseech God that your lordship may as lightly overcome in that cause which ye most coveteth, as simple as I do here cleave to another part, being overcome either with fear or else with infirmity of mind."
George Daye was at liberty to judge me as he wished. For myself, I certainly desired nothing but the victory of the truth.

26. Let him be asked if he wrote letters to William [Warham], Archbishop of Canterbury saying that he knew certainly that all the universities of the world could never prove that marriage with a dead brother's wife is against the laws of God and of nature.
I admit that I have written in that sense.

27. Whether he wrote this for any other cause than to make the Archbishop harder and less inclined to favour the king's cause.
I did not so write in order to change his opinion, but that he might refrain from urging me to assent to anything against my conscience.

28. Whether Rochester wrote to the Archbishop that he (the Archbishop) intended to deceive and betray him to his adversaries when he asked him to come

to Knowle to see the determinations of the universities and whether he asked the Archbishop not to think he would sin against the Holy Ghost?
I wrote because he had not deigned to warn me by his letters of the matter about which he had summoned me, so that I might be the better prepared to answer those who were then ready. But when I came to Knowle I prayed his lordship not to suspect I would sin against the Holy Ghost either by impugning a known truth, or by not admitting the truth, if it could be shown by the writings of the universities or by others.

29. Whether he wrote any letter to the Lady Catherine as if she despaired of the mercy of God?
   The king knows very well that the Lady Catherine, not for one time only, sent for me by his consent on account of certain scruples which offended her conscience and that long before this affair began. To remove those scruples I used many words when I was with her, and wrote some letters afterwards.

30. Whether the cause of this despair was that she committed perjury, and, as some say, received the Host, that she was never carnally known by Prince Arthur?
   I never heard from her that she despaired of mercy, or had committed perjury.

31. Why he should exhort her not to despair of the mercy of God unless he knew she despaired thereof?

THE OATH

If I wrote so, I wrote that she might put away all scruples of conscience, and establish her mind in the hope and promises of Christ.

32. Who brought unto him the articles sent from the said Lady Catherine in which mention is made that a certain chaplain of the Bishop of Bath revealed to her almoner that the Bishop of Bath, Master Thomas More, chancellor, the Bishop of Exeter, and the Bishop of Chichester[29] would favour the cause as much as she could desire?
I cannot now remember who brought the articles, nor should I have remembered them unless I had read them now.

33. Whether the Bishop of Rochester's book containing the reply against the universities, and the book of Mr. Wilson,[30] and the Bishop of Bath's book were sent to Paris to a Spaniard, Doctor of Divinity and a friend to the said Lady Catherine, by the advice of the bishops of Exeter, Chichester, Bath and Rochester?

---

[29] The Bishop of Bath (John Clerk), was one of the Queen's counsellors but soon deserted her. John Veysey, Bishop of Exeter, "lived in great splendor" (D.N.B.) and was one of the consecrators of Cranmer. Robert Sherborn, Bishop of Chichester, another magnificent prelate, was under suspicion in 1532, but he accepted all changes. Of the four mentioned in the question, only Sir Thomas More was certainly a supporter of the queen, and he made his position clear to the king, but did not otherwise express his opinions.

[30] Nicholas Wilson who was sent to the Tower with John Fisher. This question is the only evidence that he wrote a book defending the queen. No book written on her behalf is known to be the work of John Clerk. See note above, p. 155. John Fisher's published book *De Causa matrimonii* does not seem to be the one to which he here refers.

I feel sure that the book I wrote against the opinion of the universities was not sent to Paris, for at that time when the Lady Catherine asked it of me, scarcely half of it was written, neither was any of the others sent there with my knowledge and consent.

34. Whether he received any letters from Peter Ligham[31] containing these words, "I beseech the Lord Jesus to give grace and spiritual strength to show the truth, putting all fear apart, for by all conjecture that I see, there be many corrupt solicitors intending to make division and schism in taking away the pope's authority, but would God they were cut off and separated which trouble the king."
I should not have remembered these letters either, unless I had seen them now.

35. Why he kept close these letters and did not show them to the King's Council as they seem to be written against them that were of the King's Council or those in whom he trusted?
I did not understand anything in these words to express against the king.

36. What were the writings which Ligham proposed he would send by his servants?
I do not know.

37. Why he concealed the letters of one Baynes[32] of

---

[31] See above, pp. 258-159.

[32] Ralph Baynes, fellow of St. John's, a leading Hebrew scholar. He went to Paris about 1544 as professor of Hebrew. He returned under Queen Mary and became Bishop of Lichfield; deprived and died 1559.

Cambridge in which the king's cause was defamed?
I truly believe Baynes did not write them out of ill-will to the king.

38. What these words mean of Richard [Fox][33] Bishop of Winchester where he prayeth that he and the same Rochester might once speak together before he died, so that it were not in Parliament or convocation "from which God deliver us"?
I do not know what they mean unless it be that he would not thenceforth willingly mix himself with the business of those two places.

39. Whether he received two letters from the Bishop of Bath, one concerning the curates, and the other the interpretation of the Levitical law of marriage with a brother's wife, as if it meant a living brother?
Many learned and esteemed interpreters of the Old Testament have followed this interpretation that the Levitical prohibition applies to a living brother.

40. Whether he has followed in his books this interpretation of the Bishop of Bath?
Although in my writings I cited many who affirm that interpretation, I do not endeavour to rest my opinion altogether upon them, as my writings clearly show.

What was the purpose of this lengthy interrogatory? It had little relation to John Fisher's imprisonment for

---

[33] *d.* 1528. An interesting reminder of the friendship between the two men.

refusing to take the Oath to the Act of Succession. The marriage cause had been settled to the king's satisfaction; Queen Catherine had officially become the Lady Catherine, princess-dowager, and Anne Boleyn was queen. The opening questions may provide part of the explanation; if it could be proved that John Fisher had been active in negotiations with foreign princes, a charge of treason could be brought against him. Had the contents of recent letters from Chapuys to the emperor been known, such a charge would have had substance. These mysterious letters, however, did not provide the evidence required. John Fisher's answers gave no clue to the identity of the "prince" or of "E.R." or of the messenger.

The majority of the questions concern books written in support of Queen Catherine. The questions are evidence of the great amount of writing done on this subject; hardly anything has survived.[34] Nothing new is revealed, but it may have been hoped that there might be some disclosure that would implicate others, especially those whose names were given. There is the possibility that more evidence was needed against Queen Catherine. It was indeed rumoured that a Bill of Attainder was to be brought before Parliament against her and the Princess Mary. Here again, John Fisher's answers must have seemed unsatisfactory.

Perhaps the simplest explanation is the true one; these many questions suggest that the king was intent on relentlessly pursuing any who had opposed his cause. This lengthy interrogatory also strengthens the view that their opposition to the king's marriage schemes, and not the succession, was the effective reason for the imprisonment of John Fisher and Sir Thomas More.

---

[34] The reader should remember that the word "book" is not to be taken to mean always "printed book".

CHAPTER XXIV
IN THE BELL TOWER

THE seventh session of Parliament met from 3rd November to 18th December 1534. Three important Acts call for attention as they directly affected the position of John Fisher and Sir Thomas More.

The first was the Supremacy Act[1] by which it was declared that "the king our sovereign lord, his heirs and successors, kings of this realm, shall be taken, accepted and reputed the only supreme head in earth of the Church of England, called *Anglicana Ecclesia*." The qualifying clause, "as far as the Law of Christ allows" did not appear in the Act. On 15th January 1535 the king's full style was proclaimed to be, "Henricus Octavus, Dei gratis Anglia et Franciæ Rex, Fidei Defensor et Dominus Hiberniæ, et in Terra Supremum Caput Anglicanæ Ecclesiæ."

The second Act was the ratification of the Act of Succession[2] but this time with the wording of the oath; this, it was claimed, was in keeping with the tenor of the oath that had hitherto been imposed. This may be so since it contains the sentence "ye shall observe, keep, maintain, and defend this Act, and the whole contents and effects thereof." It has sometimes been thought that the oath tendered to Fisher and More had some clause in it referring to the papacy, but, as we have seen in the last chapter, the italicized phrase, as the king insisted, covered

---

[1] G. & H., p. 243.
[2] G. & H., p. 244.

the preamble of the Act, and that, by implication, was a repudiation of the pope's authority.

The third Act extended the 1352 statute of Treason[3] to cover not only things said and done, but things thought. After February 1535 it was adjudged high treason for anyone "maliciously to wish, to will, or desire by words or writing, or by craft imagine, invent, practise, or attempt any bodily harm to be done or committed to the king's most royal person, the queen's, or their heir apparent, or deprive them of their royal estates, or slanderously and maliciously publish and pronounce, by express writing or words, that the king our sovereign lord should be heretic, schismatic, tyrant, infidel, etc." If these words are read carefully, it will be seen that the least sign of opposition to the king could easily be interpreted as treason. Dr. Lingard's comment is sufficient. "It would be difficult to discover under the most despotic governments, a law more cruel or absurd."[4] A later historian has pointed out, "In the act of succession failure to take the oath involved only the pains of misprision of treason—forfeiture and imprisonment; now it could be argued that the subject who refused the oath was endeavouring to deprive the king of his title and even to brand him as a schismatic."[5] The second Act of Succession had, retrospectively, legalized the imprisonment of John Fisher and Sir Thomas More; the Act of Treason now brought them within sight of the block; refusal to take the all-embracing oath to the succession could now be interpreted as a form of treason. Once more the safeguarding word "maliciously" was to prove meaningless.

---

[3] *G.& H.*, p. 247.

[4] *History*, IV, p. 484.

[5] Mackie, *Earlier Tudors* (1952), p. 360.

It is not known how many attempts were made to persuade John Fisher to conform with the king's wishes. The early biographer is the only source for the following incidents; there is nothing in this account that is improbable and it cannot be dismissed simply because it lacks confirmation.

> Then came to him at several times Bishop Stokesley of London, Bishop Stephen Gardiner of Winchester, Bishop Tunstal of Durham, with certain other bishops to persuade him to yield to the king's demand. And yet no doubt but most of them did this against their stomachs, and rather for fear of the king's displeasure in whom they knew was no mercy, than for any truth they thought in the matter. For I have credibly heard say that Bishop Stokesley all his life after when he had occasion to speak of this business would earnestly weep and say, "O that I had holden still with my brother Fisher and not left him when time was!' And for the Bishop of Winchester, myself have divers times heard him, sometimes in the pulpit openly, and sometimes in talk at dinner among the lords of the council, and sometimes in other places, very earnestly accuse himself of his behaviour and doings at that time...[6]
>
> These bishops, I say, persuaded thus continually with this holy man, sometime one and sometime another, but all in vain; for by no means would he be won to swear one jot from that which by his learning he knew to be just and true.

---

[6] Gardiner did preach to this effect on 2nd Dec. 1554 in the reign of Queen Mary; it is impossible to decide how far his views were influenced by changing political conditions. The early biographer's reference to himself here is important as it shows that he was in a position to collect information.

At another time there came to him, by the king's commandment, six or seven bishops at once to treat with him like sort, as the other had done severally before. And when they had declared their intent and cause of coming, he made answer again in these or like words. "My lords, it is no small grief to me that occasion is given to deal in such matters as these be. But it grieveth me much more to see and hear such men as you be, persuade with me therein, seeing it concerneth you in your several charge as deeply as it doth me in mine. And therefore me thinketh it had rather been all our parts to stick together in repressing these violent and unlawful instrusions and injuries, daily offered to our common mother and holy Church of Christ, than by any manner of persuasions to help or set forward the same. And we ought rather to seek by all means the temporal destruction of these ravening wolves that daily go about worrying and devouring everlastingly the flock that Christ hath committed to our charge and the flock that himself died for, than to suffer them thus to range abroad. But, alas seeing we do it not, ye see in what peril the Christian state now standeth. We are besieged on all sides and can hardly escape the danger of our enemy. And seeing that judgment is begone at the house of God, what hope is there left, if we fall, that the rest shall stand? The fort is betrayed even of them that should have defended it. And therefore, seeing the matter is thus begun and so faintly resisted on our parts, I fear we be not the men that shall see the end of the misery. Wherefore seeing I am an old man and look not long to live, I mind not (by the help of God) to trouble my conscience in pleasing the king in this way, whatsoever become of me; but rather here to spend out the remnant of my old days in praying to God for him."[7]

Richard Wilson, the bishop's attendant, was presumably the early biographer's informant for the following incident.

> His own man that kept him in the prison, being but a simple fellow and hearing all this talk, fell in hand with him about this matter and said, "Alas, my lord, why should you stick with the king more than the rest of the bishops have done, who be right well learned and godly men? Doubt you not he requireth no more of you but only to say he is head of the Church? And me thinketh that is no great matter, for your lordship may still think as you list." The bishop, perceiving his simplicity and knowing that he spake of good will and love towards him, said unto him again in the way of talk, "Tush, tush, thou art but a fool and knowest little what this matter meaneth, but hereafter thou mayest know more. But I tell thee it is not for the supremacy only that I am thus tossed and troubled, but also for an oath [succession] which if I would have sworn, I doubt whether I should ever have been questioned for the supremacy or no. But, God being my good lord, I will never agree to any of them both. And this thou mayest say another day thou heardest me speak, when I am dead and gone out of this world."

In his isolation, but cut off, as it seems, from the sacraments of the Church, John Fisher would have been consoled by a letter sent to him by the Fellows of St. John's College. According to the early biographer a

---

[7] *Ortroy*, pp. 303-307.

deputation had waited upon him just before he was committed to the Tower. It seems that Archbishop Cranmer had proposed changes in the college statutes, and it was necessary to have the seal of the sole surviving executor of the Lady Margaret.

The master and fellows of St. John's College in Cambridge, not forgetting their great benefit received at his hands, sent up two of their company called Mr. Seton and Mr. Brandesby,[8] partly to salute him and visit him in the name of the whole house and partly to desire of him the confirmation of their statutes under his seal, which himself long before had made and drawn in writing but never yet confirmed. And therefore doubting much the time of his imprisonment to be very near at hand, their humble suit was that it would please him to allow the same statutes under his seal before he went to prison. But to that he answered that he would first read and consider them once more and then if he liked them, he would fulfil their request. "Alas," said they, "we fear the time is now too short for you to read them before you go to prison." "Then," said he, "I will read them in prison." "Nay," said they, "that, we think will hardly be brought to pass." "Then," said he, "let God's will be done; for I will never allow under my seal that thing which I have not well and substantially viewed and considered."[9]

---

[8] Dr. John Seton, one of John Fisher's chaplains, was imprisoned in 1561 as one of the "papistical clergy." He died in Rome, 1567. Nothing further is known of Richard Brandesby who became a Fellow in 1523.

[9] *Ortroy*, p. 282, note (a). Also Baker, St. John's College, I, p. 100. The text of the letter is given in Lewis, vol. II, pp. 356-358 from the copy in the early Register of letters at St. John's College. The original letter has not been preserved.

One thing here is typical; John Fisher was not to be hurried to a decision; he must have time to consider before making up his mind. Both the king and Wolsey had experienced the same caution when they sought his opinion.

It has been suggested that there is some confusion here with a deputation from the college that waited on the bishop in the Tower itself. The letter he received is not dated but the wording suggests that it belongs to the earlier part of his imprisonment; it refers to "the bitter and troublesome cares which of late" had overtaken him.

They wrote because they felt it would be base and wrong not to signify their affection for him. Their feelings were both of sorrow and of joy: sorrow because of his adversity and peril, but joy also because it was a mark of divine favour to be called upon to suffer tribulation in this world. They had never doubted that he had chosen to please God rather than man, and, in their daily prayers, they would ask God to bestow on him plenteously of his grace. "You are our father, our teacher, our preceptor and lawgiver, and above all our pattern of virtue and holiness. To you indeed we owe our sustenance and our learning, and whatever we have or know that is good. We have no way of showing our gratitude or of repaying these benefits save by the prayers we continually offer to God on your behalf." At the same time they begged him to use whatever was theirs as his own, for they were entirely at his service.

This noble tribute of devotion is unsigned; had it been, the first name would have been that of the Master, Nicholas Metcalfe, a faithful friend of many years. He was forced out of the Mastership in 1537 as a determined Romanist. Amongst the Fellows at that time were Roger Ascham, John Redman, Robert Pember, John Cheke and

Thomas Watson; they were to be divided in religion but united in that devotion to Greek studies that had become the mark of St. John's.

John Fisher did not take advantage of this offer of help from St. John's; he may not have received the letter.

At length on 22nd December 1534 he made an appeal to Thomas Cromwell. It is the last letter by John Fisher that has been preserved.

> After my most humble commendations, where as ye be content that I should write unto the king's highness, in good faith I dread me that I can not be so circumspect in any writing but that some word shall escape me wherewith his grace shall be moved to some further displeasure against me, whereof I would be very sorry. For as I will answer before God, I would not in any manner of point offend his grace, my duty saved unto God, whom I must in everything prefer. And for this consideration I am full loth and full of fear to write unto his highness in this matter. Nevertheless, sithen [since] I conceive that it is your mind that I shall so do, I will endeavour me to the best than I can.
>
> But first here I must beseech you, good Master Secretary, to call to your remembrance that at my last being before you and the other commissioners for taking the oath concerning the king's most noble succession, I was content to be sworn unto that parcel concerning the succession. And there I did rehearse this reason, which I said moved me, I doubted not but the prince of any realm, with the assent of his nobles and commons, might appoint for his succession royal such another as was seen unto his wisdom most according; and for this reason I said, that I was content

to be sworn unto that part of the oath as concerning the succession. This is the very truth, as God help my soul at my most need. Albeit, I refused to swear to some other parcels by cause that my conscience would not serve me so to do.

Furthermore, I beseech you to be good master unto me in my necessity. For I have neither shirt nor sheet, nor yet other clothes that are necessary for me to wear, but that be ragged and rent to shamefully. Nothwithstanding I might easily suffer that, if they would keep my body warm. But my diet also, God knoweth how slender it is at many times, and now in mine age my stomach may not away but with a few kinds of meats, which if I want I decay forthwith, and fall into coughs and diseases of my body, and can not keep myself in health. And as our Lord knoweth, I have nothing left unto me to provide any better, but as my brother of his own purse layeth out for me to his great hindrance. Wherefore good Master Secretary eftsoons [forthwith] I beseech you to have some pity upon me, and let me have such things as are necessary for me in mine age and especially for my health.

And also that it may please you by your high wisdom to move the king's highness to take me unto his gracious favour again, and to restore me unto my liberty out of this cold and painful imprisonment; whereby ye shall find me to be your poor beadsman for ever unto Almighty God, who ever have you in his protection and custody.

Other twain things I must also desire upon you: that one is that it may please you that I may take some priest with in the Tower by the assignment of master lieutenant to hear my confession against this holy time; the other is, that I may borrow some books to stir my devotion more effectually these holy days for the comfort of my soul. This I beseech you to grant me of your charity. And thus our Lord send you a merry Christmas and a comfortable to your heart's desire.

At the Tower, the 22nd day of December
Your poor Beadsman,[10]

Jo. Roffs.

A prisoner in the Tower had to provide for his own keep and that of any servant he was allowed to have with him; the lot of anyone without means for this must have been indeed miserable; presumably he would be allowed sufficient food to keep him alive. For himself and his servant John Fisher had to pay a pound a week (Tudor currency); Sir Thomas More was charged fifteen shillings for himself and servant; bishops as lords were apparently rated on a higher scale than commoners.

It is not known how far this appeal to the king through his secretary was successful. The prisoner was at least permitted the use of pen and paper and was thus able to record the fruits of his meditations.

---

[10] Beadsman is an antiquated term for a pensioner who is paid for by a benefactor to offer prayers for him. By using this term St. John is showing himself to be utterly dependent upon the Crown to survive. - Editorial note.

CHAPTER XXV
FOR HIS SISTER

JOHN FISHER'S half-sister, Elizabeth White, was "a nun, who was so like the said Bishop of Rochester in person, that Queen Mary knew her."[1] She entered the Dominican house at Dartford, Kent. It was for her that John Fisher wrote in the Tower *A Spiritual Consolation*, and, *The Ways to Perfect Religion*.[2] These were probably first published in the reign of Queen Mary as it would have been hazardous to have printed them while Henry VIII was alive.

The Spiritual Consolation opens:

> Sister Elizabeth, nothing doth more help effectually to get a good and a virtuous life than if a soul when it is dull and unlusty without devotion, neither disposed to prayer, nor to any other good work, may be stirred or quickened again by fruitful meditation. I have therefore devised unto you this meditation that followeth.

Her brother recommended three things: first, she should put herself in the position of someone "suddenly ravished by death"; second, "never read this meditation but alone by yourself in secret manner"; third, "that when you intend to read it, you must afore lift up your mind to Almighty God, and beseech him that by the help and succour of his grace, the reading thereof may fruitfully work in your soul a good and virtuous life, according to

---

[1] Arundel MS. 152, f. 281r.
[2] *E.W*, pp. 3 49-387.

his pleasure, and say '*Deus in adiutorium meum intende, etc.*'."

One passage will indicate the manner of the whole.

> O then, how many idle words, how many evil thoughts, how many deeds have I to make answer for, and such as we set but at light, full greatly shall be weighed in the presence of his most high majesty. O, alas, what may I do to get some help at this most dangerous hour? Where may I seek succour? Where may I resort for any comfort? My body forsaketh me, my pleasures be vanished away as the smoke, my goods will not go with me. All these worldly things I must leave behind me; if any comfort shall be, either it must be in the prayers of my friends, or in mine own good deeds that I have done before. But as for my good deeds that should be available [of benefit] in the sight of God, alas, they be few or none that I can think to be available, they must be done principally and purely for his love. But my deeds when of their kind they were good, yet did I linger them by my folly. For either I did them for the pleasure of men, or to avoid the shame of the world, or else for my own affection, or else for dread of punishment. So that seldom I did any good deed in that purity and straightness that it ought of right to have been done. And my misdeeds, my lewd deeds that be shameful and abominable be without number, not one day of all my life, no not one hour I trow was so truly expended to the pleasure of God, but many deeds, words, and thoughts, miscaped [came wrongly from] me in my life.

He was no doubt thinking over his own life when he wrote that "neither building of colleges, nor making of sermons, nor giving of alms, neither yet any other manner of business" would of themselves provide against the hour of death.

The Ways to Perfect Religion was also written for his sister "to the health of your soul and the furtherance of it in holy religion." This guide to the devout life is notable for the analogy the writer drew between the life of the hunter in the field, and the pursuit of the Christian after righteousness. John Fisher used a similar method in his Good Friday sermon in which he likened the crucified Christ to the outstretched pages of an opened book. Such analogies were popular with medieval preachers, and, presumably, with their hearers. Sometimes the comparison is strained, but, had this little work been preached, it cannot be doubted that the opening picture would have seized the attention.

It is not an academic exercise, but a description taken from life, and, it may be felt, from the writer's early experience.

> What life is more painful and laborious of itself than is the life of hunters which most early in the morning break their sleep and rise when others do take their rest and ease, and in his labour he may use no plain highways and soft grass, but he must tread upon the fallows, run over the hedges, and creep through the thick bushes, and cry all the long day upon his dogs, and so continue without meat or drink until the very night drive him home; these labours be unto him pleasant and joyous, for the desire and love that he hath to see the poor hare chased with dogs. Verily, verily, if he were compelled to take upon him such labours, and not for this cause, he would soon be weary of them, thinking them full tedious unto him.

Neither would he rise out of his bed so soon, nor fast so long, nor endure these other labours unless he had a very love therein. For the earnest desire of his mind is so fixed upon his game, that all these pains be thought to him but very pleasures. And therefore I may well say that love is the principal thing that maketh any work easy, though the work be right painful of itself and that without love no labour can be comfortable to the doer. The love of his game delighteth him so much that he careth for no worldly honour but is content with full simple and homely array. Also the goods of the world he seeketh not for, nor studiedh how to attain them. For the love and desire of his game so greatly occupieth his mind and heart. The pleasures also of his flesh he forgetteth by weariness and wasting of his body in earnest labour. All his mind, all his soul, is busied to know where the poor hare may be found. Of that is his thought, and of that is his communication, and all his delight is to hear and speak of that matter, every other matter but this is tedious to him to give ear unto, in all other things he is dull and unlusty, in this only quick and stirring, for this also to be done, there is no office so humble, nor so vile, that he refuseth not to serve his own dogs himself to bathe their feet and to anoint them where they be sore, yea and to cleanse their stinking kennel where they shall lie and rest them. Surely if religious persons had so earnest a mind and desire to the service of Christ, as these hunters to see a course at a hare, their life should be unto them a very joy and pleasure. For what other be the pains of religion but these that I have spoken of—that is to say, much fasting, crying, and coming to the choir, forsaking of worldly honours, worldly riches, and fleshly pleasures, and communication of the world, humble service, and obedience to his sovereign and charitable dealing to her sister which pains in every point; the hunter taketh and sustaineth more largely for the love that he hath to his game, than do many religious persons for the love of Christ. For albeit, the religious person riseth at midnight, which is painful to her in very deed, yet she went before that to her bed at a convenient hour, and also cometh after to her bed again. But the hunter riseth early, and so continueth forth all the long day, no more returning to his bed until the very night, and yet peradventure he was late up the night before, and full often up all the long nights. And though the religious woman fast until it be noon, the which must be to her painful, the hunter yet taketh more pain which fasteth until the very night, forgetting both meat and drink for the pleasure of his game. The religious woman singeth all the forenoon in the choir, and that also is laborious to her, but yet the hunter singeth not, but cryeth, hallooeth and shouteth all the long day, and bath more greater pains. The religious woman taketh much labour in coming to the choir and sitteth there so long a season but yet no doubt of it more labour taketh the hunter in running over the fallow and leaping over the hedges and creeping through the bushes than that can be. And would to God that in other things, that is to say, touching worldly honours, worldly riches, worldly pleasures, would to God that the religious persons many of them might profit as much in mindfulness in seeking of Christ as the hunter doth in seeking his game, and yet all their comfort were to commune and speak of Christ, as the hunters hash all their joy to speak of the poor hare and of their hunting. And furthermore would to God the religious persons would content themselves with the humble service done to their sovereign, and with charitable behaviour unto their sisters and with as good a heart and mind as the hunters acquit themselves to serve their hounds. I wis it is a thing more reasonable to love and serve reasonable creatures made in the image of Almighty God rather than to love and serve dogs which be unreasonable creatures. And rather our duty were to speak of Christ and of things belonging to his honour than of the vain worldly matters which be but very trifles indeed. And also with more attentive mind we should seek after our Saviour Christ Jesus to know our very comfort in him, wherein resteth the great merit of our souls. Then the hunters should seek after the hare which when they have gotten, they have no great gains thereby. But as I said, the cause why so many religious persons so diligently pursue not the ways of religion as do the hunters, is the want of the observation of their game which is nothing else but the lack of love. For verily as I think the earnest love and hearty desire of game maketh all labours and pains pleasant and joyous unto the hunter. And if there were in religious persons as great favour and love to the service of God as be in hunters to their game all their life should be a very paradise and heavenly joy in this world. And contrariwise without this fervour of love it can not be but painful, weary and tedious to them.

Then follow eight "considerations" or meditations on the main theme. The little work concludes with seven sentences, each a prayer to be used on successive days of the week.

O blessed Jesu, make me to love thee entirely.
O blessed Jesu I would fain, but without thy help I can not.
O blessed Jesu, let me deeply consider the greatness of thy love towards me.
O blessed Jesu, give unto me grace heartily to thank thee for thy benefits.
O blessed Jesu, give me good will to serve thee, and to suffer.
O sweet Jesu, give me a natural remembrance of thy passion.
O sweet Jesu possess my heart, hold and keep it only to thee.

These two writings for his sister are not weighted with the many quotations that are to be found in much of John Fisher's work. This may have been because he desired to be as simple as possible in his directions for a life of prayer and meditation; perhaps it may have been partly due to his lack of books in the Tower. In this he seems to have been treated less favourably than his fellow-prisoner, Sir Thomas More, who, until the last few months, was allowed the books he needed.

A small collection of miscellaneous papers in Latin and English that belonged to John Fisher have been preserved.[3] Some are fragments, while others run to a dozen or so pages. It cannot be now known if all these were removed from his cell after his death, or whether some came from Rochester. There is, for instance, a fragment on the eucharist, notes on some Psalms, a short treatise in vindication of the rights and dignity of the clergy, and a theological commonplace book. None of these adds significantly to our knowledge of the writer, but in this

---

[3] *L.P.*, VIII, no. 887. P.R.O. S.P.I., 93, ff. 99-102.

miscellany are five precious pages in his hand containing a complete draft and part of the revision of a prayer or meditation; the manuscript is sadly mutilated,[4] but these fragments bring us close to the heart of the saint.

An opening sentence suggests that he composed this prayer either in the Tower, or when he knew that such would be his fate.

> Rescue me from these manifold perils that I am in, for unless thou wilt of thine infinite goodness relieve me, I am but as a lost creature.

That is not, however, the predominant mood; soon he turns to lament his own sinfulness, then, throwing himself on the mercy of God, he prays for a renewal of the Holy Spirit "by whose gracious presence I may be warmed, heated and kindled with the spiritual fire of charity and with the sweetly burning love of all godly affections."[5]

These tattered pages give us a glimpse of John Fisher's method of composition; the interlineations, the deletions, and the marginal additions are indications of a feeling for style and expression that led him to search for the right phrase and for the best ordering of sentences that would express his thoughts.

His English works are not considerable in bulk; they consist mainly of sermons and devotional writings. He wrote no full length book, as far as is known, in his own language.

The sermon is a special class of composition of which the funeral tribute is a small part. We have seen the great importance he gave to preaching, and how, through the liberality of the Lady Margaret, he did all he could to

---

[4] See Plate XII.

[5] The full text is given in Appendix A.

foster the art amongst priests. He himself was that rare phenomenon, for his times, a preaching bishop. He was in the tradition of the Middle Ages; this is seen in the structure of his sermons and in his occasional straining at analogy; but these were not dominant characteristics; he was moving forward to a more familiar style. What he brought of his own was human sympathy and imaginative feeling. The understanding of the life of ordinary folk is shown in the homely illustrations he used: a clock that had stopped, the shadow of a tree, a torch lighting up a room, a spider's web, the blacksmith's forge, a broken bucket, the business of presenting a petition. His imaginative feeling is revealed in his descriptions of scenes used as the setting of his exposition; two come to mind at once; his account of the Field of Cloth of Gold, and the life of the hunter quoted in this chapter.

His language, at its best, is suited to the understanding of his listeners, and is clear and straightforward; at times he reaches a high level of eloquence; but there are also awkwardly constructed passages that must have been hard to follow, and the frequent quotations from the Scriptures or from the Fathers, seem burdensome to us. It is, however, not reasonable to judge sermons as if they were written compositions; we need to hear the preacher's voice, to note his gestures, and to come under the influence of his personality. His great reputation as a preacher suggests that what may seem awkward to read, may well have been impressive to hear.

There is little of his prose apart from the sermons. His letters are few in number, and most were hampered by the conventional phraseology expected in addressing the king or his secretary. The letter he wrote to the Lords on the matter of the Nun of Kent is an admirable piece of direct writing. Other passages in this volume illustrate his eloquence, as when commemorating the Lady Margaret, or his power of description as when speaking of the Field of Cloth of Gold.[6]

The theme of much of his work was the Four Last Things—death, judgment, heaven, and hell. He treats of the vanity of life and of the need for repentance. In this, too, he was the child of the Middle Ages. He did not preach smooth things; the reader of today may be repelled by the preacher's stern condemnation of sin and by his repeated warnings of the wrath to come. This is one side of his message. He was also constant in reminding the sinner of the infinite mercy of God and of the eternal joys of those who learn to love God.

It is inevitable that a comparison should be made between the writings of John Fisher and those of Sir Thomas More, but such an exercise has little value apart from literary interest. One was, first and last, a preacher. By nature he was not sociably inclined, nor had he an ever ready sense of humour. The other was an active lawyer and statesman and the centre of a happy family. His dramatic instinct led him to use forms that were outside the needs of John Fisher.

These differences may be illustrated by the work each wrote in the Tower. Sir Thomas More's greatest book, *A Dialogue of Comfort*, was the testament of a wise and devout man of affairs who had known what it was to be familiar with a king and to fall from favour. John Fisher wrote two short guides to devotion for his sister; these were his testament, the fruit of a lifetime of meditation.

It would be pointless to compare two such works; each, in its own way, is the summing-up of a man's life. Each wrote in the style that was part of his nature and so achieved the purpose for which he wrote.

---

[6] See above, pp. 111-115.

FOR HIS SISTER 343

Nor would it be profitable to attempt a comparison between the precious meditation John Fisher composed in the Tower, and the "Godly Meditation" written by his fellow-prisoner.[7] The thoughts of both saints were turned towards God.

---

[7] See my *Saint Thomas More*, pp. 337-8.

XXI - John Fisher
Hans Holbein the Younger (attributed)
This depicts Fisher towards the end of his life. Depictions of him as a Cardinal are posthumous, as he never wore Cardinal's apparel. He was made the Cardinal of the Church of San Vitale. He is still the only martyr to have been a Cardinal.

CHAPTER XXVI
THE RED HAT

THERE is not sufficient information available to enable a connected account of John Fisher's imprisonment to be given. From the letters Sir Thomas More wrote to his daughter Margaret, it is possible to follow his fortunes in some detail, but there is no such precious record of the fourteen months during which John Fisher was a prisoner. What knowledge we have has to be pieced together from official papers.

From these we learn that his brother Robert brought him news of the Acts of Supremacy and Treasons. Richard Wilson, the bishop's attendant, stated that,

> touching the Act of Supreme Head, about Candlemas last Robert Fisher came and told him of it in the Tower, when "he took up his hands and blessed him, saying, Is it so?" Robert Fisher also told him of an Act "by reason whereof men should come to the Tower.... For now, said he, speaking is made high treason, which was never heard of before, that words should be high treason. But there was never such a sticking at the passing of the Act in the Lower House as was at the passing of the same," said he, and that they stuck at the last to have one word in the same, and that was maliciously, which, when it was put it was not worth . . . , for they [judges?] would expound the same statutes themselves at their pleasure.[1]

---

[1] L.P., VIII, no. 856; the same reference applies to other answers by servants.

Robert Fisher died in the spring of 1535, and the bishop had then to rely on Edward White, his brother-in-law.

Another Rochester servant, John Pewnall or Fawconer,[2] gave some information about the bishop's serious illness in the early months of 1535. John Fisher wrote about his sickness to Antonio Bonvisi, a life-long friend of Sir Thomas More. Bonvisi took the advice of Dr. John Clement who had once been a tutor in Sir Thomas More's household and had become a physician of note; he had attended Wolsey after his fall from power. Clement's opinion was that the bishop's "liver was wasted and he should take goat's milk." Bonvisi sent into the Tower gifts of food and wine for both the prisoners.

On 20th April, three Carthusian priors, John Houghton of London, Augustine Webster of Axholme, and Robert Lawrence of Beauvale were sent to the Tower for refusing to acknowledge the king as Supreme Head. They were joined by the learned Bridgettine, Richard Reynolds, and by two secular priests, Richard Feron of Teddington, and John Hale of Isleworth. They were charged on 28th April with high treason and condemned. Feron was pardoned, but the others suffered at Tyburn on 4th May.

That morning, Margaret Roper was allowed to visit her father; as they watched the beginning of the dread journey, Sir Thomas More said, "Lo, dost thou not see, Meg, that these blessed fathers be now as cheerfully going to their deaths as bridegrooms to their marriage?"[3]

It is not known if John Fisher was also a witness; he may have been so for the presence of Margaret Roper with her father was probably arranged in the hope that her compassion might influence him; so too it may have been

---

[2] He was the bishop's falconer, or purveyor of game to the household.

[3] *Roper*, p. 80.

thought that the sight of what lay before him might break the bishop's resolution. Richard Wilson recalled John Fisher's remark after the execution. "They be gone. God have mercy on their souls," and that, "when they were alive, Fisher said, referring to the monks under examination, 'I pray God that no vanity subvert them.'"

Two days later, the bishop told George Gold, the lieutenant's servant, "he saw not so great peril in the statute, unless it were done or spoken maliciously, and he marvelled much that the monks were put to execution, saying that they did nothing maliciously nor obstinately."

Shortly afterwards three more of the London Carthusians were arrested and sent to the Marshalsea prison and later to the Tower. They were Humphrey Middlemore, William Exmewe, and the Sebastian Newdigate on whom John Fisher had conferred the subdiaconate almost exactly four years earlier.[4]

Thomas Cromwell and other members of the council visited John Fisher three days after the execution of the Carthusians and their fellow martyrs. There is no official record of what took place, but references to it are made in later interrogations. It is clear that the purpose was to get, if possible, the crucial evidence needed—a definite denial of the validity of the king's new title.

Richard Wilson gave the following account.

> On Friday after Ascension Day last, Mr. Secretary [Cromwell] and others of the Council, came to examine Fisher on the Act of the Supreme Head, and this respondent [Wilson] standing in the chamber without the partition, heard some part of the examination. Mr. Secretary said they were sent for two things, first touching the Act of Supremacy; the

---

[4] See above, p. 119.

second point respondent did not hear. Mr. Secretary read the Act, and Fisher replied that he could not consent to take the king as Supreme Head. The Act was also read to him making it treason to deny the king to be Supreme Head. After supper respondent told his master that he thought Mr. Bedyll's[5] reasons weak when he said the king was head of his people, and the people was the church, with some further observations. The bishop asked if he thought he had been too quick with Mr. Bedyll, and respondent said no.

In reply to a later question Wilson said,

> At supper, Fisher, in answer to his questions, said he had not made answer "but the council was gone even as it came." Then said my master to this respondent, "Sir, that last day before this that the Council was here, the council should ask me two questions or two points. And this respondent said, Yes, for he heard Mr. Secretary say then and purpose that he had come then principally for two things, one was touching the Act of Supreme Head, and the other this deponent could not hear." Then said his master that the council bore him in hand that they purposed to ask him two questions, of which one was whether he would accept the king as Supreme Head, "and I remember no such thing." Nor I neither, said this deponent then. But a while after he came to his master as he was saying evensong and said, Yes, that he had

---

[5] Thomas Bedyll was clerk to the council: he was one of Cromwell's dependable agents and had been closely concerned with the action against the Carthusians. Their attitude and that of John Fisher must have been beyond the comprehension of his plodding mind.

answered that he did not think the king might be Supreme Head, but his master denied having said so. The next day he remarked to his master that he had been a long time with the council yesterday.

These two answers call for careful study. Had John Fisher denied the king's new title before these councillors, they would have got what they wanted—evidence for a conviction under the Act of Treasons. The fact that they examined Wilson on this point at such length shows that they had not got what they wanted, and they hoped that the servant could report the kind of denial that was essential in order to bring John Fisher to trial.

The Indictment—to which further reference will be made—states that on 7th May John Fisher had made such a denial. If it was not before the council (and he was convinced he had not done so), to whom was it made? The answer lies in an important passage in William Rastell's account.[6] Having failed to get the incriminating evidence by a frontal attack, an indirect method was used.

> The king, then, knowing how this bishop so behaved himself in talk and communication, that none of his crafty councillors could get him in a trip [slip of the tongue] to speak directly on the one side or the other in this matter of the supremacy, he and his devilish devisors invented then a farther fetch [trick]

---

[6] *Harpsfield*, pp. 232-5. This incident is not accepted by *Ortroy* (p. 325 n.) and is doubted by Bridgett and Gairdner. This is a formidable body of opinion. Chambers, in a long and carefully reasoned note (Harpsfield, pp. 363-8) makes a good case for accepting Rastell's account, and I am inclined to agree with him. Father Philip Hughes (Clergy Review, May 1935, p. 416) considered Chambers' reasoning to be convincing. Pollard (art. "Richard Rich" in D.N.B.) accepted Rastell's account of this incident and of its use in the trial.

which was this: he on the 7 May sent one of his subtle councilors to this bishop in the Tower again with a very secret message from the king which ye shall hear.

"The king," quoth this mischievous messenger to this blessed bishop, "hath sent me, his trusty councillor and servant to your lordship with a very secret message; that is, that I should deliver unto you from his highness, on his behalf, that albeit all the bishops of this realm except yourself, and all the clergy also, except very few, and all the whole Parliament, as well Lords as Commons, have agreed and granted to his supremacy, yet his majesty, for the satisfaction of his own conscience is marvellous desirous to know your lordship's opinion thereon, because he assuredly, by great and long experience, hath known your lordship and esteemeth you no less than you be indeed, that man that, as well for your person as for your godly virtue and pure conscience are one of the chief flowers of the realm this day living, and so fully known, reputed and taken, not only within this realm but in all outward parts throughout all Christendom. Wherefore the king for this cause most heartily and most entirely requireth your good Lordship to certify him by me his sure and secret messenger, in his behalf, what your full opinion is in this matter by your conscience and learning. And further," quoth this crafty caitiff, "the king willed me truly and sincerely to assure you, and faithfully to promise you, on his honour, and the word of a prince, that whatsoever your lordship shall by me his messenger certify to be your opinion in this matter, although it be directly against the laws made for the king's Supremacy, shall there none advantage thereof be taken against your lordship, and that you shall not be impeached for your said declaration of your mind [a gap here in the manuscript]."

The bishop did not perceive that this device was laid to catch him in a snare. But thought verily that the king meant as truly and as plainly as this message and tale told by this messenger imported.

Wherefore the bishop, thinking assuredly that no manner of hurt nor harm should come unto him by sending his opinion in this matter by this messenger to the king was willing thereunto as well for that he was glad to show himself willing to do to the king his sovereign lord all such pleasure and service as he possibly could, saving his life and conscience, as for that he had some hope that the king, the rather by knowing his opinion herein, would not execute any further rigour by his new laws and statutes against any man that denied his supremacy only according to his conscience.

This bishop therefore for these causes and trusting upon the king's assured promise thus made unto him by this messenger and taking also faithful promise of this messenger that neither hurt nor harm should come unto him for disclosing his opinion and mind in this matter, and trusting also upon this messenger's oath that none should know of his answer but only the king—the bishop, I say, for these causes plainly and frankly in few words willed this messenger to certify the king from him that he believed directly in his conscience and knew by his learning precisely that it was very plain by the holy scripture, the laws of the church, the general council, and the whole faith and general practice of Christ's Catholic Church from Christ's ascension hitherto, that the king was not, nor could be, by the law of God, supreme head of the church of England.

And when the king was by this messenger ascertained that this bishop had thus plainly declared his opinion against his supremacy, then was he very glad thereof, because he had hereby some plain matter to lay to the bishop's charge, to arraign him and condemn him for speaking against his supremacy, where before this time by no means any such advantage could be caught against the bishop.

Rastell did not name "this crafty caitiff," but the early biographer wrote that it was Richard Rich, the same who tried to trap Sir Thomas More into a similar assertion.

By the end of May news had reached England that John Fisher had been created a cardinal, Clement VII died on 26th September 1534; his successor was Alessandro Farnese who took the title of Paul III. He was of the same age as John Fisher. It was on the 10th May that the pope created the imprisoned bishop, cardinal-priest of the title of St. Vitalis. When he heard of this, Sir Gregory Casale, who was Henry's agent in Rome,[7] protested that such an appointment was an insult to his king, and, at an audience with the pope, Sir Gregory (according to his own account) declared that "no greater blunder had ever been committed." The pope then explained his reasons for honouring John Fisher.

Since cardinals had to be created, he was led to choose one from England for two reasons: first,

---

[7] Henry still kept contact with Rome in the hope that the new pope might reverse his predecessor's verdict, or come to a compromise. The king's anger when Fisher was made a cardinal may have been partly due to the realization that no great change could be expected.

because he had seen letters from the most Christian king [France] in which he expressed his wish that matters could be arranged with the king of England and that satisfaction could be given him in the affair of the marriage. Hence he thought that, in creating Fisher a cardinal, he would obtain a proper agent to treat of these affairs, and would do a good thing pleasing to his majesty. Secondly, that he was thinking much of a council,[8] and since a certain constitution exacts that cardinals of all nations should be present in the council, it had seemed to him necessary to make some Englishman a cardinal. He had not Rochester in his mind more than another, but when it was said that the writings of Rochester were held in great esteem, especially in Germany and Italy, and when Campeggio and others spoke so highly of him, it appeared it would be a good thing and give pleasure to the king to make him a cardinal.[9]

A stronger reason, one that he could hardly put to Henry's own agent, was that this elevation to such a high position in the Church might lead to John Fisher's release. It was in this sense that the pope conveyed a message to Francis of France in the hope of enlisting his support. On 6th June, the Bishop of Faenza, papal nuncio in Paris, reported to Rome that,

> he had spoken at length to the French king of the pope's concern about Fisher, and begged him to use his influence with the king of England for his liberation. Francis replied that there was no need to speak of Fisher's virtues which were known to the

---

[8] Paul III was responsible for calling the Council of Trent (1545).
[9] *S.P.*, VII, p. 425.

whole world, and that no one had written better than he against the Lutherans. His holiness might be sure he would do all he could for his liberation, but he doubted his success, for he feared this [cardinal's] hat would cause him injury, according to what he had heard from England where they had been using strange measures against the Carthusians. He added that the king of England was the hardest friend to bear in the world; at one time unstable, and at another obstinate and proud, so that it was almost impossible to bear with him. "Sometimes," said Francis, "he almost treats me like a subject. In effect he is the strangest man in the world, and I fear I can do no good with him, but I must put up with him as it is no time to lose friends."[10]

Francis had had dealings with Henry for more than a quarter of a century; he knew his man; the pope did not.

It was George Gold who told John Fisher that there was a rumour that he was to be a cardinal. "Then said Mr. Fisher, 'A cardinal! Then I perceive it was not for nought that my Lord Chancellor [Audley] did ask me when I heard from my master the pope, and said there was never man that had exalted the pope as I had.'" In his own replies to an interrogatory, the bishop said, "that George aforementioned brought him word since the last sitting of the council here [the Tower] that he heard say of Mistress Roper that this respondent was made a cardinal. And then this respondent said in the presence of the same George and Wilson that 'if the cardinal's hat were laid at his feet, he would not stoop to take it up, he did set so little by it.'"[11]

---

[10] *L.P.*, VIII, no. 837.

[11] *L.P.*, VIII, no. 858.

The early biographer gives the following account.

> Whereupon shortly after the cardinal's hat was sent towards him. But when it came to Calais, it was there stayed till such time as the king was advertised thereof and his pleasure known. Who, as soon as he heard of it, sent speedily in great anger to the lord deputy commanding him in any wise to suffer it come no nearer till his further pleasure known. And immediately sent Mr. Thomas Cromwell, his secretary, to this good father in his prison to advertise him what was done, only to the intent to know what he would say to it and how he would take it. Mr. Cromwell being come into his chamber and entering into talk with him of many matters, asked at last in this manner, "My lord of Rochester, if the pope should now send you a cardinal's hat, what would you do? Would you take it?" "Sir," said he, "I know myself far unworthy of any such dignity, that I think of nothing less than such matters; but if he do send it me, assure yourself I will work with it by all means I can to benefit the church of Christ, and in that respect I will receive it on my knees." Mr. Cromwell making report afterward of this answer to the king, the king said again with great indignation and spite, "Yea, is he yet so lusty? Well, let the pope send him a hat when he will. But I will so provide that, whensoever it cometh, he shall wear it on his shoulders, for head shall he have none to see it on."[12]

The king's comment is confirmed in a letter from Chapuys to the emperor on 15th June.

---

[12] *Ortroy*, p. 311.

As soon as the king heard that the Bishop of Rochester had been created a cardinal, he declared in anger several times that he would give him another hat, and send the head afterwards to Rome for the cardinal's hat. He sent immediately to the Tower those of his council to summon again the said bishop and Master More to swear to the king as head of the church, otherwise before St. John's day (24th June) they should be executed as traitors. But it has been impossible to gain them, either by promises or threats, and it is believed they will soon be executed. But as they are persons of unequalled reputation in this kingdom, the king, to appease the murmurs of the world, has already on Sunday last caused preachers to preach against them in most of the churches here, and this will be continued next Sunday. And although there is no lawful occasion to put them to death, the king is seeking if anything can be found against them, especially if the said bishop has made suit for the hat. To find out which, several persons have been arrested both of his kinsmen and of those who live in the prison.[13]

If further confirmation were needed of the king's wrath, it is found in the immediate proceedings taken against John Fisher.

---

[13] *L.P.*, VIII, no. 876. Edward White was a kinsman; the others arrested were the servants.

CHAPTER XXVII
INTERROGATIONS

JOHN FISHER and Sir Thomas More did not meet in the Tower, but were kept rigorously apart. Each must have been often in the thoughts and prayers of the other; each must have wondered how the other fared in the interrogations they both had to suffer. They managed to pass a few notes; one was intercepted and sent to the council, and in consequence the servants were subjected to a searching examination. Sir Thomas More said later that he regretted the notes had been burned, for had they been produced, the council would have seen that they contained nothing incriminating.

Those questioned on 11th June[1] were Richard Wilson, servant to "Mr. Fisher, doctor of divinity, late bishop of Rochester," John a Wood, servant to Sir Thomas More, George Gold, servant to the lieutenant of the Tower (Sir Edmund Walsingham), John Pewnoll, falconer at Rochester, William Thorneton of Thames Street who supplied the bishop's food, and Edward White, brother-in-law to John Fisher.

The councillors were intent on getting information on two points:

1. *Had anything been written or said against the Supremacy, or on the "king's matter"?*
   This might provide the essential evidence against either or both prisoners.

---

[1] The answers take up nearly six pages in *L.P.*, vol. VIII, no. 856; fifty-four questions were asked. Some of the information has been used in the previous chapter.

2. *Had John Fisher had any correspondence with Rome about his being created a cardinal?*
If there had been such letters, he would have come under the new laws.

Richard Wilson had to undergo the longest examination. As we have seen, William Rastell called him a "false knave," but the early biographer noted that "he was very closely shut up also and terribly threatened to be hanged.'"[2] Neither he, nor any of the other servants revealed anything to the purpose of the councillors; there was, in fact, nothing incriminating to be revealed. Subsequent separate interrogations of John Fisher and Sir Thomas More bore out the substantial truth of the servants' answers.

John Fisher was questioned on 12th June by Thomas Bedyll and Richard Layton.[3] His answers were written down and each page bears his signature.[4] The questions have not been preserved so some of the answers cannot be fully understood, but those that are important are given here.

> When the Act by the which words were made treason was a-making Robert Fisher his brother came to him to the Tower and said that there was an Act in hand in the Common House by the which speaking of certain words against the king should be made treason.

---

[2] *Ortroy*, p. 293. The Latin version adds that after his master's execution, Wilson fled to the Low Countries and became a priest.

[3] He was to be Thomas Cromwell's most unsavoury agent in the suppression of the monasteries. When Dean of York he pawned the Minster plate.

[4] *L.P.*, VIII, no. 858 summarizes the answers; they are here given in full.

And because it was thought by divers of the said house that no man lightly could beware of the penalty of the said statute, therefore there was much sticking at the same in the Common House, and unless there were added in the same that the said words should be spoken maliciously, he thought the same should not pass. And then this respondent asked him whether men should be bound to make any answer to any point upon an oath by the virtue of the same Act, like as they were by the other Act of Succession. And he said, No.[5]

There hath been letters sent between him and Master More to and fro upon four or thereabouts from either of them to other, since they came to the Tower, touching the matters specified in these interrogatories. And, declaring the contents and effect of the same as far as he can remember, saith, that he remembered not the effect of any of the letters that either he sent to Master More, or that he received of Master More before the first being of the council here with this examined, but he doth well remember that there were letters sent to and fro between him and Master More before that time. And the first occasion of writing between them proceeded first of Master More, and now being better remembered, saith, that the effect of the first letter that Master More did write unto him after they came to the Tower was to know the effect of this deponent's answer which he had made to the council in the matter for the which he was first committed to the Tower. And then this respondent signified unto him by his letters what answer he had

---

[5] See above, p. 256, for Wilson's version: he put the talk between the brothers at too late a date; it must have been in November or December 1534 when Parliament was sitting.

made them. Examined whether he doth remember the effect of any other letters that went between him and Master More before the first being of the council with them saith, No. And further examined what letters went between them since that time saith, that soon after that the council had been here first to examine this respondent, George, Master Lieutenant's servant, showed this examined a letter which Master More had addressed to his daughter Mistress Roper, the effect whereof was this, that when the council had purposed[6] unto him the matter for the which they came for, he said that he would not dispute the king's title, and that Master Secretary gave him good words at his departure;[7] and that is all he can remember of the effect of the same letter. And by the occasion of that letter this respondent wrote to Master More a letter to know a more clearness of his answer therein, which letter he did send him by the said George. And thereupon he received a letter again from the said Master More by the hands of the said George concerning his answer, but what the same was, he saith, he hath not in remembrance. And after a deliberate time, about a three or four days, this respondent calling to his remembrance the words that his brother Robert Fisher had spoken unto him long before, viz., how that the Commons did stick and would not suffer the said statute to pass unless the word *maliciously* were put in it, wrote a letter containing the same words in effect, adding this, that "if this word *maliciously* were put in the said statute,

---

[6] "Purpose" here and later is the earlier form of "propose".

[7] Perhaps *Rogers*, no. 210, where mention is made of "master secretary's great good mind and favour towards me"; not dated, but probably autumn of 1534.

he thought it should be no danger if a man did answer to the question that was purposed unto him by the council after his own mind, so that he did not the same *maliciously.*" But, he saith, he nothing required or demanded in the said letters the advice or counsel of Master More therein, as he is sure that the same Master More himself would testify if he be examined. And thereupon, as this deponent thinketh, Master More supposing that this respondent's answer and his should be very nigh and like and that the council thereby would think that the tone of them had taken light of the other, would, that the same suspicion should be avoided, and thereupon wrote a letter to this respondent accordingly.

Soon after the taking away of Master More's books from him, the said George came to this deponent and told him that Master More was in a peck of troubles, and that he desired to have either by writing or by word of mouth certain knowledge what answer this respondent had made to the council. And thereupon this respondent wrote unto him a letter that "he had made his answer according to the statute which condemneth no man but him that speaketh maliciously against the king's title. And that the statute did compel no man to answer the question that was purposed him, and that he besought them that he should not be constrained to make further or other answer than the said statute did bind him but would suffer him to enjoy the benefits of the same statute." Which was all the effect of the said letter as far as this deponent doth remember.

They [the letters] were all burned as soon as he read them and to the intent that the effects thereof should have been kept secret if it might be. For he was loth to be reproved of his promise made to Master Lieutenant that he would not do that thing for which he might be put to blame. Albeit, if that there were more in the said letters than is before touched, he is sure it is nothing else but exhortation either of other to take patience in their adversity, and to call God for grace, and praying for their enemies, and nothing else that should hurt or offend any man earthly, as he saith.

There was certain communication between Wilson and him about the time they read the said statute, and saith that he threppened [maintained obstinately] upon this respondent that the council had purposed unto this respondent two points, and this respondent said, that he remembered not that it was but one which was this, how the council was sent hither to know his opinion touching the statute of Supreme Head, and no other did he remember that they should purpose unto him. And said further, that Wilson said, that he stood behind the door and heard partly what this respondent did answer unto them, and how he heard Mr. Bedyll's reasons that he made then.

After that the said Wilson had read the said statutes to this respondent once or twice, this respondent caused them to be burned because he thought that if Master Lieutenant had found them with this examinant he would have made much business thereupon.

He saith that he doth not remember that ever he declared to Wilson or to any man what an answer he was disposed to make, whatsoever communication were between them thereof.

He received no such letters[8] to his knowledge or remembrance but one that Erasmus did send unto him, which this respondent's brother Robert Fisher showed first to Master Secretary ere it came to him.

Then follows the answer concerning how he heard the news of his being made a cardinal. This has already been quoted. He was next asked, judging from the answers, if he had had any letters bout his appointment. To this he gave a brief denial.

He wrote oftentimes letters touching his diet to him that provided his diet, as to Robert Fisher while he lived, and to Edward White, and a letter to my Lady of Oxford[9] for her comfort, and letters of request to certain of his friends that he might pay Master Lieutenant for his diet, to whom he was in great debt, and he was in great need. He received certain money of each of them according to his request, and no other answer, as he saith.

Examined whether there were any such confederacy or compaction between this respondent and his servant Wilson and the said George that said conveying of letters and messages to and fro should be kept close if they were examined thereof, saith, they were agreed so together to keep the same as secret as they might.

---

[8] For lack of the question it is not known what kind of letters were meant—perhaps letters from friends. A letter from Erasmus would certainly be welcomed by the prisoner; unfortunately it has not been preserved.

[9] It has not been possible to trace a connexion here. The Earl of Oxford was a strong supporter of the king.

These answers are of interest not only for the information they give, but also for the light they throw on John Fisher himself. The straightforwardness of the replies and the care he took not to go beyond the facts are in keeping with what we know of his character. What may be regarded as his simplicity of outlook, even guilelessness, is shown in his frank explanations of the deceptions practised on the lieutenant of the Tower and the scruples he had while doing so. Even the councillors must have seen that their prisoner had not even the elements of a conspirator in his nature.

It was probably about this time that John Gostwick, the Receiver for First-Fruits (and other things), went down to Rochester to make the final arrangements for the disposal of the bishop's possessions. The story is told by the early biographer.

> These commissioners being come to Rochester, according to their commission, entered his house and first turned out all his servants. Then they fell to rifling his goods, whereof some part was taken to the king's use, but more was embezzled to the uses of themselves and their servants. Then they came to his library of books which they spoiled in most pitiful wise, scattering them in such sort as it was lamentable to behold. For it was replenished with such and so many kind of books as the like was scant to be found again in the possession of one private man in Christendom. And of them they trussed up thirty-two great pipes (casks),[10] beside a number that were stolen away. And whereas many years before he had made a deed of a gift of all those books and other household stuff to the college of St. John's in Cambridge, the poor

---

[10] Each of over 100 gallons.

college was now defrauded of their gift and all was turned another way. And where likewise a sum of money of three hundred pounds was given by one of his predecessors, a Bishop of Rochester, to remain for ever to the said see of Rochester in custody of the bishop of the time being for any sudden occasion that might mischance to the bishoprick, the same sum of £300 with a hundred more laid to it, was found in his gallery locked in a chest and from thence carried clean away by the commissioners.

Among all other things found in his house I cannot omit to tell you of a coffer standing in his oratory, where commonly no man came but himself alone, for it was his secret place of prayer. This coffer being surely locked and standing always so near him, every man began to think that some great treasure was there stored up. Wherefore because no collusion or falsehood should be used to defraud the king in so great charge as this was thought to be, witnesses were solemnly called to be present and so the coffer was broken up before them. But, when it was open, they found within it, instead of gold and silver which they looked for, a shirt of hair and two or three whips wherewith he used full often to punish himself, as some of his chaplains and servants would report that were there about him and curiously marked his doings. And other treasure than that found they none. But when report was made to him in his prison of the opening of that coffer, he was very sorry for it and said that, if haste had not made him to forget that and many things else, they should not have found it there at that time.[11]

---

[11] *Ortroy*, p. 316.

The early biographer mentions three times the theft of the St. John's College library. We can share his indignation for in this barbarous fashion one of the finest collections of books in the country was looted and dispersed—a crime that was to be repeated untold times during the next decade.

CHAPTER XXVIII
THE TRIAL

ON 1st June 1535 a special commission was appointed to try cases under the Act of Treasons. The Lord Chancellor (Sir Thomas Audley) had as his colleagues, the Duke of Suffolk (the king's brother-in-law), Henry Courtenay, Marquis of Exeter (beheaded 1538), Thomas Manners, Earl of Rutland, Henry de Clifford, Earl of Cumberland, Thomas Boleyn, Earl of Wiltshire (father of Anne Boleyn), Thomas Cromwell (beheaded, 1540), William Paulet, later Marquis of Winchester, Sir John Fitzjames (Chief Justice), and several of the judges.[1]

The first case before them was tried on 11th June when the three young Carthusians, Humphrey Middlemore, William Exmewe, and Sebastian Newdigate were condemned. They were executed at Tyburn on 19th June.

On 4th June, Thomas Bedyll with three others saw John Fisher in the Tower and put to him three questions; these are here given with the answers.

1. Whether he would obey the king as Supreme Head of the Church of England?
    He stands by the answer he made at his first examination, but will write with his own hand at length.[2]

---

[1] *L.P.*, VIII, no. 856.

[2] No such statement has been preserved.

2. Whether he will acknowledge the king's marriage with Queen Anne to be lawful, and that with the Lady Catherine invalid?
He would obey and swear to the Act of Succession, but desires to be pardoned answering this interrogatory absolutely.

3. For what cause he would not answer resolutely to the said interrogatories?
He desires not to be driven to answer, lest he fall in danger of the statutes.[3]

Sir Thomas More was questioned on the same day. To three questions similar to those put to John Fisher, he declined giving any answer. He was also asked about the letters that had passed between them.

Had written divers scrolls or letters since then [i.e. since coming to the Tower] to Dr. Fisher, and received others from him, containing for the most part nothing but comfortable words and thanks for meat and drink sent by one to the other. But about a quarter of a year after his coming to the Tower he wrote to Fisher saying he had refused the oath of succession, and never intended to tell the council why; and Fisher made him answer showing how he had not refused to swear to the succession. No other letters passed between them touching the king's affairs till the council came to examine this deponent upon the Act of Supreme Head; but after his examination he received a letter of Fisher desiring to know his answer. Replied by another letter stating that he meant not to

---
[3] *L.P.*, VIII, 867.

meddle, but to fix his mind on the passion of Christ; or that his answer was to that effect. He afterwards received another letter from Fisher stating that he was informed the word maliciously was used in the statute, and suggesting that, therefore, a man who spoke nothing of malice did not offend the statute. He replied that he agreed with Fisher, but feared it would not be so interpreted. Did not report to Fisher his answer to the council with the advice to make his answer different lest the council should suspect confederacy between them. After his last examination sent Fisher word by letter that Master Solicitor [Sir Richard Rich] had informed him it was all one not to answer and to say against the statute what a man would, as all the learned men of England would justify. He therefore said he could only reckon on the uttermost, and desired Fisher to pray for him as he would for Fisher.[4]

This answer must have proved a disappointment to the councillors.

On 17th June John Fisher was brought to trial. The indictment was that he "did on the 7th day of May in the 27th year of the said king's reign at the Tower of London, in the County of Middlesex, contrary to his allegiance, falsely, maliciously, and traitorously speak and utter these words in English to divers of his majesty's faithful subjects, viz., the king our sovereign lord is not supreme head in earth of the Church of England."[5]

There is no official record of the trial comparable with the records of the trial of Sir Thomas More. William Rastell's account is the only one of any substance. The

---

[4] *L.P.*, VIII, no. 867.

[5] *L.P.*, VIII, no. 886.

early biographer used it but had nothing of moment to add.

Rastell first described the journey from the Tower to Westminster Hall. His account is given here in full.

> He was the seventeenth day of June, being Thursday, in the year of our Lord God 1535 and in the seven and twenty year of Henry 8, with a great number of bills, and glaives and halberts and the axe of the Tower borne before him, the edge from him, brought from the Tower of London, part by horseback, part by water, because he was yet so little recovered of his feebleness and infirmity that he was not able to walk or go any thing, to the court of the King's Bench in Westminster Hall before divers of them that were appointed by the king commissioners for this matter.

After giving lists of the commissioners and of the jury, Rastell continues.

> Then came forth for witness against him only he that had been . . . the messenger from the king to this bishop in the Tower, who there openly before the judges and the jury and the whole presence, where were a great number of people gathered to see this woeful tragedy, deposed upon a book that the bishop had by plain and express words declared unto him in the Tower that he knew by his learning and believed in his conscience that the king was not, nor could be, supreme head in earth of the church of England.
> And when this bishop heard this mischievous man depose this, he said unto him, "Sir, I will not deny that I so said to you, but for all my so saying I committed no treason. For upon what occasion I so said, and for

what cause, you yourself know right well." And thereupon the bishop declared openly, not only the message that this man came with to him in the Tower from the king, but also all their communication and talk, and further the earnest and assured promise that this messenger made unto him on the king's behalf with also his own solemn oath that he would utter the answer to none but to the king . . . "Now, my lords," quoth the bishop, "what a monstrous matter is this, to lay now to my charge as treason the thing which I spake not until then; besides this man's oath, I had as full and as sure a promise from the king by this his trusty and sure messenger as the king could make me by word of mouth, that I should never be impeached nor hurt by mine answer that I should send unto him by this his messenger, which I would never have spoken had it not been in trust of my prince's promise and of my true and loving heart towards him, my natural liege lord, in satisfying him with declaration of mine opinion and conscience in this matter, as he earnestly required me by this messenger to signify plainly unto him."

Whereunto this shameless beast, this mischievous messenger, said that true it was that he declared unto him that message from the king and by the king's commandment made him that assured and faithful promise from the king, and sware unto him also as he had said. "But all this," quoth this wicked witness, "do not discharge you any wit."

"O my lords," quoth the bishop, to his judges, "How can this only testimony burden me, that ought, as the case standeth by all equity, all justice, all worldly honesty, and all civil humanity, to be no wit charged here withal, though in my so doing I had committed treason? And besides this the very statute that maketh the speaking against the king's supremacy treason, is only and precisely limited where such speech is spoken maliciously. And now all ye, my lords," quoth he, "perceive plainly that in my uttering and signifying unto the king of mine opinion and conscience, as touching this his claim of supremacy in the church of England, in such sort as I did, as ye have heard, there was no manner of malice in me at all, and so I committed no treason."

To this was it answered to the bishop by some of his judges, utterly devoid of worldly shame, and affirmed by some of the residue, both that the word maliciously in the statute was of none effect, for that none could speak against the king's supremacy by any manner of means but that the speaking against it was treason; and also that message or promise to him from the king himself neither could, nor did, by rigour of our law in any wise discharge him, but that in so declaring his mind and conscience against the king's supremacy, though it were even at the king's own commandment and request, he by the statute committed treason, and nothing might discharge him now of the cruel penalty of death appointed by the statute for speaking against the king's supremacy, howsoever the words were spoken, but only the king's pardon, if it would please his grace, to grant it him.

Upon this point and only by this witness of the king's own messenger sent to the bishop were the twelve men charged to find the holy, learned bishop guilty of treason. But before the inquest of twelve men went from the bar to agree upon their verdict, there was laid to the bishop's charge by some of his judges, high pride and great presumption, that he and a few

THE TRIAL

other did dissent and vary in this matter of the king's supremacy from the whole number of the bishops, lords, learned men and commons, gathered together in the Parliament with divers other things. Unto all which he answered in effect as the holy fathers Carthusians and Doctor Reynolds had done, wherein he showed himself excellently and profoundly learned, of great constancy and of a marvellous godly courage, and declared the whole matter so learnedly and therewith so godly, that it made many of them there present, and some of their judges also, so inwardly to lament, that their eyes burst out with tears to see such a great famous clerk and virtuous bishop to be condemned to so cruel a death by such impious laws and by such an unlawful and detestable witness, contrary to all human honesty and fidelity and the word and promise of the king himself.

But pity, mercy, equity, nor justice had there no place. For the twelve men gave their verdict that he was guilty of treason, which they did by the persuasion and threats of some of his judges and of the king's learned counsel.

The verdict was to be expected; indeed it had been assumed. He was condemned to be hanged, drawn and quartered. So he returned to the Tower.

Rastell continued:

> When this cruel judgment was thus given against him at Westminster Hall, he was, part on horseback and part by foot, from thence conveyed again to the Tower of London with a great number of officers and men bearing halberds and weapons about him and before him and behind him, with the axe of the Tower

borne all the way before him, the edge towards him, as the fashion is in England when any condemned of treason is brought from judgment.

And when he came to the Tower gate, he turned him unto those that thus had brought him from the Tower to Westminster and from thence to the Tower again, and said unto them, "I thank you, masters all, for the pains ye have taken this day in going and coming from hence to Westminster and hither again." And this spake he with so lusty a courage and so amiable a countenance and his colour so well come to him as though he had come from a great and honourable feast. And his gesture and his behaviour showed such a certain inward gladness in his heart that any man might easily see that he joyously longed and looked for the bliss and joys of heaven, and that he inwardly rejoiced that he was so near unto his death for Christ's cause.[6]

Did Sir Thomas More witness the return of his fellow prisoner? Or that last journey to the block five days later? We do not know. His own trial was delayed for a fortnight; was it in the hope that, even yet, the knowledge of the fate of John Fisher might shake his resolution? Rather it must have brought him an access of grace to face what lay before him.

---

[6] *Harpsfield*, pp. 236-42. Chapuys said that "he was followed by a crowd of men and women in great grief who demanded his blessing when he crossed the water [the moat of the Tower]." *L.P.*, VIII, no. 1075.

CHAPTER XXIX
THE MARTYRDOM

WILLIAM RASTELL was present at the execution of John Fisher on 22nd June; his testimony is therefore of primary importance, and is best given in his own words rather than in the expanded version of the early biographer.

> For he thus being brought again to the Tower, and there remaining four days in his old prison, very feeble and sickly of body, but of constant courage and lusty heart, glad to die for the truth of Christ's Catholic faith. The twenty-second day of June next following, being Tuesday and the day of St. Alban, the first martyr of England, and the day before the even of the Nativity of St. John Baptist, about five a'clock in the morning, the Lieutenant of the Tower came to this holy man in his chamber, yet in his bed asleep and waked him, and showed him that he was come to him with a message from the king. And after some circumstance unto him used, with persuasion to remember that for age he could not long live, and therefore ought the rather to be content to die, he told him that the king's pleasure was that he should suffer in that forenoon.
> "Well," quoth the bishop, "if this be your errand hither, it is no news unto me; I have looked daily for it. I pray you, what is it a'clock?"
> "It is," quoth the Lieutenant, "about five."
> "What time," quoth the bishop, "must be mine hour to go out hence?"

"About ten of the clock," said the Lieutenant.

"Well, then," quoth the bishop, "I pray you, let me sleep an hour or twain. For I may say to you, I slept not much this night, not for fear of death, I tell you, but by reason of my great sickness and weakness."[7]

With which answer the Lieutenant departed from him till about nine a'clock. At which time he came again to the bishop's chamber, and found him upward, putting on his clothes, and showed him that he was come for him.

"Well," quoth the bishop, "I will make as convenient haste as my weak and sickly body will give me leave. And I pray you, reach me there my furred tippet to put about my neck."

"O, my lord," quoth the Lieutenant to him, "what need you be now so careful of your health? Your time is short, little more than half an hour."

"I think none otherwise," quoth the bishop, "but, I pray you, yet give me leave to put on my furred tippet, to keep me warm for the while until the very time of execution; for I tell you the truth, though I have, I thank our Lord, a very good stomach and willing mind to die at this present, and I trust in his goodness and mercy, he will still continue it and increase it, yet will I not hinder my health in the mean time not a minute of an hour, but will preserve it in the mean season with all such discreet ways and means as Almighty God of his gracious goodness hath provided for me."

It is not known when the king remitted the most savage part of the sentence and decided that John Fisher should be beheaded and not hanged, drawn and quartered. One tradition says that he was not told until the very

---

[7] Stapleton records that he "had asked for milk for his breakfast."

morning of his execution. It was believed that this change was made because it was feared that if he were dragged on a hurdle at the heels of a horse the four miles to Tyburn, he would have died on the way. The king, as we shall see, took great credit to himself for this act of mercy.

At this point in the narrative the early biographer added the detail that, before he left his cell, "taking a little book in his hand, which was a New Testament lying by him, he made a cross on his forehead and went out by the prison door with the Lieutenant, being so weak, that he was scant able to go down the stairs."

William Rastell's version varies a little.

> Then was he carried down out of his chamber between twain in a chair, and so to the Tower gate, where he being delivered to the sheriffs of London,[8] he was with a great company of halberds, bills and glaives, carried in a chair by four of the sheriffs' officers, the sheriffs riding next after him, from thence not far off to a plain besides the Tower of London commonly called Tower Hill, otherwise called East Smithfield, where he was brought near to the scaffold on which he should be beheaded.

The early biographer adds an account of an incident that is confirmed from other sources.[9]

> And as they were come to the uttermost precinct or liberty of the Tower, they rested there with him a space, till such time as one was sent before to know in what readiness the sheriffs were to receive him.

---

[8] Humphrey Monmouth, patron of Tyndale; and, John Cotes, Mayor, 1542-3.

[9] Such as *L.P.*, VIII, no. 985.

During which space he rose out of his chair, and standing on his feet, leaned his shoulder to the wall, and lifting his eyes up towards heaven, he opened his little book [N.T.] in his hand and said, "O Lord, this is the last time that ever I shall open this book. Let some comfortable place now chance me whereby I, thy poor servant, may glorify thee in this my last hour." And with that looking into the book, the first thing that came to his sight were these words: *Haec est autem vita ceterna ut cognoscant te solum verum Deum et quem misisti Iesum Christum. Ego te ciarificavi super terram, opus consummavi quod dedisti mihi ut faciam et nunc clarifica me tu, Pater, apud temetipsum, claritate quam habui priusquam,* etc. And with that he shut the book together and said, "Here is even learning enough for me to my life's end."[10]

As William Rastell was in the crowd round the scaffold, he would not be a witness of this delay, but his reference to the time of the execution shows that there had been such a delay lasting the best part of an hour. His account continues:

And when he came to the foot of the scaffold, they that carried him would have helped him up the stairs of the scaffold. But then he said unto them, "Nay, masters now let me alone, ye shall see me go up to my death well enough myself; without help." And so went up the scaffold stairs without help, to no little marvel of them that knew his weakness and debility by reason of his age and infirmity.[11]

---

[10] *Ortroy,* p. 340.

[11] Stapleton adds the detail that he cast aside "the staff of his old age."

THE MARTYRDOM 379

And when he came up upon the scaffold, which was about eleven of the clock, he that should behead him, came unto him, as the fashion is, and kneeled unto him, and prayed him to forgive him his death. To whom the blessed bishop answered, with a bold courage and a loving cheer, that he forgave him heartily, and said, "I trust on our Lord thou shalt see me die even lustily."

Then was his gown taken off from him and his tippet, and he stood up there in the sight of the people (where was a wondrous number of people gathered to see this horrible execution, of which myself was one a long, lean, slender body nothing in manner but skin and bare bones, so that the most part that there saw him marvelled to see any man bearing life, to be so far consumed, for he seemed a lean body carcase, the flesh clean wasted away and a very image of death, and, as one might say, death in a man's shape, and using a man's voice. And therefore more monstrous was it that the king or any man could be so cruel to put such a man to death, yea, though he had been an offender, for very shortly he must have died by nature. And surely, I think, if he had been in the great Turk's land, and guilty of a great trespass there, he would never for pity have put him to death, being already so near the pit's brink. For it is the most cruel thing that can be, to put any to death that is presently dying. Wherefore in this point I think that this King Henry passed all the Turks or Tyrants that ever was read or heard of.

When this holy, innocent bishop, with his deadly carcass, stood up thus on the scaffold, then spake he to the people in effect as follows, "Christian people, I am come hither to die for the faith of Christ's Catholic Church. And I thank God, hitherto my stomach hash served me well thereto, so that yet hitherto I have not feared death. Wherefore I desire you help me, and assist me with your prayers, that at the very point and instant of my death's stroke, and in the very moment of my death, I then faint not in any point of the catholic faith for any fear. And I pray God save the king and the realm, and hold his holy hand over it, and send the king a good counsel."

These words, or words of like effect, he then spake with a cheerful countenance and with such a stout and constant courage as one no wit afraid but glad to suffer death. And these words spake he so distinctly and perceivably and also with such a strong and very loud voice that it made all the people astonished, and noted it in a manner as a miracle to hear so plain, strong and loud a voice come out of so old, weak and sickly a carcass; for the youngest, strongest, and healthfulest man there present could not have spoken stronglier, louder, plainer, nor better to be perceived.

Then after these few words, or the like, spoken by him, he kneeled down on both his knees and said certain prayers, and as some reported, he said then the psalm or canticle *Te deum laudamus*, etc., to the end, and *In te domine speravi, non confundar in æternum*. Then was he blindfolded with an handkerchief about his eyes. And then, lifting up his hands and heart devoutly towards heaven, he said a few prayers, which were not long, but fervently devout. Which done, he laid him down on his belly, flat on the floor of the scaffold, and laid his lean neck upon a little block, so that his body was on the one side of the block and his head on the other side, so that his neck was just upon the middle of the block. And then came quickly the executioner and with a sharp and heavy axe cut asunder his neck, and so severed the head from the body, his holy soul departing to the bliss of heaven.

* * *

Then took the executioner away his bishop's clothes and his shirt and left the headless body lying there naked upon the scaffold almost all day after. Yet one[12] at last for pity and humanity cast a little straw upon the dead body's privities. And about eight a'clock in the evening commandment was come to bury the body to certain men that tarried there about the scaffold with the body all that afternoon with halberds and bills. Whereupon one of them took up the dead body without the head upon his halberd and carried it to a churchyard of a parish church there hard by called Barking,[13] where, on the north side of that church wall, he and his fellows with their halberds digged a grave (for other grave had he none but this that they digged with their halberds) and therein without any reverence, they vilely threw this holy, innocent bishop's dead body, all naked, flat upon his belly, without any winding sheet or any other accustomed funeral ceremonies, and then covered it quickly with the earth, and so, following herein the commandment of the king, buried it very contemptuously.[14]

---

[12] Was this William Rastell?

[13] All Hallows, Barking.

[14] *Harpsfield*, pp. 242-246. The place of the first burial is confirmed in Grey Friar's Chronicle (Camden Society), p. 38. It seems likely that the remains of the two saints were not disturbed in later reconstructions of St. Peter ad Vincula.

*   *   *

The head was parboiled and set up on London Bridge where the heads of the young Carthusians were already exposed. It was said that people marvelled that the head remained "very fresh and lively," and, because of this, it was thrown into the Thames a fortnight later. It then made place for the head of a fellow martyr, Sir Thomas More, who was executed on 6th July. His body was buried at the belfry end of the chapel of St. Peter ad Vincula within the Tower. John Fisher's remains were brought from the churchyard of All Hallows and reburied in the same resting place. This was probably done because the place of his unprovided burial was already drawing many who wished to pay tribute to the memory of the dead bishop.

The dust of the two saints is united.

CHAPTER XXX
FOUR HUNDRED YEARS

THE fate of the tomb of John Fisher is but one example of the systematic attempt to obliterate his memory. He had prepared for his burial in the chapel of St. John's College, but after his death the Fellows of the College were not able to carry out his wishes. In 1773 the slabs of limestone prepared for the tomb were discovered when rubbish was being cleared out of a disused chapel; the partly executed design followed that of Torregiano's tomb for the Lady Margaret in Westminster Abbey; the recumbent figure had not been carved.

The stall ends of the choir in the chapel had carved on them a fish with an ear of wheat in its mouth[1]; by Thomas Cromwell's orders (he was the new chancellor of the University) these were defaced, as well as the inscription that was above the intended Fisher Chapel: *Faciam vos Piscatores hominum.*

These were minor steps in the vilification of the dead bishop.

On 25th June 1535 a circular[2] was issued in the name of the king instructing the bishops to cause their clergy to preach in support of the title of Supreme Head; they were also ordered to erase the "Bishop of Rome's" name from all service books, and "to set forth the treasons of the late Bishop of Rochester and Sir Thomas More." It will be noted that this was a week before the trial of Thomas

---

[1] See title-page.
[2] *L.P.*, VIII, no. 921.

More. Letters from some of the bishops have been preserved showing that they hastened to carry out the royal will.

Then, early in December, a proclamation was issued to suppress "specially one book imprinted comprising a sermon made by John Fisher late Bishop of Rochester, who according to the laws of this realm was justly attainted and convicted of divers and sundry manifest and detestable high treasons." All copies were to be surrendered within forty days. This too was quickly enforced; thus on 15th December the Court of Aldermen of the City of London resolved that "the proclamation last made concerning a sermon made by John Fisher late Bishop of Rochester, in derogation and diminution of the royal estate of the king's majesty, shall be put in print so that every parish may have one of them to be openly published by the curate in the pulpit upon Sunday next and the same after to be fixed to tables [boards] and set up upon their several churches at the costs of the churchwardens of their several parishes."[3]

The sermon referred to was probably the one preached by John Fisher early in June 1532,[4] though there may have been a later one not recorded; so effective was this interdiction that not a copy has survived.

The strong hand of the king and the vigilance of Thomas Cromwell were sufficient to drive into silence any who would have spoken in praise of the two martyrs in their own country. The problem of how to satisfy foreign criticism was more troublesome. England was in no condition to face attack; discontent within the country and also in Scotland and Wales might encourage a foreign adventurer, and there was the possibility that Francis or

---

[3] *Repertory*, 3, fo. 145.

[4] See above, p. 258.

Charles might seize the opportunity for intervention. Henry's safety lay in the fact that each monarch was too busy watching the other to take risks; but Henry could not be sure of that, and the speedy denunciation issued by the pope was at the same time an encouragement to such a venture.

It was impossible to ignore the dismay and horror expressed on the Continent at the execution of a cardinal of the Church, and of a former Lord Chancellor whose name was honoured by the learned throughout Europe. One expression of that feeling may be taken as typical of innumerable tributes. It came fittingly from Erasmus. In a letter dated 31st August he wrote, "You will learn from a letter which I enclose the fate of Thomas More and the Bishop of Rochester. They were the wisest and most saintly men that England had."[5]

In a special consistory the cardinals in Rome expressed their abhorrence, and the pope at once wrote to Ferdinand of Hungary (King of the Romans), and to Francis of France to implore them to execute justice on the king of England. A passage from the letter to the king of France reveals the pope's deep feeling.

> But as for us, my son, and for this Holy See, what shall we first mourn in such a wound of the universal church? The innocence and holiness of that man, or his learning, both famous and spread throughout the whole world, for the defence of the Catholic faith? The dignity both of a bishop and of a cardinal, violated with the same stroke of the sword? The kind and cause of his death? The kind of death, indeed, in itself cruel, and suited to culprits and criminals, which was meted out to the most holy man? All those for certain

---

[5] *Allen*, XI, no. 3049.

we must bewail, but the cause of his death is most to be lamented, since this most holy man laid down his life for God, for the Catholic religion, for justice, for truth, while he was defending not merely the particular rights of one man alone, as Thomas of Canterbury formerly did, but the truth preserved by the universal church.[6]

A direct reply to this was written by Stephen Gardiner. Much of this answer is contemptible scoffing. There is not a sentence that attempts to justify Henry's action. In his letter the pope referred to the cruel way in which John Fisher had been put to death. Gardiner made much of this comment which was probably based on the terms of the sentence.

And amongst other things this is to be laughed at, that this Holy See in the number of his lamentations maketh mention of the kind of his death, the which of truth, in that bitter choice (when a man must needs die) was the most easy, and as the case required, most noble, and such as, taking away the natural fear of death, had very little feeling, or any pain .. he was not burned, he was not put to death with lingering torments, but lost his life with a sudden stroke of a sword, the which sort of death in such bitterness is easiest.

Why, Gardiner asked, had not the pope shown his anxiety earlier and tried to get the prisoner released? Why all this fuss now about the death of a traitor?

---

[6] Gardiner, *Obedience in Church and State*, etc., ed. P. Janelle (1930), p. 13. Gardiner's reply is given on pp. 22-65.

> In time past, when Rochester did write many things against the adversaries of that See and in his own country lived without giving occasion for complaint, he then lived miserably at home, like a man unknown and little spoken of, and then this was allowed for good reason, of that Holy See, "What have we to do with these rude and barbarous ultramontanes?' But now in the last end of his life, when he, against all laws as well of God as of man, resisted his prince and the ordinance of God, and being thus a traitor, was imprisoned therefore, he was then incontinently esteemed of that Holy See worthy to be a cardinal; whereby may not every man see plainly that this Holy See did make sport with this prisoner's distress, than go about his deliverance?

When Bishop Fox of Hereford went to meet the German princes at Smalkalde in the autumn of 1535 he took with him a copy of Gardiner's reply, so presumably it was intended for Protestant consumption.[7]

Another line of defence had to be taken up in Rome and Paris. Thomas Cromwell himself defined the position to be adopted by the English representatives in those cities. One passage from the instructions sent to Sir Gregory Casale in Rome sufficiently illustrates the case put forward in justification of the king's action.

> The great iniquity of these men, who were thought so upright, was made manifest by witnesses, by letters in their own handwriting sent by the one to the other, and by their own oral confession. These and many other such matters at last compelled the most just prince to cast into prison these rebels, these enemies of

---
[7] *L.P.*, IX, no. 213.

their country, these disturbers of public peace, these impious and seditious men.

Here the reader may be assured that Thomas Cromwell was referring to Bishop John Fisher and to Sir Thomas More!

> In prison they were treated more gently and humanely than their crimes deserved. The king allowed them to converse with their relatives; their own favourite servants were permitted to wait on them; such food was granted to them and such dress as their own relatives and friends judged most suited to their temperaments and the preservation of their health. But in spite of this mercy of the king, all good faith, all obedience, all love of what is right, utterly forsook these rebels and traitors; for when, after long and mature deliberation, with absolute unanimity certain laws and statutes were made in Parliament for the common good of the kingdom, and in perfect accordance with the true Christian religion, these men alone refused to acquiesce, always hoping that with time something might happen to favour their impiety, while they pretended that they had laid aside all thought of human affairs and were intent solely on the contemplation of divine things. In the meantime they gave all their thoughts and vigils, how they might elude and refute by their fallacies and juggling arguments these holy laws. Of their impious and perfidious minds there are most manifest proofs: their own handwriting in coal and chalk when ink was wanting to them; their secret messages sent backwards and forwards. They could not deny the letters that had passed between them and been burnt. The most

clement king might not longer tolerate such atrocious guilt, and committed them to open trial and judgment. They were found guilty of high treason and rebellion and condemned.[8]

This deliberate perversion of the facts reveals the lengths to which the king and his secretary were prepared to go in an attempt to justify themselves even at Rome. When Bishop Foxe went on an embassy to Germany he was instructed to inform the princes that John Fisher and Thomas More "were of such traitorous hearts as even when in prison to plan an insurrection within the realm, as proved by a great number of honest men."

In their emphasis on treason, the king and his secretary were careful not to explain that they were using the term in its new sense—"maliciously to wish, will or desire." Foreign courts would assume that treason in England meant definite acts showing an intention to overthrow the constituted government of the country. So too, the unlettered people in the parish churches up and down the land, would think of treason as they had always done, as an attempt to get rid of the king.

Yet this travesty of the truth could not drive out of the popular mind the belief that two good men had been ruthlessly put to death. Those who knew the facts might keep silent under the terror, but in their hearts they were not deceived.

Henry VIII was succeeded in 1547 by his boy-son Edward VI; the new Ordinal of 1550 and the Act of Uniformity of 1552 took England further away from Rome, and the bitter factions amongst the rulers of the State brought the country to the verge of chaos.

---

[8] *S.P.*, VII, no. 436.

With the accession of Mary Tudor in 1553, it was again possible to speak openly of John Fisher and Thomas More. It is not necessary here to tell the story again of how William Rastell brought together the writings of his uncle and had them printed in one magnificent volume in 1557, the year before the deaths of Queen Mary and Cardinal Pole.

John Fisher's English writings were not so extensive, nor had he a devoted disciple to gather them together; this has probably meant the loss of some of his sermons and shorter writings. The sermons on the Penitential Psalms were reprinted in 1555 by Thomas Marsh, and the sermon against Luther (1521) in 1554 and again in 1556. A modernized version was printed in 1714. It is probable that *A Spiritual Consolation* was also published in Queen Mary's reign, but no printer's name is given nor is the edition dated.

It was during the reign of Queen Mary that the unknown early biographer happily collected together the records of the life of John Fisher. The result is not a work as notable, in a literary sense, as the lives of Thomas More by William Roper and Nicholas Harpsfield, but it deserves to be better known.

In 1560, John Cawood, one of the printers of the 1557 edition of Sir Thomas More's English works, published an English translation of John Fisher's *Tractatus de orando deum*. It is not known with certainty when he wrote this little work. The English title describes its scope. "A godly treatise declarying the benefites, fruites, and great commodities of prayer, and also the true use thereof, written in Latin fourtie years past by an Englysh man of great vertue and learnyng." It was not thought wise to give John Fisher's name now that Anne Boleyn's daughter was on the throne.

The translation was by Viscount Montague of Cowdray (1526-1592), a steadfast Catholic who served Queen Elizabeth loyally but who did not hesitate to oppose anti-Catholic legislation.

If the "fourtie years past" is accurate, this would date the composition as about 1520, but the translation omits one passage that suggests a later date. John Fisher deplored "this wretched age" when there was "scarce anything left in the church but open iniquity and feigned sanctity."

An edition of the original Latin was brought out by Dr. Richard Hall at Douai in 1576. This was reprinted at Rome and Paris in 1631, and another English translation (by a Benedictine) at Paris in 1640. Dr. Hall stated that he had received the book from one of John Fisher's household. Was this Richard Wilson?

On the Continent the *Confutatio* was reprinted in 1537, 1545, 1558 and 1564. A volume containing many of John Fisher's Latin works was published in 1597 at Wurzburg in Bavaria. It contained Henry VIII's *Assertio Septem Sacramentorum*, with the note, "Roffensis tamen hortatu et studio edita."

A passage has already been quoted in this chapter from Paul III's letter to Francis of France in which the pope declared that "this most holy man [John Fisher] laid down his life for God [and] for the Catholic religion." This declaration may be regarded as the first step toward canonization. In 1583 Gregory XIII approved of the painting on the walls of the English College in Rome of the representations of fifty-four victims of the first series of persecutions; by so doing the pope recognized them as martyrs.

The first edition of Sander's *De Schismate Anglicana* (1585) contained a list of English martyrs up to that date.

Other lists or catalogues followed during the seventeenth century, as well as collections of short lives. In 1640 Urban VIII granted faculties to the Archbishop of Cambrai to study the evidence of these martyrdoms, but the disturbed times prevented this inquiry from being completed.

With the restoration of the hierarchy in 1850, the cause of the English martyrs was again brought forward, but a generation passed before Leo XIII in 1886 confirmed "the honour given to the Blessed Martyrs John Cardinal Fisher, Thomas More and others put to death in England for the Faith from the year 1535 to 1583."

A widespread desire that John Fisher and Thomas More should be canonized gathered strength as the fourth centenary of their martyrdom approached. In June 1930 the cause was opened and the long and careful examination of the evidence began. On 29th January 1935 the results of this inquiry were submitted to the Sacred Congregation. It is usual for proof of miracles to be required, but for these two martyrs Pius XI granted a dispensation.

The final stages of canonization calls for three Consistories, private, public and semi-public. One who was present at the second consistory gives a vivid impression of the feeling of triumphant joy that was in the hearts of all.

> I had stood with the Postulator, Padre Agostino della Vergine, in the background on the Pope's right. After the procession had formed and was going out of the hall, we indulged in a mild exhibition of gate-crashing and followed Archbishop Hinsley's tall figure through the Sala Ducale into the room where the Cardinals were assembled, while the Holy Father was unvesting. Monsignor Caccia Dominioni and

Monsignor Respighi noticed us, and so, when the Pope had taken leave of the Cardinals, there were we planted in his path, determined to thank him once again for all his goodness to us and for all his interest in the cause. He took the Archbishop's hands in his, as we tried to say what was in our hearts. The Cardinals pressed round us in a circle, adding their thanks to the Pope and their congratulations to us. Then the Holy Father put his arms about Monsignor Hinsley's neck and embraced him: for us there was a special, smiling blessing: and so he passed on to his private apartments, and we stood up with that exhaustive feeling which follows such a moment, and tried to reply coherently to the Cardinals who were still bent on showing their gracious pleasure—nay delight—at this further step towards the consummation of all our hopes.[9]

The final ceremony took place in St. Peter's on 19th May 1935.
Four hundred years earlier, Reginald Pole had written:

What other have you, or have you had for centuries, to compare with Rochester in holiness, in learning, in prudence, and in episcopal zeal? You may be, indeed, proud of him, for, were you to search through all the nations of Christendom in our days, you would not easily find one who was such a model of episcopal virtues. If you doubt this, consult your merchants who have travelled in many lands; consult your ambassadors; and let them tell you whether they have anywhere heard of any bishop who has such a love of his flock as never to leave the care of it, ever

---

[9] Mgr. Reginald L. Smith in *Clergy Review*, May, 1935.

feeding it by word and example; against whose life not even a rash word could be spoken; one who was conspicuous not only for holiness and learning, but for love of country?[10]

The Collect for the Votive Mass of Saint John Fisher reads:

God, who didst fill thy blessed bishop John with such great courage that he cast away his life in the cause of truth and justice, enable us through his intercession and example to give up our life in this world for the sake of Christ, so that we may find it again in heaven.

Finis

---

[10] *De Unitate Eccl.*, lib. iii.

APPENDIX A
A PRAYER COMPOSED BY ST. JOHN FISHER[1]

HELP me, most loving father, help me with thy mighty grace. Succour me with thy most gracious favour. Rescue me from these manifold perils that I am in, for unless thou wilt of thy infinite goodness relieve me, I am but as a lost creature. Thy strict commandment is that I should love thee with all my heart, with all my soul, with all my mind, with all my power. And thus, I know, I do not, but am full far short and wide therefrom; which thing I perceive by the other loves that I have had of thy creatures heretofore. For such as I sincerely loved, I loved them so that I seldom did forget them. They were ever in my remembrance and almost continually mine heart was occupied with them and my thought ran ever upon them as well absent as present. Specially when they were absent I much desired to have their presence and to be there where they were, or else my heart were never in any rightful quiety.

But alas, my dear father, I am not in this condition towards thee. For I keep thee not in my remembrance nor bear thee in my thought nor occupy my heart with thee so often as I should, but for every trifle that cometh to my mind I let thee slip and fall out thereof. And for every fantasy that stirreth in my heart I set thee aside, shortly forget thee. I suffer many a trifling thought occupy my soul at liberty, but with thee, my dear father, I have lightly

---

[1] Reprinted by permission of Dr. David Rogers and the editor of *The Month*. The transcription was made by the Rev. J. F. McMahon, M.S.C. of Australia. The difficulty of transcription will be appreciated by studying Image XI (before page 138) which gives the conclusion of the MS.

done, and forthwith turn me to the remembrance of thy creatures and so tarry with thee but a short while, the delight in thy creatures so pulleth and draweth me hither and thither, my wretched desires so blind me. This false world so deceiveth me that I forget thee, which art my most loving father and art so desirous to have my heart and love. What are thy creatures but creatures made by thee? Thou made me and them of naught and thou far incomparably passeth all them. And what are my desires, when they are set on thy creatures and not in an order to thee, what are they but wretched and sinful affections?

And finally what is this world but a miserable exile, full of perils and evils far unlike that glorious country where thou art resident and sheweth thy most excellent Majesty in wonderful glory? There thou art clearly seen to all thy blessed angels and saints of thy most highly triumphant court. They be there ever present before thy blessed face and behold thy Majesty continually face to face. O my dear father, here should be mine heart, here should be my desire and remembrancy. I should long to have sight of thy most blessed face, I should earnestly desire to see thy country and kingdom, I should ever wish to be there present with thee and thy most glorious court. But this, alas, I do not. And therefore I sorrow at my grievous negligence, I weep for my abominable forgetfulness, I lament my vileness, yea, my very madness, that thus for trifles and vanities forget my most dear and loving father. Alas, woe is me! What shall I do? Whither may I turn me? To whom shall I resort for help? Where shall I seek for any remedy against the worldly and earthly waywardness of my heart? Whither should I rather go than to my father, to my most loving father, to my most merciful father, to him that of his infinite love and mercy hath given me boldness to call him father?

Whose son Jesu my saviour hath taught me thus to call him, and to think verily that he is my father, yea, and a more loving father than is any natural father unto his child. These are his words speaking unto the natural fathers of this world when ye that are infect with evil can liberally give unto your children good gifts, how much rather your heavenly father shall give a good spirit to them that ask it of him. These works, most gracious father, are the words of thy most dearly beloved son, Jesu, wherein he teaches us that thou art our very father and maketh promise on thy behalf that thou shalt give thine holy spirit unto them that ask thy son or thee studiously. Thou wiliest that we should believe him and faithfully trust his words. For thou testified of him that he was thine entirely beloved son and bade us hear him and give a full faith unto his words. Wherefore we may be certain and sure of three things. The first is that thou art our father, the second that thou art a more kind and loving father unto us than are the carnal fathers of this world unto their children. The third, that thou wilt give, to such as devoutly ask it of thee, thy most holy spirit. We may be well assured that for thine inestimable goodness, and for the honour of thy name and everlasting truth thou wilt not disappoint these promises, for as much as they were made by thy most entirely beloved son Christ Jesu whom thou sent into this world to make the truth certain and to confirm the same unto us by the blood which he shed for us on his cross.

O father, then, whither shall I turn in my necessity rather than to thee which have me call thee by this name, a name of much love and tenderness, of much delight and pleasure, a name which stirreth the heart with much hope and constancy and many other delectable affections. And if nothing were told me but only this name, it might suffice to make me steadfastly trust that thou, which hast commanded me to call thee by this name father, will help me and succour me at my need when I sue unto thee; but much rather because my saviour thy son Christ Jesu hath assured me that thou art a more kind and more loving father unto me than was mine own natural father. This assurance made by thy most entirely beloved son should specially move both thee and me. First it should move me to have an hope and a confidence that thou wilt deal with me according to the same promise. Second, it should also move thee to perform this promise effectually and so to show thyself a kind and loving father in this my petition. My petition, most dear father, is agreeable to that same promise made by thy most entirely beloved son any saviour Jesu. I ask none other thing but thy good and holy spirit to be given unto me according to that same promise which he promised.

I know, most gracious father, that thou art here present with me albeit I see thee not. But thou both seest me and hearest me and no secrecy of any heart is hid from thee. Thou hearest that I now ask thine holy spirit and thou knowest that I now pray therefor and that I am very desirous to have the same. Lo! dear father, with all the enforcement of my heart I beseech thee to give thine holy spirit unto me. Wherefore unless thou wilt disappoint the promise of thy son Jesu thou canst not but give me this holy spirit; so by this means I shall be fully relieved of that my misery whereof I complained unto thy goodness at the beginning. Thy most holy spirit he shall make me to love thee with all my heart, with all my soul, with all my mind, with all my power, for he is the author of all good love, he is the very furnace of charity and he is the fountain of all gracious affections and godly desires. He is the spiritual fire that kindles in the heart of them where he enters all gracious love; he fills their souls in whom he is received with the abundance of charity; he makes their minds sweetly to burn in all godly desires and gives unto them strength and power courageously to follow all ghostly affections and specially towards thee. Wherefore, dear father, when thou hast strictly commanded me thus to love thee with all my heart and thus would I right gladly do (but without thy help and without thy holy spirit I cannot perform the same), I beseech thee to shed upon my heart thy most holy spirit by whose gracious presence I may be warmed, heated and kindled with the spiritual fire of charity and with the sweetly burning love of all godly affections, that I may fastly set my heart, soul and mind upon thee and assuredly trust that thou art my very loving father and according to the same trust I may love thee with all my heart, with all my soul, with all my mind and all my power. Amen.

APPENDIX B
SAINT JOHN FISHER'S RELATIVES

THE facts of John Fisher's parentage have been given in Chapter I. A note amongst those collected by the early biographer reads:

> His mother had by one White three sons and a daughter, viz. John White, a merchant of the Staple, who dwelt in Beverley ..., Thomas, who dwelt in Lyn, a merchant also, Richard White, priest, bachelor of divinity and view of Bugden [Buckden] in Huntingdonshire, imprisoned in the time of Henry 8 by Gooderich, bishop of Ely, for religion; and a nun, who was so like the said bishop of Rochester in person, that Queen Mary knew her.[2]

In *L.P.* VIII, no. 888, a record of moneys due to John Fisher includes the names of Robert Fisher, Ralph Fisher, Edward White, John White, Robert White, and Henry White.

Robert Fisher, John Fisher's brother, was, as we have seen, his steward at Rochester and looked after him in the Tower. Edward White is also referred in official papers as a brother-in-law; he seems to have been imprisoned for a short time in connexion with the letters passed between the two prisoners. His employment at Rochester may mean that his wife, John Fisher's sister, had died earlier.

---

[2] *Ortroy*, p. 42.

APPENDIX B

This information can be summarized in the following table.

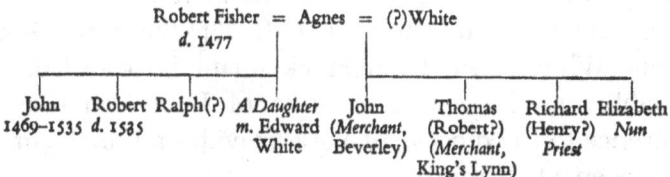

It is possible that the early biographer's informant had not remembered the Christian names correctly.

The statement that Richard White was vicar of Buckden seems sufficiently definite to be accepted, but, on investigation, it presents several problems.

Buckden was in the diocese of Lincoln, and the registers show the appointment to Buckden of Henry (not Richard) White, M.A. (not B.D.) by John Longland, Bishop of Lincoln on 29th January 1532 (*Register*, 27 fol. 239). Unfortunately the registers were not carefully kept at this period, and the next appointment to Buckden is dated 6th December 1554, without any reference to the occasion of the vacancy, or the name of the previous vicar.

The visitation book of 1552 shows that the vicar of Buckden had not preached there for eighteen months nor had he provided a substitute. His name is not given. This may not have been Henry White at this date.[3]

There was a Henry White at Cambridge who took his B.A. in 1508/9.

---

[3] I am indebted to Mrs. Joan Varley, archivist of the diocese of Lincoln, for this information.

THE LIFE OF ST. JOHN FISHER

Turning to the Rochester registers, we find that a Henry White of *the diocese of York* was ordained deacon on 17th May 1516 (f. 73v) on his tide of Freckenham, Suffolk, which was a peculiar of the Bishops of Rochester. Under the date 2nd October 1516 (f. 73r) the resignation of Henry White, B.A., from Freckenham is recorded. It is possible that he was a relative of John Fisher as the reference to the diocese of York provides a link. He might have been a half-brother.

There is no information available giving a link between Henry White of Freckenham and Henry White of Buckden. It would certainly be of interest if John Fisher's half-brother had been at Buckden during the period (July 1533 to May 1534) when Queen Catherine was living at Buckden Palace (which belonged to the Bishop of Lincoln).

The note about Bishop Goodrich of Ely also raises difficulties. Buckden was not in his diocese, nor was Freckenham.

Something can also be said of Elizabeth White. She was a member of the Dominican house at Dartford; she was receiving a pension in 1539 with, amongst others, Agnes Roper, who may have been a sister of William Roper. In 1557 she was living at the former house of the Dominicans at King's Langley. She refused to take the new oath of Supremacy under Elizabeth in 1559, and left the country, going to Antwerp. In 1560 it was reported that "the sister of the Bishop of Rochester, now in the island of Zeeland" was "in a very poor monastery and an unhealthy locality." That is the last known of her.[4]

---

[4] See "Sisters of the Martyrs" by the Rev. L. E. Whatmore, in *The Life of the Spirit-Blackfriars*, December 1945.

www.ingramcontent.com/pod-product-compliance
Lightning Source LLC
Chambersburg PA
CBHW011128070526
44583CB00023B/2951